Maxixe 30-38
Nationalism 180
Villa-lobos 186
Gu range 72-76

Choro

Penny Pan
04/07

Profiles in Popular Music
Glenn Gass and Jeffrey Magee, editors

Choro

A Social History of a
Brazilian Popular Music

Tamara Elena Livingston-Isenhour and
Thomas George Caracas Garcia

Indiana University Press | Bloomington and Indianapolis

This book is a publication of

Indiana University Press
601 North Morton Street
Bloomington, IN 47404-3797 USA

http://iupress.indiana.edu

Telephone orders   800-842-6796
Fax orders   812-855-7931
Orders by e-mail   iuporder@indiana.edu

The paper used in this publication meets the minimum requirements of American National
Standard for Information Sciences—Permanence of Paper for Printed Library Materials, ANSI
Z39.48-1984.

Manufactured in the United States of America

Library of Congress Cataloging-in-Publication Data
Livingston-Isenhour, Tamara Elena.
Choro : a social history of a Brazilian popular music / Tamara
Elena Livingston-Isenhour and Thomas George Caracas Garcia.
p. cm.—(Profiles in popular music)
Includes bibliographical references (p.   ), discography (p.   ), and
index.
ISBN 0-253-34541-3 (cloth : alk. paper)—ISBN 0-253-21752-0 (pbk. : alk.
paper)
1. Choros—History and criticism.   2. Popular instrumental music—Brazil—
History and criticism.   3. Dance music—Brazil—History and criticism.   I.
Garcia, Thomas George Caracas.   II. Title.   III. Series.
ML3487.L58 2005
781.64'0981—dc22

2004026035

1   2   3   4   5   10   09   08   07   06   05

Tamara Livingston-Isenhour: **TO MY BEAUTIFUL DAUGHTER LARISSA**

Thomas Garcia: **TO THE MEMORY OF FREDERICK CHARLES HESSE GARCIA**

CONTENTS

Ethnographies and social histories of music require a delicate balance between objective observation and subjective interpretation. This work departs from the norm in the fields of historical musicology and ethnomusicology in that it represents the combined results and conclusions of two independent researchers both working in the same subject matter. Thomas Garcia completed his dissertation entitled "The Brazilian *Choro:* Music, Politics and Performance" in 1997 at Duke University. Two years later, Tamara Livingston defended her dissertation, "Choro and Music Revivalism in Rio de Janeiro, 1973–1995" at the University of Illinois at Urbana-Champaign. Although we knew of each other's work, we did not meet in person until 2001 at the annual meeting of the Society for Ethnomusicology in Detroit. Since our work complemented each other's so well in terms of subject material and scope, the thought of writing two separate books, which would necessarily have to cover similar ground in order to introduce and situate the subject at hand, seemed absurd. Instead, we proposed to combine our work and our writing styles and perspectives to produce a unified work about choro. It was a challenge, in that our different backgrounds and writing styles meant that we would have to rework much of our material. Nevertheless, we looked at it as an opportunity to bring added depth to the material that perhaps might have been lacking had we each written separate books. We hope that by presenting a few words from each of us about our backgrounds and experiences, we will provide the reader with a better idea of our theoretical and subjective approaches to the material in this book.

Thomas Garcia

I was raised in a house dominated by the trappings of a serious academic and a serious musician: thousands of books and a grand piano. My father was a professor of Portuguese at the United States Military Academy, and my mother is a concert pianist. My father was also a great fan of classical music and had an extensive record collection. There was always music in my house, usually classical and often Brazilian. I do not remember a time when I was not in some way aware of Brazilian music. Both my parents are Brazilian, and I was raised in a bilingual and bicultural home. I was born in Brazil but came to the United States as an infant.

I began my musical studies very young, and by 12 years of age found that my favorite composer was Heitor Villa-Lobos. My mother frequently played the piano music of Villa-Lobos (with whom she studied at the Instituto Nacional de Canto Orfeônico) as well as other Brazilian piano music. Her practice and teaching schedule limited my access to her piano, and I opted to study guitar instead. I played most of the guitar *Preludios* and *Estudos* by Villa-Lobos through high school and was always looking forward to learning new pieces. I took a brief hiatus from serious guitar for several years while I worked on degrees in tuba at the Juilliard School but found myself continually drawn back to the guitar. While at Juilliard I began working with the great guitar and lute teacher Patrick O'Brien, who recognized in me the heart of a musician and the mind of a scholar. He encouraged my first serious study of Villa-Lobos's music, and for several years he and I dissected the repertory. I read that Villa-Lobos was heavily influenced by choro, so I started looking at choros to perform and had friends and relatives in Brazil send sheet music. I built up a respectable repertory of solo guitar choros, but I knew little about choro history and tradition.

After many years as a freelance guitarist in New York City, I found myself drawn back to school. After I earned a master's in musicology at the University of Massachusetts, for which I wrote a thesis on Villa-Lobos's early guitar music, I went to Duke University and pursued a Ph.D. in performance practice. I was absolutely certain about the subject of my dissertation: the late guitar music of Heitor Villa-Lobos. My dissertation prospectus was entitled "Performance Practice Issues in the Late Guitar Music of Heitor Villa-Lobos: The *Preludios* and *Estudos*." I felt that traditional musicological scholarship had been dominated by a Eurocentric approach that has left many important musical genres, traditions, and composers virtually unexplored, specifically Brazilian music and Latin American music in general.

Since most of the available research done on Villa-Lobos (most of which was done by Brazilian scholars) mentions the importance of choro in his music, my plan was to include a chapter that would define choro. I felt I needed to explain the musical, political, and performance issues surrounding choro; provide a basic primer of choro style and genre; and explore the history and biographies of some of the most important figures of the choro tradition. And this all was to be accomplished in one chapter. It was a daunting if not impossible task, considering it was intended to be only a part of a larger work. I discussed the quandary with my dissertation advisor John Druesedow. In the middle of a rant I exclaimed my frustration at the lack, in Portuguese, English, or any other language, of a good source on the history of choro. Without missing a beat, he said, "So write one!" I asked, "Are you serious?" His reply: "You bet." I had defended my prospectus and had every intention of writing my dissertation on Villa-Lobos, but my advisor argued that doing the work necessary to understand choro would indeed go a long way toward helping people understand Villa-Lobos and his relationship to choro.

Another issue was that my degree was in performance practice and required a performance component in the form of a recording. This meant that in addition to doing the archival work required to study a genre in its historical context, I would have to listen to historical and contemporary recordings and live performances and spend some time in the bars and restaurants where choro is traditionally located. I already had funding to spend significant time in Brazil doing my fieldwork, so there would be little adjustment in terms of the logistics. I decided to focus my work in Rio de Janeiro, the cultural capital of Brazil and the place of origin of choro. I also planned to travel throughout Brazil in search of choro, which took me from the south through the center to the northeast of the country. I spent a total of twenty months in Brazil between 1992 and 1997.

I ended up meeting a large number of choro musicians and performing in formal and informal choro gatherings. I also had the good fortune to be invited to give solo recitals at the Museu Villa-Lobos and the Museu da República, both in Rio de Janeiro, where I performed choros by some of the greats of the tradition (Pernambuco, Nazaré, Zequinha de Abreu) and pieces by Villa-Lobos based in some way on the choro tradition. These eventually became the core of the recording portion of my dissertation document. I also found there was a lack of choro scores, either for solo guitar or in lead-sheet format, and resolved to address this issue as part of the dissertation.

When completing my fieldwork, I was faced with an important decision: Where to start and where to end? Starting was easy: I began at the beginning, in the 1870s. But where to end the project? In the 1990s, choro was a rising star, partly as a result of a strong revival movement in the 1970s and 1980s. But there was a large gap from the late 1950s to the 1970s. I resolved to end my discussion with the early 1950s, a time when choro ceased to be part of the day-to-day musical life in Brazil.

Tamara Livingston-Isenhour

One of my fondest early memories of music involves my mother playing *Saudades do Brasil*, a set of pieces by French composer Darius Milhaud, on the piano. His attempts to capture the sensuality and syncopation of Brazilian popular music of the late nineteenth century intrigued me before I ever considered studying Brazilian music. Years later, I chose the classical guitar as my preferred instrument and dutifully made my way through the guitar repertoire of Villa-Lobos. Like many guitarists, I fell in love with his evocations and stylizations of Brazilian popular music. I especially enjoyed the compositions called choros, although I had never heard of the genre before. When I entered the Ph.D. program in ethnomusicology at the University of Illinois, I considered writing what I assumed would be a historical account of choro, since the sources available to me suggested that it was rarely if ever performed anymore (this was during the late 1980s and early 1990s, before it became popular again). My surprise and delight upon hearing a recording of contemporary choro that I happened to find in a local record store was so strong that I resolved to go to Brazil to find out more about the performance and practice of choro.

My dissertation research was carried out from January to May 1994 and from August to November 1995 in Rio de Janeiro. Shortly after my arrival in Rio de Janeiro in January 1994, my host and colleague Samuel Araújo arranged for me to attend an informal gathering of choro musicians in the Santa Teresa neighborhood of Rio de Janeiro. I will never forget the emotion I experienced when I first heard choro played live in the very city in which it developed. What I had heard before only on recordings was happening right in front of my eyes, unmediated by stage or recording studio and indescribably enriched by my delight in watching the body language and nonverbal interaction between the players. I was absolutely entranced by the intimacy of the performance, the way the instruments interlocked, the elaborate bass lines played by the guitar, and the variety of melodies played by the flute and bandolim.

Initially at least, I had a difficult time finding more choro: Concerts were rarely listed in the newspapers or magazines, I never heard choro on the radio, and most record-store employees shook their heads or shrugged their shoulders when I asked if they had any choro recordings. My breakthrough came when I discovered a choro group that played regularly at a bar in the neighborhood of Botafogo, where I was living. After I explained my research, I was welcomed by the musicians, who hoped that I would bring attention to their work. The contacts I made in this group, especially with guitarist Josimar Monteiro and *pandeiro* player Darly Guimarães, opened up a whole network of choro musicians, fans, critics, and researchers.

Through these people, I learned not only that choro was alive and well in the city of Rio de Janeiro but that it had undergone a rebirth (*renascimento*) in the 1970s. Many of the younger musicians told me they had been aspiring rock-and-roll guitarists until they discovered the instrumental possibilities of choro by hearing the great musicians of the past playing during the revival. When I returned from my first trip to Brazil, I reflected on the way people spoke about choro and about the revival. I was frequently told that choro was dying out until it was rescued or revitalized by the revival, that choro represented authentic Brazilian nationality in its blending of African and European characteristics, that choro was an important part of the cultural heritage and cultural memory of the nation. I sensed there was a desire among younger musicians to make choro their own by modernizing it, which conflicted with the aesthetics of many older musicians who preferred to preserve or carry on the tradition. It struck me that there were parallels between the discourse of choro revivalists and the discourse in other ethnic and folk music revivals. This led me to investigate the idea that perhaps musical revivals were manifestations of broader underlying social processes that would account for their similarities across cultural lines. When I returned to Rio de Janeiro the following year, I focused on choro in the 1970s and early 1980s, investigating the revival as both a musical and a sociopolitical phenomenon.

The personal accounts related above show some interesting points of convergence. Both authors are trained as classical guitarists and thus are particularly sensitive to the role of the guitar in choro. Both are formally trained in music and music research and have found the need to combine historical and ethnographic approaches: Garcia is grounded in historical musicology but is interested in aspects of performance practice of popular musics, and Livingston-Isenhour is an ethnomusicologist but is interested in the historical aspects of urban popular musics. In writing this book, we have combined techniques and approaches from both historical musicology and ethnomusicology. We sincerely hope that the reader finds our collaboration and synthesis of approaches to be as rewarding and engaging as we have.

Acknowledgments

The list of people to whom we owe a debt of gratitude is enormous. We would like to thank our many friends and colleagues in Brazil who made this work possible, including Jorge Hesse Leão, Hamilton de Holanda, Luciana Rabello, Egeu Laus, Ricardo Tacuchian, Gilson Peranzetta, Reco do Bandolim, Samuél Araújo, Sérgio Pinna, Josimar Monteiro, Darly Guimarães, Jorge Simas, Dolores Tomé, Maria Helena Diniz, David Chew, Nicolas Souza Barros, and the late Dr. Assis. Our special thanks to Marco de Pinna for his enthusiastic support and for sharing his extensive choro collection with us. We would like to express our gratitude to the Museu Villa-Lobos, the Biblioteca Nacional, and the Museu da Imagem e do Som in Rio de Janeiro and to our American friends and colleagues Cliff Korman and Mike Marshall. Finally, we thank our families and our spouses, John Isenhour and Regina Enéas Garcia, for their patience and support.

Choro

Introduction

This book is about the Brazilian popular music known as choro. We consider the many facets of this music, including style, repertoire, composers, players, and instruments. We look at the social history of choro, including the communities that have supported and lovingly cultivated it for over a century. Brazilians often speak of choro as a quintessentially Brazilian music; in this book we take a close look at the relationship between choro and notions of what it means to be Brazilian, and suggest reasons why choro occupies a unique position in the Brazilian soundscape. We also look at choro within a broader context of national and international politics and forces. Using examples of choro compositional techniques, performance practice, repertoire, and performance venues and contexts, we demonstrate how social and political contexts are embedded in style and genre to produce a sonic experience at once entertaining yet profoundly meaningful.

Our intent was to write this book for a broad audience in a manner that, we hope, will make this material accessible to people with various degrees of interest and purposes in mind. For the teacher of world music, we include concise descriptions and examples of the music that can easily be presented to students, including a compact disc of music discussed in the text and lists of additional sources of information. For the music researcher, including ethnomusicologists and historical musicologists, we hope to have provided sufficient analytical and ethnographic details to sustain interest and make a contribution to the literature in Brazilian music. Last but not least, we hope that anyone with an interest in Brazilian music will find this book engaging and useful in furthering knowledge about the subject area.

We begin our study with the development of choro from its origins in Rio de Janeiro as a participatory playing style to its emergence as a genre in the late nineteenth and early twentieth centuries. In the 1880s, groups based on the *terno,* or trio of guitar, *cavaquinho* (a small four-stringed guitar), and flute, formed to play popular European dances for parties and social occasions. Many of these groups consisted of skilled amateur musicians who held day jobs in industry or government service. In the evenings and on weekends, they gathered to play music, socialize, and engage in spirited instrumental competitions to see who could improvise the best or most creative accompaniment or melodic variation. At about the same time, artists, writers and intellectuals were beginning to consciously forge a new Brazilian style as a reaction against the elite's heavy reliance upon European culture for everything from fashion to language, music, and dance. In the 1920s, choro became part of this pursuit when it captured the eyes and ears of intellectuals and critics who eagerly proclaimed it to be a distinctly Brazilian popular music. With the rise of cinema at the turn of the century, recording in the 1910s, and radio in the 1930s, choro musicians were in demand, as much for their musical skill as for their symbolic value as representatives of a newly emergent national culture. Professional groups were organized to accompany recording vocalists and, in the 1930s, to act as studio musicians for live radio broadcasts. These groups (called *conjuntos regionais*) codified certain styles and repertoires and became so associated with Brazilian national sentiment that the government of Getúlio Vargas often used them in the 1930s and 1940s to further nationalist policies. Although choro continued to be played in amateur gatherings, or *rodas,* mass media carried the sound of professional choro musicians to even the most remote corners of the nation, where this formerly regional style of music became synonymous with a unified national and musical identity.

After a decline in the dissemination of choro by the mass media in the 1950s and 1960s, choro was revived in the 1970s, supported by an unlikely coalition of the military dictatorship and middle-class, university-educated whites. Revivalist choro style and repertoire emulated that of the earlier professional *regionais,* leading to an eventual fracturing of styles into progressive and traditional. In the 1980s and 1990s, choro continued to be influenced by styles, players, and repertoires from the revival and incorporated new younger players who continue to innovate within the stylistic realm of choro. Since its inception, the impact of choro on Brazilian composers of concert music has been so striking that we devote an entire chapter to the study of choro within the Brazilian classical music tradition. As the music on which young instrumentalists are still encouraged to cut their teeth, choro retains its status as a serious popular music that is technically and musically challenging, enjoyable to perform, and still quintessentially Brazilian.

What is choro? If one asks a Brazilian choro musician this question, one is likely to get a variety of answers, including some that are so vague as to apply to almost any kind of music. To some it is "a state of mind," to others, "a conversation between instruments." Some will describe it to Americans as "Brazilian jazz," or worse, "Brazilian blues." Despite these confusing responses, a set of discrete features helps define and characterize both the style and the genre.

First, the term "choro" has been used, with varying degrees of specificity, to refer not just to a style of playing and a genre of music, but also to an instrumental ensemble (based on the combination of guitar, cavaquinho, and flute or other melody instrument) and a social gathering at which such music is performed. Musicians and others who are closely associated with choro are known as *chorões* (singular: *chorão*). Historically, choro referred to small groups of instrumentalists, either the terno or larger groups based on the terno. Late-nineteenth-century choro ensembles typically featured a soloist (usually a flautist or other wind player) who played highly ornamented versions of familiar melodies. The other instruments improvised harmonic and rhythmic accompaniment and provided occasional melodic counterpoint. Bass lines and harmony were provided by the cavaquinho and *violão* (six-string guitar); later the seven-string guitar (in standard Spanish guitar tuning with an additional bass string tuned either to a B or C) became a popular instrument in choro. Although many flute and wind players were able to read and write musical notation, most early choro musicians were musically illiterate. As a result, choro style was characterized by a certain degree of improvisation in both melody and accompaniment, regardless of the presence of a musical score.

CHORO STYLE

Choro style is grounded in the particular relationships among the instruments of the ensemble. From homophonic dance forms in which the melody is supported by a simple constant metrical structure, *chorões* created spontaneous multilayered forms with rhythmic and melodic counterpoint playing against the main melody. Although almost any instrument or type of ensemble can play in the choro style, choro has come to be strongly associated with the timbres and capabilities of the flute, cavaquinho, guitar and *pandeiro* (Brazilian tambourine). The instruments fulfill four basic sonic requirements: the melody, the center, the bass line, and the rhythmic line. Each line or role requires different and varying levels of specialization. Although each instrument of the choro ensemble is associated with a functional role, there is a great deal of flexibility and spontaneity in an actual performance, and instruments often temporarily switch roles during a piece.

THE MELODY

In choro, a single soloist, often the flute or *bandolim* (the Brazilian variant of the mandolin), plays the melody the majority of the time. Choro melodies are based on compositions by known authors (as opposed to being of anonymous or collective authorship, as in some folk or traditional music), some of which are published as sheet music. That known authors compose pieces, however, does not mean that one is expected to play them exactly as notated. Indeed, many musicians learn pieces without ever consulting music scores, and most players do not use music notation in the roda. Furthermore, the soloist is expected to take a certain amount of liberty in playing a melody; it is an unwritten rule that one should never play *only* what is written.[2]

Most genres played by choro musicians, such as polkas, waltzes, and choros, utilize relatively simple formal structures, usually binary or ternary with repeated sections, or rondo form (ABACA). The soloist is expected to present the melody in a recognizable form the first time through; on the repeats, most soloists add some improvisation, usually subtle rhythmic or melodic variations. Sometimes the soloist will exchange melodic riffs with the accompanists. Unlike jazz, in which the melody is used as a springboard for extended improvisatory solos, the melody in choro is almost always recognizable. If a soloist does venture an extended solo, he or she will almost always return with a restatement of the melody. Melodies that are already harmonically rich or extremely chromatic may be ornamented only slightly. The comments of choro musician Jacó do Bandolim about his improvisatory style sums up the opinion of many old-guard choro musicians on the role of the soloist:

> I improvise when I interpret music. But I improvise not for the sake of improvising, but to augment the scale and the sentiment of the composition. I am not completely tied to what the composer has done nor am I obligated to reproduce it exactly. I reproduce it in a manner that pleases me, in the way a painter reproduces nature that appears one way to everyone else and another way to himself. Thus, it is not the desire to improvise, to be original. It is rather the desire to encounter in musical phrases the richness in a composition, which, when it is well done, is subtle and refined in all its details, and that presents me with innumerable possibilities.[3]

When the musicians want to extend a piece to allow for more improvisation or to give others an opportunity to play the melody, there are several possibilities. Some pieces lend themselves to continuous repetition of the chord progression of the first, or A, section (in rondo form), thus allowing for extended improvisation. In other cases, any of the sections or the whole piece may be repeated several times. Most choros are composed with aural tags or cues that communicate to the other players what is about to happen. Examples are a distinctive preparatory three-sixteenth–note pickup played by the soloist that musically identifies the piece about to be played and codas or distinctive section endings that signal the accompanists to move on to the next section in the manner of a first and second ending. If a piece in progress does not have internal tags, the soloist generally signals the end through visual cues, such as a nod of the head or an extended glance.

THE CENTER

The role of center (called *centro* by choro musicians) is considered a key element by traditional choro musicians. The cavaquinho (an instrument resembling a small guitar with four steel strings that is played by strumming with a plectrum originally made from tortoiseshell or quill) functions as the center instrument in most choro ensembles. Its role is to provide the rhythmic and harmonic underpinning to the music that is fundamental to the basic flow and texture of choro. The guitarist is released from having to continuously provide chordal and rhythmic accompaniment, allowing him or her to concentrate on creating an interesting bass line instead. The cavaquinho may also engage in riff-style comping, or the insertion of short repeated rhythmic figures as filler or background accompaniment.

Although the cavaquinho may be played as a solo instrument, its primary function is to provide chords strummed on the off beats or in syncopated patterns. The strumming consists of alternating up and down strokes, a pattern which can be broken to give emphasis to one chord or another. This style of articulation gives the instrument a percussive quality, and since percussion instruments were not part of the early choro ensemble, the cavaquinho was important as both a harmonic and a rhythmic instrument. The percussive quality of the strummed strings is intensified by the instrument's high pitch (it is tuned an octave higher than the guitar) and its relatively strident tone. Players are expected to improvise rhythms, and variation in repeated sections is the norm. Typical rhythmic figures are highly syncopated (see Example 1.1).

Example 1.1. Typical cavaquinho accompaniment rhythms.

The guitar may also fill the center role, especially in cases where there are two or more guitars in an ensemble. The harmonic accompaniments of the guitar are plucked in block chords or arpeggiated in a rhythm that tends to be less complex than that of the cavaquinho. A typical guitar accompaniment often incorporates the constant sixteenth-note pattern of the pandeiro with a strong articulation of the beat, usually provided by the thumb of the right hand. The guitarist playing a steady sixteenth-note pattern may occasionally emphasize notes other than the downbeats to sustain interest. Novice guitar players often assume the center voice in order to learn accompanying techniques while actively participating. They may begin their involvement in choro by playing a less active line, consisting simply of repeated eighth notes and even quarter notes. The result is a more constant, less syncopated rhythm that complements but does not compete with the cavaquinho, which can be accented in different ways to create levels of rhythmic interest. In this context, chordal arpeggiation and chord inversion to provide smooth voice leading in the lowest part of the accompaniment are additional techniques at the disposal of the guitarist. The guitar may also play the pandeiro rhythm combined with typi-cal Afro-Brazilian rhythmic figures in any combination at the discretion of the player which, when merged with the cavaquinho line, creates the hallmark con-stant sixteenth-note rhythm of choro (see Example 1.2). These rhythmic figures are often played with various articulation techniques: muting the string with the right arm, producing a violin pizzicato effect; muting the strings with the left hand, cre-ating a variety of timbres; including or omitting open strings to change the sustain of the chord; and legato articulation of the lowest note with the left hand com-bined with the cessation of plucking with the right.

Example 1.2. Guitar combining pandeiro rhythm with Afro-Brazilian rhythms (Bar 5, second beat). Note the inversions of the chords, creating a smooth line in the bass.

THE BASS

A hallmark feature of choro style is an elaborated, usually improvised, bass line played on the lower strings of the six- or seven-string guitar. In the terno, the guitar is expected to provide both a chordal rhythmic accompaniment and a bass line. The bass line, or *baixaria* (from *baixo,* bass), is created using a number of stylistic re-sources: filling in the tonic and dominant chords with scalar runs, utilizing a walk-ing bass (i.e., stepwise motion reinforcing the beat), inserting melodic or rhythmic responses to the soloist or cavaquinho player, and improvising contrapuntal melodies, riffs, and pedal points (see Example 1.3). The earliest recording that ex-hibits this characteristic dates from 1914: the waltz "Falena" by Chiquinha Gon-zaga, recorded for Casa Edison by Chiquinha Gonzaga e seu Conjunto,[4] in which the guitar exhibits a prominent bass line with stepwise descending scalar passages between bass notes typical of choro style. Cadential riffs, or standardized endings, are an important identifying feature of choro style.

Example 1.3. Baixaria lines from "Bicho carpinteiro" and "Descendo a serra." Arrangement by Thomas Garcia.

In fast choros, the harmonic rhythm tends to be quite active with an average of two chord changes per measure (in 2/4 time). In this case, the guitarist may choose to play a walking bass line only on the downbeats. In slower choros, the guitarist will frequently fill in spaces between chord changes with melodic phrases or riffs. The guitarist responsible for the bass line needs to be quite skilled in order to improvise runs and keep up with the harmonic rhythm. Other guitarists, however, may join in and simply play the basic chords, perhaps in different registers so as not to duplicate exactly each other's contributions. Guitarists with greater skill who are not responsible for the bass line may switch roles several times during the course of the music for added interest: For example, they may join the bass-line player to play certain passages in harmony (usually in thirds), then revert back to playing chords.

THE RHYTHM

The rhythmic line in choro is played by the pandeiro, a tambourine made with a circular frame and a plastic or skin head tuned by a tension mechanism. The jingles
consist of two metal curved discs with the curved edges pointing in rather than out
as in a tambourine. A combination of left- and right-hand strokes and use of the
head and jingles can produce a variety of sounds. The right hand strikes the instrument with the thumb, a block of fingers, the base of the hand, or the open palm. A
"roll" is produced when the tip of the thumb is dragged around the perimeter of
the head, creating a series of vibrations. The left hand holds the instrument and
helps oscillate it to shake the jingles. Fingers of the left hand are also used to
dampen the head from underneath, thereby changing the pitch and tone color.

Early choro ensembles did not regularly include percussion instruments. Instead, the rhythmic line was assumed by instruments that played the center and
bass and was reinforced by a melodic line that was often subdivided into sixteenth
notes, the basic rhythmic unit of choro. Since the 1910s, the pandeiro has been a
standard component of the choro ensemble and is considered indispensable for
playing traditional choro style. It is also a standard instrument for Carnaval samba
(*samba enredo*), roots samba (*samba de morro*), and samba derivations, including
popular samba (*pagode*).

The rhythmic aspects of the melody, the center, and the bass are typically reinforced and complemented by the pandeiro, which generally plays a constant
sixteenth-note pattern in 2/4 time (see Example 1.2). A good pandeiro player will
emphasize the offbeats (either the second or third sixteenth note of each beat),
thereby adding a rhythmic drive to the music. To accompany particular pieces, the
pandeiro may also emphasize the second downbeat by releasing the finger that
dampens the head of the instrument from underneath. This technique imitates the
pattern played by the large *surdo* drum found in samba and creates yet another
layer of rhythmic interest in the choro ensemble. Although the pandeiro player
mostly plays time or maintains a steady pulse in choro, there are occasions when
one may play "against time" or "against the groove," a common technique used in
instrumental breaks and codas. Stops are another common feature in choro; the
pandeiro may suddenly stop the constant rhythm, only to resume when the melody
returns. The rhythm guitar and percussion instruments (such as the small hand-held
drum called *tamborim*) play a syncopated variation on this rhythm: Each player
strives to play a slightly different rhythmic pattern so as to "fill in the spaces"
without duplicating each other's efforts.

Many of these performance characteristics are illustrated in the example of
the choro "Flôr amorosa" by Joaquim Antônio da Silva Calado, arranged as a typical choro ensemble might play it.[5] As demonstrated in Example 1.4, one of the
guitars assumes an elaborated bass line, while the other plays rhythmic chords.
The rhythmic patterns within the accompaniment create a constant sixteenth-note

motion, one of the principal distinguishing characteristics of the choro style and genre. Some of the accompaniment notes are accented, but there is still a feeling of evenness because the divisions of the beat are steady and constant. Choro ensemble performance often includes improvised countermelodies as part of the accompaniment texture; a typical countermelody in "Flôr amorosa" is given in Example 1.5.

The interlocking nature of the melody, center, bass, and rhythmic roles are fundamental to creating the sounds distinct to choro. They also provide a clear means of musical interaction, so that individual players may engage in a "conversation between instruments" that balances personal expression with social and musical unity. This ideal balance of musical and social forces is the driving force behind the choro jam session, or roda, in which individual and group expression blend to create an immensely pleasurable sonic experience for players and fans.

Example 1.4. Excerpt from "Flôr amorosa," by Antônio Calado, scored for terno (flute, cavaquinho, and two guitars). Arrangement by Thomas Garcia.

Example 1.5. Model of choro countermelody to "Flôr amorosa."

THE SPIRIT OF CHORO: MALÍCIA

An important, but difficult to define, stylistic marker of early choro was *malícia*, or an attitude of spirited competition in which one musician strives to outwit the other. "Malícia" refers to the choro soloist who enjoyed throwing off his accompanists with unexpected modulations or virtuosic improvisations. It was said, however, that the delight of audiences was even greater when the accompanists showed greater malícia by maintaining their cool and playing through the complex sections with panache and finesse. Malícia has specific ties to Afro-Brazilian culture and is considered a fundamental attribute of *capoeira*, an Afro-Brazilian martial art originally developed by slaves as a means of lethal fighting without the use of weapons.[6] J. Lowell Lewis defines malícia in this context as "deception, trickery, cunning, double-dealing, dissimulation and indirection." It is the distrust of surface appearance, the pretense of doing something one way then its subversion by doing the opposite. It is the essence of the capoeira move called "the blessing" (*benção*), in which the player presents himself to his opponent as if desiring to shake hands and instead delivers a sharp blow with his heel or the flat of the foot, mocking the custom that slaves be required to ask for the master's blessing.[7] In capoeira and in slave culture in general, malícia allowed slaves to covertly rebel and resist domination when open rebellion was not possible or desirable. In nineteenth-century Rio de Janeiro, Afro-Brazilian practitioners of capoeira (*capoeiristas*) were frequently hired as mercenaries to do the bidding of those with money; they were both feared and respected by the populace. In the early twentieth century, malícia and its counterpart *malandragem* (the lifestyle of the lower-class Afro-Brazilian hustler and rogue) were often referred to in the lyrics of urban samba.[8] Malícia is a constant thread weaving together various Afro-Brazilian cultural forms and serves as a reminder of the Afro-Brazilian heritage of choro.

The repertoire of early choro musicians consisted of dance music imported from Europe, especially the waltz and the polka, serenades, and other local popular genres. Over time a new genre arose, also known as choro, which combined aspects of choro performance practice with the formal and harmonic structure of the polka. Thus, we can speak of norms and tendencies in harmony, melody, rhythm, form, and structure that define the choro genre, many of which are direct outgrowths of choro performance practice.[9] In terms of harmony, the early choro was thoroughly grounded in contemporary European practice. Indeed, the choro has never been harmonically progressive. Its attraction was in its expressive and rhythmic character and its showcasing of instrumental virtuosity. As in choro style, the distinguishing features of the choro genre are found in the melodies and the rhythm.

Choros are easily identified by their melodies, many of which are idiomatic to the instrument for which they were originally composed. Melodies with wide leaps, arpeggios based on the harmonic progression, and chromatic sequences are common. A majority of choros begins with a preparatory three-sixteenth–note pickup (see Example 1.6a and 1.6b) typically played by the melodic soloist. As many choro musicians recognize a tune more easily from its opening bars than from its title, Garcia suggests that this practice may have developed from the need to provide an aural cue for the key, mood, and tempo of the piece for accompanists who played

Example 1.6. Some typical choro openings.

a. Saudade do Cavaquinho

b. Não me toques. . .

c. Saxofone, porque choras?

d. Nenê

e. Escorregando

solely by ear. Some choros have extended pickups, up to an entire bar (see Example 1.6d and 1.6e). Another characteristic of the choro is long, sweeping melodic lines covering a broad range (see Example 1.6c and 1.6d).

Choro harmonies, especially in the late nineteenth and early twentieth centuries, were based on standard European harmonic progressions such as I-IV-V7-I in major keys and i-III-VI-ii°-V7-i in minor keys or on variations derived from these progressions. The chord changes were typically predictable, allowing accompanying instrumentalists playing by ear to easily improvise within the tonal plan. When choro became more professional in the 1920s and 1930s, the level of training and proficiency among chorões increased. After this point, choros were no longer restricted to triads and seventh chords, and many began to incorporate dissonance and an extended harmonic vocabulary.

Most choros are modeled on the form of European dances from which the genre developed. Sections of regular and approximately equal length are typical and may be arranged in simple structures such as AABB, ABA, and, most commonly, ABACA (rondo form). Within these structures, harmonic motion is predictable. For example, a choro in rondo form in a major key will typically have the A section in the tonic key; the B section in the dominant, parallel, or relative minor or the tonic key; and the C section in the subdominant or dominant key. For a piece in a minor key, the C section is typically in the parallel or relative major.

Choro is, of course, more than its musical components. In the following pages, we hope to provide the reader with two things: a basic understanding of choro as a musical art form and an insight into choro as an historical process, a social phenomenon, and a local practice with national and even global significance.

Structure and Organization of the Book

We begin our study of choro with a look at its musical and social antecedents. Two African-influenced early forms of popular music, the *lundu* and the *maxixe,* had a strong stylistic influence on choro and are important not only as musical antecedents but as social antecedents for the negotiation of issues of race and class. Our analysis of these genres in chapter 2 looks at their respective musical development and considers their role within a broader political context of identity construction based on racist ideas of miscegenation. This background is critical for understanding how and why choro became an important emblem of Brazilian national identity in the 1920s and its position within the politics of race and class in subsequent years. Another important musical antecedent to choro was the *modinha.* Originating as a lyrical salon genre, it was taken up by street musicians and chorões and was incorporated into their repertories. The modinha lent a lyrical quality to some choros, and its overtly sentimental nature is incorporated into slow, more introspective choros.

The choro roda is of prime importance in any consideration of choro history, tradition, and ethos. Indeed, musicians and fans say that the heart and soul of choro is in the roda, where instrumentalists are free to converse musically and socially in an atmosphere of camaraderie and mutual respect. In chapter 3, we discuss the important social and musical features of the roda and its impact on the shaping of choro tradition and consider its role in the choro community. The close, interdependent nature of the social and musical aspects of choro is exemplified by the term "chorão." Although it was used in most cases to refer to a highly accomplished choro musician, it was sometimes bestowed upon a respected host of musical gatherings or given to fellow bohemians who just as likely as not had no musical talent but exhibited instead great generosity and love for the bohemian life. In this chapter we describe the social chorão as well as the musical variety. We also examine past and present rodas, including ethnographic descriptions of rodas we experienced.

Chapter 4 examines the rise and development of choro between 1870 and the 1920s, beginning with the etymology of the term "choro" and the relationships between urban choro and rural music-making of plantation slaves. We introduce the reader to the earliest composers of choros and their social milieus, focusing on salon composer and flautist Joaquim Antônio da Silva Calado and bandleader Anacleto de Medeiros. Whereas Calado's compositions often require a high level of musical ability and tend to reflect his formal conservatory training, Medeiros's works were written specifically for the amateur groups he worked with. These composers represent two sides of choro: the erudite and the popular.[10] The works of pianists and composers Chiquinha Gonzaga and Ernesto Nazaré represent a third facet. Chiquinha was a regular at rodas de choro and was also heavily involved in popular theater. As a result, her choros and other popular compositions exhibit characteristics from both the erudite and the popular realms of music. She is also notable as a female composer in a genre and milieu dominated by men. Nazaré was the leading choro pianist and composer of his day, and his music was far more sophisticated than that of his contemporaries because of his classical training. His choros, which he usually labeled as tangos, spanned class divisions during a period of great social and musical changes.

The advent and growth of sound recording in the 1910s and 1920s and the development of radio in the 1930s created a demand for highly skilled, musically literate, versatile studio musicians versed in popular music. The transition from the informal terno format to the professional *conjunto regional* is the subject of chapter 5. This process occurred against the backdrop of the momentous Semana de Arte Moderna (Week of Modern Art), during which composers of classical music, artists, and writers gathered to discuss and formulate the development of a postcolonial national culture, one that would declare its independence from European culture. The sentiments expressed in the Semana confronted the racist tendencies of the elite classes in the controversy surrounding the trip black choro musician and band-leader Pixinguinha made to Paris. The Parisians' eager acceptance of Pixinguinha as a cultural ambassador posed a dilemma for Brazilian elites. On the one hand, French acceptance of an aspect of Brazilian culture was important to intellectuals and elites, but on the other hand, it implied that Brazilian culture was essentially black rather than white, a point that most elites and intellectuals found untenable.

Pixinguinha also unwittingly exposed the tensions between proponents of a xenophobic national culture and those who embraced cosmopolitan culture and ideals. When Pixinguinha returned from Paris and formed a jazz band based on bands he had heard abroad, he was accused of having betrayed Brazilian national culture. This narrow definition of Brazilian culture intensified in the years to come, encouraged by the nationalist policies of dictator Getúlio Vargas. Chapter 6 explores the role of choro within the rubric of Brazilian popular music during the Vargas years, a time when popular music was frequently used for nationalist purposes to consciously forge a unified Brazilian identity. Both choro and samba (an Afro-Brazilian song and dance form strongly associated with Carnaval) were supported (and in the case of samba, controlled) by regional and national governments as musical emblems of Brazilian culture. We suggest that the tension evident in national discourse in the 1920s about the corrupting nature of cosmopolitan (especially North American) music continued in the 1930s and 1940s with the division of popular musics into two kinds: national and foreign. This division was reflected in live radio shows in the practice of featuring a *regional* for Brazilian popular music and a separate dance-band ensemble (*orquestra*) for "foreign" numbers. Whereas governing officials, intellectuals, and the elite strongly supported the *idea* of a national culture, racism continued unabated and professional black composers and musicians were rare.

The 1950s ushered in a new era marked by the end of Vargas's cultural policies with his suicide in 1955. Television replaced radio as the predominant and most effective mode of mass communication. The professional *regionais,* which had been indispensable in the past as accompanists and studio musicians for live shows, were displaced by prerecorded radio shows and music, and many groups were completely eclipsed by the excitement caused by the advent of television. Nevertheless, the period was a fertile one for the development of instrumental virtuosi, especially on instruments that had previously played minimal roles in choro, namely the bandolim and the cavaquinho. In chapter 6 we also consider the lives and works of influential musicians such as guitarist Garoto, bandolinist Jacó do Bandolim, cavaquinho soloist and virtuoso Waldir de Azevedo, and flautist Altamiro Carrilho. Not only did these musicians take their instruments to new levels of mastery, they also composed new repertoires to show off the capabilities of their instruments.

The advent of new, foreign popular musics, such as rock and roll, and the decline of live radio as an important aspect of popular culture was accompanied by a concern among many educated Brazilians that choro was quickly disappearing from the musical soundscape. Choro was framed as an important part of Brazilian heritage, important as much for its historical significance as for its use in repelling foreign cultural domination. Choro musician Jacó do Bandolim and radio announcer and personality Almirante played important roles as tireless advocates of the choro genre. For the majority of Brazilians in the 1950s, however, choro was music of the past, as irrelevant to the glorious future just around the corner for Brazil as a mule-drawn cart in the middle of a new gleaming superhighway. What had been declared during the Vargas years as national culture was now seen as irrevocably and hopelessly backward. Brazil in the 1950s had its eye firmly on the future, and choro and samba were both considered to be music of the old inferior Brazil.

The national mood changed drastically when the heavy borrowing upon which the grandiose national infrastructure projects in the 1950s were based propitiated an economic disaster. In 1964, Brazil's fragile democracy, which had lasted less than a decade, collapsed, and a series of military generals ruled the country for the next twenty-one years. Protests and general unrest characterized the mood of the nation in the 1960s and early 1970s. By the mid-1970s, the brutally repressive tactics of the regime had created a general climate of paralyzing fear. Realizing that its grip on the people was a tenuous one, the regime was very concerned at this time with building support among the middle class. Their support of choro, long considered a middle-class music, was an important part of this effort. In chapter 7, we examine the broad-based movement in the 1970s, centered in Rio de Janeiro, to revive choro. With support from above, the revival quickly began to pick up momentum, and soon choro clubs arose in practically every state in the nation. Once the general public began to take an interest in choro, the debate on whether choro should be "modernized" began to surface. At issue was the belief shared by many musicians and critics that "traditional" choro represented cultural stagnation; in order for Brazil to be a First World modern nation, it needed to produce "modern" music along the lines of American and British rock and American jazz. Finally, in the mid-1980s, Brazil returned to democracy. Unfortunately, the economic decline that had begun in the 1950s took a strong turn for the worse. Government funding for choro dried up completely, and it seemed that choro might slip into obscurity once again. Nevertheless, the large number of young musicians who participated in the revival kept the tradition alive, and by the 1990s, choro was again firmly established in the Brazilian soundscape. In chapter 8, we provide an ethnography of choro in Rio de Janeiro from the mid-1990s to the present day (2004) based on the direct experiences of the authors as well as a consideration of choro and its influences on musicians in the United States and elsewhere. An important facet of choro of the 1990s and later is its dissemination through the World Wide Web and websites such as that of the Agenda do Samba e Choro. We also consider

American musicians, such as mandolinist Mike Marshall and Cliff Korman, who champion the cause of choro to an English-speaking audience.

In chapter 9, we consider the impact of choro on Brazilian composers within the Western art-music idiom. In Brazil, divisions between "high" and "low" culture have never been as strongly demarcated as in Europe or the United States. As a result, the interchange between popular and erudite music has been constant and mutual. Since the late nineteenth century, Brazilian composers have consistently incorporated elements of popular and folk musics into their music. Many composers were choro musicians themselves or had firsthand experience with the music. Heitor Villa-Lobos is one such example, having been a guitarist who frequented certain rodas de choro. It is not surprising that Villa-Lobos incorporated a variety of influences from the choro tradition in his compositions. In this chapter, we consider the influence of choro on past and present Brazilian composers, including Villa-Lobos, Mignone, Guarnieri, Gnattali, and Tacuchian.

A Note on Source Materials

The material presented in this study is based on a variety of sources and types of data. Both authors have conducted extensive and numerous formal and informal interviews with musicians, fans, composers, and others involved in choro. Livingston-Isenhour recorded more than thirty-four hours of live choro music at shows, rehearsals, and rodas. Garcia was a participant-observer in numerous rodas de choro. Both authors spent a great deal of time in archival repositories in Rio de Janeiro, including the Biblioteca Nacional, the Museu Villa-Lobos, the Museu Edison Carneiro, and the Museu da Imagem e do Som. These findings were supplemented by holdings in private archives, including the collections of Marco de Pinna, Olga Prauger de Coelho, Dolores Tomé of Brasília, and the archives of the Clube do Choro in the home of the late Dr. Assis in Brasília.

Race, Class, and Nineteenth-Century Popular Music

The Modinha, the Lundu, and the Maxixe

The emergence and development of choro in the late nineteenth century was affected by three forms of Brazilian popular music, each of which influenced choro in terms of style, practice, and social meaning: the *modinha,* the *lundu,* and the *maxixe.* The modinha is a lyrical song style that originated in the salon but became popular among wandering serenaders accompanying themselves on guitar. The lundu, an early song and dance genre, and the maxixe, an instrumental dance form that arose concurrently with choro, exhibit African influences and were cultivated among slaves, freed slaves, immigrants, and lower-class mulattos (of mixed African and European blood). The wildly popular maxixe made an especially strong impression on polite society, with its close couples dance style and sinuous movements of the hips and lower body. These three genres were critical not only to the stylistic development of choro but also to its social positioning and meanings in the years after its emergence first as a style then as a genre.

Any consideration of early Brazilian popular music must take into account the economic and social context of nineteenth-century Brazil, including racial discourse before and after slavery. The formulation of a national identity based on concepts of racial blending, or miscegenation, was one of the most important and influential intellectual currents to develop in postcolonial Brazil. By the 1930s, choro was upheld by intellectuals as the perfect example of musical miscegenation, in which the European sensibilities of the modinha were combined with the African rhythmic vitality of the lundu and maxixe. Before this time, the lundu and the maxixe had already been the subject of discussions about race and Brazilian identity, and the popularization of the once-elite salon modinha had served as a site for the negotiation of social class.

While European traditions dominated nineteenth-century classical and popular music in terms of harmonic vocabulary, melodic style, forms, and musical instruments, African musical traditions lent the single most important factor in the development of a distinctly Brazilian music: rhythmic complexity. Strong African influence is evident in many other aspects of Brazilian culture, such as dance, language, cuisine, and religious beliefs. Indeed, the entire economy of Brazil, from its founding as a Portuguese colony in 1500 to the late nineteenth century, depended upon the importation of large numbers of slaves, primarily from four regions of Africa: Mozambique, Angola, the Congo area, and the Gold Coast (Nigeria/Benin). Although the slave population represented numerous language groups and tribal associations, their musical practices tended to share a rhythmic complexity that was absorbed and blended into Brazilian popular music. The degree of blending over time is such that it is difficult to identify with certainty specific African sources for many of these musics, although many scholars have devoted their research to this subject.[1]

The Portuguese claimed a vast territory when they established the new colony of Brazil. Much of the interior was inaccessible, and early settlements arose in close proximity to the coast. The inhabited portion of the colony was a thin line on the more than 4,600 miles of coastline. The earliest attempts at large-scale agricultural plantations were made in the northeast of Brazil, but Portuguese settlers found it difficult to deal with the harsh tropical climate. At first they used the native population as a source of impressed labor, but the indigenous peoples did not respond well to captivity and many fled deep into the interior to escape oppression. Portugal had long before established trading posts in Africa, and the proximity of Brazil to the West African coasts made the importation of African slaves a practical and economical solution to the labor problem. Brazil surpassed all other New World colonies in the sheer number of African slaves imported. By conservative estimates, a total of almost 3.5 million slaves were brought to Brazil, compared to the 250,000 brought to the United States, and the number of Africans in Brazil even surpassed the number of indigenous peoples living in the territory before colonization.[2] By the late 1810s, slaves constituted as much as 30 percent of the Brazilian population.[3]

The degree and strength of African traits apparent in much of Brazilian culture today is an artifact of the way slaves were treated in Brazil. Slave families were often kept intact, and tribal groups were maintained, allowing Africans to retain some aspects of their former identity. Perhaps most importantly, slaves were permitted to speak in their native languages, a factor which allowed a great many aspects of their cultures to survive. As a result, Nagô, a Yoruban-based language, is still used today in Bahia in liturgical and ritual settings, and Kimbundu (a Bantu language of northern Angola) survives in daily use, albeit in creolized form. Although Catholicism was mandated, slaves managed to maintain their native religions by superimposing the names of Catholic saints on African deities, which eventually resulted in the creation of entirely new African-derived religions, of which *candomblé* is the most important. In this system, Xangô (pronounced "Shango"), the god of lightning and storms, was identified with St. Michael or St. Jerome (depending on the region of Brazil). Although the importation of slaves was officially abolished in 1850, children born of slave mothers were not considered free until the Law of the Free Womb of 1871. Finally, in 1888, the Golden Law freed all slaves in Brazil, thus ending almost four centuries of slavery.

Miscegenation and National Identity

With the creation of the new independent nation of Brazil in 1822, intellectuals, writers, and artists took upon themselves the task of fashioning a unified, distinct Brazilian cultural identity from the disparate factions left over from colonialism. They turned to the idea of miscegenation, or the blending of the African, European, and Indian races as it was occurring in Brazil, as the factor that distinguished Brazilians from all other nationalities. Even though the idea of miscegenation seemed to be a great equalizing force, strong racist notions were at its heart. Miscegenation was understood not only as a process by which all the different races would be joined together but also as a means of tempering and eventually eradicating the undesirable races with the influence of white European blood. The process was known as *branqueamento,* literally, "whitening." During the course of the nineteenth century, the contradictions between race, ethnicity, class, and national identity that were inherent in miscegenation were played out in reactions toward popular music, specifically the modinha, the lundu, and the maxixe.

Miscegenation was both a natural response to conditions in colonial Brazil and a process that was encouraged by governing authorities. During the first century of colonization, few women emigrated from Portugal to Brazil. The colonial government, anxious to ensure steady population growth in the colonies, came to recognize a kind of common-law marriage between white men and black women called *mancebia* (the term is also translated as "concubinage"), and even the Church sanctioned mixed-race marriages. In the northeast state of Bahia, where the scarcity of white (or near-white) women was pronounced, extramarital sexual contact between the races was common. Many of these developed into semipermanent unions outside of marriage that resulted in a great number of offspring of mixed blood. In 1819, there were almost as many people of mixed blood in Brazil as there were whites.[4] By the turn of the twentieth century, Rio de Janeiro had approximately 600,000 inhabitants, of whom 30 percent were black, 30 percent were mulatto, and 40 percent were white.[5] In the north and northeast, some Europeans had conjugal relations with the indigenous populations, resulting in mixed-bloods known as *caboclos*. The number of caboclos, however, was small compared to the number of mulattos. Indeed, few Brazilians before the great immigration from Europe of the nineteenth and early twentieth centuries could claim a total lack of African blood, and at least 75 percent of Brazil's current population has some black ancestry.[6]

As a distinguishing feature of Brazilian society, miscegenation was considered by many to be the cornerstone of a unique identity.[7] Nevertheless, some members of the intellectual elite strongly resisted the idea; they were not convinced that miscegenation would produce an essentially "white" race. They believed in notions of racial superiority advanced in European works and readily adopted theories set forth in works such as Arthur Comte de Gobineau's sociological treatise *Essai sur l'inegalité des races humaines*[8] and Georges Vacher's *L'aryen, son rôle social*.[9] Not long after these works appeared, Brazilian intellectuals produced their own derivative works, such as Manoel Bonfim's 1903 essay "O Parasitismo Social e Evolução" in *A America Latina*,[10] in which the author argues that Latin America is racially inferior to Europe and the United States. Graça Aranha's novel *Canaã*[11] which was published in 1901, is premised on the inherent inferiority of people of mixed blood, and Oliveira Viana's sociological work *Populações meridionais do Brasil*[12] accepts and supports the idea of the superiority of whites. Many blamed the country's lack of progress not on the folly of the government or the instability of the single-crop economic system (based first on sugar and later on coffee) but rather on the racial mix of the nation. Vianna Moog, one of Brazil's foremost sociologists, notes that the pervasiveness of these theories lies not in their rationalization but in deep-seated prejudice:

> In order to believe in the doctrine, or rather, in the myth of racial superiority and inferiority, no proof was required, whether biological, sociological, anthropological, or historical. Everything was taken for granted. For some time there was the theory that the reason the United States, despite being settled later than Brazil, progressed farther and faster was because Anglo-Saxon society remained relatively pure racially, and the Portuguese, having taken interracial mixing to the extreme, caused slower development due to the inferiority of the mixed races. This theory was widely accepted in Brazil as well as Europe and the United States. Even government documents claimed that Brazil could not compete with the United States because it did not possess the "superior aptitudes of that race."[13]

Although miscegenation was considered by some to be the immediate cause of Brazil's woes, others believed it held the future key to the eventual resolution of the "race question." According to the theory of branqueamento, the process of miscegenation carried out over the years would naturally culminate in the creation of a unique light-skinned race, and the Indian and the Black would cease to exist as racial groups in Brazil. The logic of this argument rests in social Darwinism: Because the indigenous and African races were genetically weak and inferior, the dominant white race, with its civilizing influences, would eventually prevail. As proof, the rapid decline in indigenous populations and the perceived drop in birth rates of African slaves were produced as "scientific evidence" that the Aryan race was stronger. In order to hasten the branqueamento process, European immigration was actively encouraged by the government in the late nineteenth and early twentieth centuries. Immigrant labor forces were badly needed to replace slave workers, and the addition of European heritage to the gene pool was considered an additional benefit. By the 1880s, the theory of branqueamento was noted and approved by Europeans and Americans, a fact that legitimated it beyond doubt among the Brazilian elite. An example of the high profile given to foreign perceptions of Brazil is a statement Theodore Roosevelt made after a trip to Brazil, which was translated into Portuguese and boldly printed on the front page of the prestigious Rio de Janeiro newspaper *Correio da Manhã* in 1914:

> In Brazil . . . the idea looked forward to is the disappearance of the Negro question through the disappearance of the Negro himself—that is, through his gradual absorption into the white race. This does not mean that Brazilians are or will become the "mongrel" people that they have been asserted to be by certain French, English and American writers. The Brazilians are a white people, belonging to the Mediterranean race, and differing from the northern stocks only as such great and civilized old races as the Spaniards and Italians, with their splendid historic past, differ from these northern stocks. The evident Indian admixture has added a good, and not a bad, element. The very large European immigration of itself tends, decade by decade, to make the Negro blood a smaller element of the blood of the whole community. The Brazilian of the future will be in blood more European than in the past, and he will differ in culture only as the American of the North differs.[14]

Despite the lack of scientific evidence to support it, the theory of branqueamento did much to assuage the fears of white elites and intellectuals about the future of Brazil. As paradoxical as it may seem, they approved of the idea of miscegenation even as they practiced racism. In this way, elites and intellectuals began to construct a national sentiment on the notion of a future ideal society in which racial divisions would be nonexistent. Many Brazilians even today refuse to admit that racism exists in Brazilian society.[15] The reality of social segregation for blacks and dark-skinned mulattos tells a different story, however. Although race was never overtly cited as a factor, a system that tied social advance to lightness of skin, social milieu, and cultural affectations was firmly set in place, thereby institutionalizing pre-abolitionist prejudices and practices. The old saying that "money whitens" points to the Brazilian social reality that "[l]ightness of color in itself is not sufficient to place a person in the upper class, but it always improves one's position over a darker person."[16] The range of skin colors found in Brazil (from very dark to light) and the intersecting and interdependence of the concepts of race and class in Brazilian society necessitate a consideration of both race and class in discussions of musical and, hence, social phenomena. It is important to contextualize the rise of popular musics among the nascent middle class of nineteenth-century Brazilian society within this framework.

Popular Music, Race, and Class

The attitudes of the elite concerning race and class were most evident in their reactions to popular music. Even well into the twentieth century, popular music associated with African or Afro-Brazilian culture was denigrated not just as "black" music but also as low-class music. In practice, however, men and women of the lower and middle classes, regardless of color, participated in and aided the development of African-influenced popular music and dance throughout the nineteenth century and earlier. The strength of popular culture that emanated from the urban middle classes was such that it propelled Brazil's most famous African-influenced popular music of all, samba, to the status of national icon in the 1920s and 1930s. In the eyes of intellectuals and the government, samba was a prime example of the racial harmony produced by years of miscegenation.

The gradual acceptance of miscegenation as the basis for national identity had a strong effect on the social perception of choro as well: As a balanced combination of European harmonies and melodies with African rhythms, it represented the perfect harmonious blending of the races to many Brazilians. The use of popular music as a site for the negotiation of national identity actually began much earlier than the advent of choro in the late nineteenth century and samba in the early twentieth century. The complex relationship between race and class is evident in the practices and elite perceptions of three Brazilian popular music genres: the modinha, the lundu, and the maxixe. These musics had a strong influence on choro style and practice, and their role in the discourse of national identity set the stage for the professionalization of choro in the 1920s and 1930s.

The Modinha and the Seresta

Among the musical antecedents of choro is the lyrical sentimental song genre called modinha. Musicologist Gérard Béhague believes that the modinha and another early song genre, the lundu, are the foundation upon which a large part of subsequent Brazilian popular music was built.[17] It was first cultivated in the early part of the eighteenth century, and although the genre crossed the Atlantic several times and was popular in both Portugal and Brazil, Brazilian musicologists often cite it as the earliest distinctly Brazilian genre. The word "modinha" is the diminutive of the Portuguese "*moda,*" literally meaning song or melody. In Portugal, the moda was generally associated with art song, which was popular at various times among all social classes. The modinha developed in colonial Brazil and was distinguished from its Portuguese antecedent by the use of the guitar rather than keyboard as an accompanying instrument. The Brazilian form was taken to Portugal in 1775, when the Brazilian mulatto singer Domingos Caldas Barbosa presented himself at the court performing modinhas, to the delight of the ladies.[18] These songs were tremendously successful first in Brazil and later in Portugal, where they were published in the *Jornal de Modinhas* in Lisbon from 1792 to 1795.[19] In the late eighteenth and early nineteenth centuries, Portuguese composers wrote modinhas in great numbers to entertain the court and please cosmopolitan Lisbonites. The *modinha de salão,* or salon modinha, was distinguished by a structure more rigid than the Brazilian variant. When the Portuguese king Dom João VI went into exile to Brazil with his court in 1808, he took the salon modinha with him.

Two basic types of modinhas developed in nineteenth-century Brazil: One was characterized by simple sentimental melodies and was preferred by serenaders and street singers of the lower classes, and the other exhibited elaborate melodies resembling Italian opera arias and was sung in upper-class salons. Both types in Brazil had a quality of improvisation and spontaneity in musical and poetic structure, but over time the simpler type began to predominate. Modinhas tended to be based on uncomplicated sectional forms such as ternary (ABA), rondo (ABACA), and strophic (verse and refrain). Although modinhas with syncopated melodies existed both in Portugal and Brazil, the syncopation was of Moorish rather than sub-Saharan African influence.[20] As a result, the syncopation is subtle and is quite distinct from the West African and African diaspora varieties.

Composers embraced the two modinha styles, and some produced works in both. Early-nineteenth-century pieces, which were composed before the great immigration from Italy later in the century,[21] tended to be uncomplicated. One of the most popular composers of modinhas was Padre José Mauricio Nunes Garcia (1767–1830), a mulatto priest whose music was popular in the Portuguese court in exile in Rio de Janeiro between 1808 and 1822.

Throughout the nineteenth century, the salon modinha was influenced by European art song. The influence of Italian opera arias was especially strong toward the latter half of the century, when Brazil experienced a flood of migrants from Italy. Although elites looked toward France for language, fashion, and literature, they looked to Italy for opera, which they considered to be the most highly developed European musical art form. Italian arias were an essential part of the salon; they were learned and sung by "ladies of society," and even slave and free black musicians were com-

Example 2.1. "Beijo a mão," by José Mauricio Nunes Garcia, a simple-style sentimental modinha. Arrangement by Thomas Garcia.

pelled to learn Italian arias and songs. Additionally, Brazilian classical musicians frequently went to Italy to complete their studies. Modinha lyrics were often written by the leading literary figures of Rio de Janeiro, and some of the best-known Brazilian classical composers took up the elevated modinha form, including Januário da Silva Arvellos,[22] Nunes Garcia, Henrique Alves de Mesquita, Francisco Antônio de Carvalho, Francisco José Martins, and João Francisco Leal.

The upper classes preferred the piano to the guitar to accompany the modinha, but the accompaniment style remained essentially guitaristic, and the vast majority of the modinhas published in nineteenth-century Brazil could be accompanied by either guitar or piano. Publishing companies marketed the genre to different audiences: Modinhas with piano accompaniments were intended for upper-class markets, while the popular genre—the *modinha da rua,* the songs of the lower classes accompanied by *viola* (folk guitar)—continued to be cultivated anonymously by street singers and musicians.

Example 2.2. "Vive amor dentro em meu peito," a modinha in the elaborate, Italian aria style.

Despite the efforts of publishing companies, the salon modinha began to wane in popularity by the end of the Second Empire and the declaration of the republic in 1889.[23] It was impossible for the upper classes to disassociate the modinha from its common poorer cousin, and they eventually abandoned it for other, more fashionable genres of salon music. For the lower classes, however, the modinha had become a permanent part of the repertoire of popular musicians and singers, always accompanied by the guitar. So little music of the common people was ever published (with the rare exception of songs occasionally published with lyrics and harmonies in chord symbols) that the repertory of these colonial and imperial *sereteiros,* or serenaders, is for the most part lost. Those songs that did survive were preserved in oral transmission by sereteiros, who were also closely connected to the early choro tradition.

Although it continued to be performed by lower classes until the end of the nineteenth century, other genres—most notably choro, lundu, maxixe, and (later) samba, all of which have African-based rhythms—supplanted the modinha in popularity. In the early twentieth century, however, there was a small but important movement led by choro guitarist João Pernambuco (1883–1947, discussed in further detail in chapter 5) and Catulo de Paixão Cearense (1866–1936) to "reform" and restore the modinha to its former state. Catulo was a singer and poet who set new lyrics to modinhas and choros by well-known composers such as Ernesto Nazaré and Anacleto de Medeiros. The result was the creation of a body of modinhas with some of the rhythmic complexity of choro; indeed, many of these "reformed" modinhas were in fact simply choros with added lyrics. Tinhorão suggests that by Catulo's time, the popular modinha was perceived as "folkloric" by the upper classes but was essentially irrelevant to their cosmopolitan tastes:

> What Catulo called the "reform of the modinha" was not actually reform, but rather its adaptation to the tastes of nationalistic exoticism, which the salon public began to cultivate from the first decade of the twentieth century, within an attitude that made the folkloric fashionable. It was, however, with the common people that the modinha lived in the beginning of the century its last great moment as a genre of popular song, sung to the light of the moon in serenades in the small cities of the interior, in the poorer neighborhoods, and [in] the suburbs [that were] a distance from the great centers.[24]

Catulo performed his reformed modinhas with the best and most famous chorões of the day, including guitarist and composer João Pernambuco, flautist Patápio Silva, guitarist Quincas Laranjeiras, guitarist and composer Sátiro Bilhar, and composer Heitor Villa-Lobos.[25] Catulo was also a part of the Velha Guarda (the Old Guard)[26] and was perhaps best known for his work with Bilhar, a guitarist and modinha composer. The reform movement Catulo and Pernambuco led did succeed in reviving the modinha for a time, although it never achieved the degree of popularity it had held during the colonial and imperial phases of Brazilian history. Nevertheless, Catulo's efforts ensured that the modinha would leave an indelible mark on choro style and repertoire by merging the two genres.

The modinha was also an important antecedent to choro in terms of instrumentation. The flute and guitar were regularly used to play popular modinhas in the latter part of the nineteenth century. Along with the cavaquinho, these instruments came to be played in accompanying ensembles called terno (trio) or *pau e corda* (literally wood and string, referring to the combination of wooden flutes and plucked string instruments, which were the basis of the early choro ensembles). Besides being played by serenaders, modinhas were often performed by groups of choro musicians, who had developed their own performance practice that included some use of African-derived rhythms. In the beginning of the twentieth century, the modinha returned again to the salon, this time carrying with it stylistic modifications influenced by choro, when it came to be known as *canção,* or song.

In his 1936 book of remembrances of popular musicians of the past, Alexandre

Gonçalves Pinto includes forty-one chorões who were also noted singers of modin- has.[27] A few were known for their voices, and their participation in the choro social circle was based on their ability to sing, not their instrumental prowess. Some are described as having a "voice of gold"; others are praised solely for their social qualities. Many choro guitarists were known for their ability to accompany modin- has, illustrating the close link between the traditions. In these contexts, the only discernible difference between choro and modinha was the vocal part; the har- monic language and musical style were often identical.

The *seresta* is part of the modinha tradition, and the differences between these genres are hard to define. In many cases a distinction was drawn according to perfor- mance location: the modinha was performed indoors and the seresta was done al fresco. Art music composers tend to use the appellations modinha and seresta inter- changeably. An excellent example is Villa-Lobos's "Seresta No. 5" for soprano and guitar, subtitled "Modinha." Whether one was considered a seresteiro or a chorão depended on one's talents (instrumental or vocal) and the occasion (serenading, per- forming for a festival, or playing for fun in a roda).[28] At the turn of the century, choro, seresta, and modinha, all of which used the same instrumental core, were closely re- lated; the same musicians played all three genres, at times interchangeably.

The fact that the upper classes rejected the modinha after it was taken up by seresteiros is not surprising, given the seriousness with which the upper class ac- tively tried to maintain its distance from the lower classes. Racism and prejudice were strong factors in the disdain for the popular; magazines and popular literature of the day are filled with racist caricatures of both blacks and lower-class European immigrants. Nineteenth-century popular music, including the maxixe, the choro, the *corta-jaca* dance, and the popular *pianeiros,* or piano players who performed in movie theaters and music stores, were all seen as manifestations of low culture and thus not worthy of the attention of the elite.

Brazilian popular music owes a great debt to the modinha. Its lyricism influ- enced instrumental and song genres such as choro, lundu, seresta, and canção, and the image of the seresteiro singing popular songs in the moonlight accompanied by guitar is indelibly inscribed on the Brazilian romantic imagination. The modinha has the distinction of being the only popular Brazilian music that originated as a salon genre, which is to say the only popular genre that did not develop from popular or folk idioms. Although it has disappeared as a distinct genre, it lives on in the senti- mental and lyrical melodies of certain choros and popular songs.

The Lundu

The lundu arose in the early eighteenth century from the music of Bantu slaves. As it developed in Brazil, it became the earliest Brazilian popular music genre to combine African rhythm with European harmony, melody, and instrumentation. Over time, the appellation "lundu" was used to indicate three separate phenomena: the dance, the song, and the instrumental genre. As was the case with the modinha, the vocal lundu took on two forms: one popular among the lower classes and the other suitable for the salon. Most often, a melodic instrument such as flute was accompanied by guitar; this form was a precursor to later African-influenced popular genres, including the maxixe and the choro.

The lundu dance shares its roots with samba; in its earliest form it was a dance accompanied exclusively by drums and voices. It was a courtship dance involving a man and a woman, with movements suggesting advance and retreat. From its beginnings, it exhibited syncretic elements, including stamping and snapping the fingers above the head, gestures common in the Spanish-influenced fandango.[29] Accounts by foreigners traveling in Brazil in the nineteenth century describe the dance as "lascivious," citing undulating body movements and "sexually suggestive" gestures, such as the *umbigada,* or the touching of one dancer's navel to another's.[30] The lundu quickly spread among poor whites, mulattos, and immigrants in Salvador and Rio de Janeiro, and foreign visitors in the early nineteenth century often noted its popularity. The longevity of the lundu dance is striking; throughout the nineteenth and into the twentieth century, long after the vocal and instrumental forms had disappeared, blacks and mulattos continued to cultivate it.[31]

Vocal lundus began to be published as sheet music in the late eighteenth and early nineteenth centuries. It is unlikely that the lyrics of these songs, which were intended to be consumed by the upper classes, had much to do with the songs that originally accompanied the dance.[32] Instead, lyrics were sentimental or nostalgic in character, similar to the modinha. The vocal lundu shared many stylistic characteristics with the modinha, including the use of syncopation, shifts between the major and minor modes, and use of a flattened leading tone. Unlike the modinha, however, the lundu from its inception had a strong African rhythmic element. Musicologist Mozart de Araújo notes the musical similarities between the salon lundu and the modinha and their different social origins and associations:

> Born into opposite cribs—she [modinha], a white child of the court and he [lundu], a black street urchin. Despite this social antagonism concerning their origin, they present connections which are so intimate within Brazilian society that in certain moments and principally in the last decade of the seventeen hundreds, it was possible to encounter modas or modinhas which were almost lundus, and lundus that were almost modinhas.[33]

Domingos Caldas Barbosa—the Brazilian mulatto singer who introduced the modinha to the court at Lisbon in the late 1770s—was known for singing the *lundu-canção,* or lundu song, and was responsible for introducing this popular song style to the concert stage. The exotic origins of the lundu song interested com-

Figure 2.1. Sketch of the lundu dance, circa 1840.

posers and theater musicians, and by the 1820s it had become popular in the theaters of Rio de Janeiro. According to Tinhorão:

> Thus, when the new variant of black-white acculturation in the field of *batucada* dances [African-influenced rhythmic dances] became popular with the name *lundu,* the authors of *entremezes* (intermezzi) had no doubt about taking it to the stage, which caused a scandal in a minority of the white public.[34]

Throughout the early part of the nineteenth century, the sung lundu with piano accompaniment enjoyed increasing popularity among the upper classes. Its popularity reached Portugal, where it became a respected salon genre known as the *doce lundu chorado*. By the late nineteenth century, there was little to differentiate the modinha and the lundu as salon genres: In the course of their mutual development, the lundu had lost rhythmic complexity and the two genres had moved stylistically closer (see Figure 2.2). The acceptance of the lundu by the upper classes was an important step in the assimilation of black music into colonial and imperial society.

In addition to the dance and song forms, an instrumental form of lundu was popular in the late nineteenth century. It was most often a rendition of a popular lundu song with the melody played by a flute or clarinet accompanied by the small five-course guitar called the *viola* and later by the larger six-string *violão*. Although it did not demonstrate the melodic tendencies of a true instrumental genre, the instrumental lundu was a precursor of other representative popular genres of the twentieth century, such as the maxixe and the choro.

The Maxixe

The Maxixe

The Brazilian maxixe
Is a mischievous dance,
Full of twists and turns,
In which the mulatta is clever and shameless
And the man never stops moving!
In which everything moves
From here to there
And the one who moves the most
Is the most pleasing.
It's not just moving the legs,
But the rest of the body as well.[35]

From its emergence in the late 1870s to its decline in the 1920s, few genres of popular music were as wildly popular, and as controversial, as the maxixe, a fast-paced couples dance in which the dancers' bodies are pressed together and the legs are often intertwined, similar to the contemporary lambada. Some believe the maxixe to be the link in the stylistic continuum between the old lundu dance and the modern urban samba.[36] Indeed, for many years it was a mainstay of Carnaval celebrations and was danced in Carnaval clubs throughout the city of Rio de Janeiro until it was supplanted permanently by the samba. The maxixe was even taken to Paris, where it became one of the first forms of Brazilian popular music to be legitimized abroad. Although its popularity was fairly short lived compared to that of the modinha and the lundu, Tinhorão argues that it was the first great contribution of the lower classes of Rio de Janeiro to the popular musics of Brazil.[37]

The etymology of the word "maxixe" to refer to the dance is uncertain. Ac-

Figure 2.2. *Esta noite, a lundu de salão,* by J. F. Leal. From *Coleção de modinhas de bom gosto compostas, e arranjadas para piano-forte* (Vienna: J. Kress, 1830).

32 cording to one popular belief, a certain Carnaval-group dancer is said to have invented a new dance by adding quick improvised steps and lundu-like movements to the polka. Whenever he danced, the musicians played the polka at a faster tempo to accommodate his fancy new steps. The dancer went by the name "Maxixe," a bitter fruit popular in many Brazilian dishes of African origin. Another commonly held belief is that the name comes not from the dancer but from the nature of the dance itself, in which the male is clearly the dominant partner. From *dança do macho* comes *machice* or *machiche*, which over time adopted the orthography of the fruit.[38]

The habanera rhythm is a characteristic feature which the maxixe shares with other Latin American dances, such as the Argentine *tango* and *milonga*. The Afro-Cuban habanera was popular in nineteenth-century Brazil and directly influenced the development of the maxixe.[39] The other important precursor to the maxixe was the polka. It arrived in Rio de Janeiro in the 1840s and quickly became popular among all social classes. Historic accounts indicate that when danced by the lower strata of Brazilian society, the polka involved a tightly embracing couple with exaggerated movements of both legs and torso. Tinhorão believes that the maxixe was born as chorões who accompanied the dance naturally adapted the rhythms of the polka to include the Afro-Brazilian rhythm to better support the movements of the dancers (Example 2.3).[40]

Example 2.3. Afro-Brazilian rhythm.

The adoption and adaptation of the polka in Brazil has parallels throughout the New World that led to the development of the *danzón* in Cuba, the *beguine* in Martinique, and ragtime in the United States. These dances involved stylistic fusions of the European polka and various African music and dance traits. In Brazil, this fusion was evident in the choreography as well as the music. The maxixe is the first of many stylistic adaptations of the Brazilian polka. It was "[the] Brazilian dance that utilized fully the Negro element of the batuque, incorporating it into the Hispanic-American (habanera) and European (polka) stylizations."[41] As European music was played by ear according to local tastes, it developed into new forms such as the polka-lundu, the maxixe, and finally the choro.

Structurally, the maxixe is similar to the polka. Melodic lines tend to be built on eight-bar phrases within a rondo form, typically ABACA. Arthur Ramos correctly states that the maxixe was not a specific form but rather a style of playing sectional dance forms.[42] The maxixe is distinguished from the polka by its rhythm and fast tempo. Since it is instrumental in nature, melodies often exhibit fast runs and arpeg-

CHORO

gios; sixteenth notes are the most common note value for the melody (in 2/4 time). A strong bass line on the beat and syncopation in the accompaniment is typical.

Few popular dances caused as much moral outrage among the self-proclaimed guardians of culture as the maxixe. Shortly after it took the dance clubs of Rio de Janeiro by storm, it was publicly condemned as a lower-class, vulgar, and lascivious dance that took place in halls frequented by loose women and unscrupulous men. These impressions were shared among members of the press: The very first printed reference to the maxixe dance, which occurred in a *cariocan* newspaper in 1881, defined the word "maxixe" as slang that was synonymous with *forrobodó* (another Afro-Brazilian popular dance; slang for "confusion") and *chinfrim* ("confusion," "vulgar").[43] The maxixe and other genres exhibiting overt African rhythmic influences[44] were seen as the reason for the moral decline of Brazilian society that moved it away from genteel European models into decadence (see Figure 2.4).

Undoubtedly, an aspect that incited public outrage over the maxixe dance was the way the male dancer held his partner, often with his hand on her buttocks. As shown in the engravings below, the male dancer held the female very tightly against his body, cheek to cheek or with foreheads pressed together, as they engaged in very fast, sometimes interlocking footwork. The sensuous movements included a rippling movement of the hips. Even more disturbing to the upper class

Figure 2.3. Two sketches of the maxixe dance. Note the hand position of the male dancer in both sketches.

Figure 2.4. Illustration relating class behavior with the maxixe and other popular dances. The left panels shows partner dances in polite society, which contrast sharply with partner dances among the lower classes, shown in the right panels. The left panels depict a delicate invitation, polite behavior after the dance, and sophisticated dancing to refined music. The right panels depict calling a partner by saying "psst," impolite behavior before and after dancing, and lascivious dancing to African music. Note the instruments and household items used in lower-class parties to play along with the music. From Raúl Pederneiras, *Scenas da vida carioca* (Rio de Janeiro: Jornal do Brasil, 1924).

O Marechal Hermes expulsando o maxixe das bandas militares!

Figure 2.5. Caricature of the minister of war banning the maxixe.
Shown in the lower left is the maxixe fruit, dejected by its banishment.
From *Fon-Fon* 1:25 (September 28, 1907).

was the fact that young white women could and did dance the maxixe with black partners (see Figure 2.3). Periodically members of cultured society became so morally outraged by the maxixe that they insisted the police close down the dance halls where it was practiced. In 1907, the minister of war even banned the maxixe from performance by military bands because of the "character" it encouraged.

Despite the attitudes of the elite, or perhaps in part because of its notoriety, the dance was quickly adopted by instrumental ensembles of the day. The improvisation that characterized the original maxixe style gave way to stylized forms of the dance and music as it was assimilated by the middle class and high society. One such stylized form was the *maxixe de salão*, a more restrained version of the dance than the one practiced in the dance halls and bars. In 1895, the maxixe attained a degree of social respectability with the opening of an operetta called *Zizinha maxixe* that included popular maxixes with added lyrics. Unlike the lundu song, vocal maxixes were just a novelty; they were little more than lyrics set to standard popular-dance tunes. *Zizinha maxixe* also featured twenty-three pieces by the female composer Chiquinha Gonzaga,[45] including "Corta-jaca" (also known as "O gaúcho"), a piece that quickly became part of the standard choro repertoire.[46] By 1901, the maxixe had gained enough respect to support the publication of a newspaper in Rio de Janeiro called *O Maxixe*,[47] and in 1906, a theatrical revue called *O Maxixe* opened at the prestigious Teatro Carlos Gomes.[48]

At the time of the maxixe's greatest popularity, French culture dominated artistic and intellectual thought in Brazil. It was not uncommon for Brazilians of sufficient means to go France for their education, and just as Brazilians eagerly adopted French culture, Parisians eagerly embraced Brazilian culture. The maxixe was quickly adopted in Paris for its exoticism and sensuality. Known as the *matchitche,* the dance spawned derivatives including the Apaché (Apache dance), named after the American Indian tribe because it suggested savagery, which remained popular in Parisian bohemian society for some time. Once established in Paris, this dance and other cultural forms entered the international cosmopolitan arena, appearing in vaudeville acts, films, and later on television.[49]

Although the maxixe dance was eventually accepted in the salon (albeit in a somewhat tamed version) and became popular in theater productions, the term "maxixe" was avoided in that milieu. Instead, the more acceptable euphemism "*tango*" or "*tango brasileiro*" was often used in its place. By the 1910s, however, the terms "maxixe" and "tango" were used interchangeably. These genres shared certain stylistic features, but social considerations most affected the choice of terminology, especially in published versions of the music. Composers and publishers also resorted to other labels, fearing a harmful effect on sales of their music to the upper classes should they use the term "maxixe." The pianist and composer Ernesto Nazaré (discussed in greater detail in chapter 4) labeled many of his compositions *tango brasileiro,* but his "tangos" exhibit all the characteristics of maxixe in rhythm, melody, and tempo markings. The tempo of most Argentinean tangos is decidedly unhurried to accompany the sensual and dramatic, yet moderately paced, couples dance. In contrast, the maxixe is driven by the constant syncopated rhythmic accompaniment and is played at a pace fast enough to keep up with the quick, almost frantic pace of its footwork. Despite Nazaré's claims that his pieces were "not low-class like the maxixe," his tangos were, in reality, highly stylized and sophisticated salon versions of the same dance. Indeed, musicologist Mario de Andrade praised Nazaré for his contributions to Brazilian popular music, calling him the "heralder of the maxixe, which is to say, of the genuinely Brazilian urban dance."[50]

The practice of using different names for the same genre depending upon the audience was common in Brazil. It reflected not only fluidity in terminology but also an acute awareness of social associations and implications. Besides labeling certain choros and maxixes as *tangos brasileiros,* the samba song was often called *canção* (literally, song) in an attempt to minimize its Afro-Brazilian origins. The extent to which early musicologists went to disassociate certain popular genres from any African influence is truly astounding. A notable example is the work of musicologist Baptista Siqueira, who claimed that the samba was originally an Amerindian dance of certain native groups from the backlands of the Northeast.[51] It is unfortunate that this kind of study, which substituted the image of the "noble savage" Indian for that of the "deformed and vulgar" black man, was common in post-abolition Brazil; such work illustrates the degree to which prejudice against blacks was ingrained in white elites and intellectuals.

In the 1930s, the maxixe dance began to decline in popularity, supplanted by the urban samba and new imports such as the foxtrot and Charleston that had been introduced by American jazz bands that were becoming popular in Rio de Janeiro. The maxixe, however, remained in the choro repertory as an instrumental genre, and maxixes continue to be composed today.

In this chapter, we discussed three forms of popular music that had a strong effect on the rise and development of choro as a style and a genre. Even though they are no longer performed in their original contexts, the modinha, or seresta, and the maxixe have survived as discrete genres within the choro repertoire. The lyricism of the modinha has had a profound influence on almost every aspect of slow sentimental Brazilian song, and the practice of accompanying such songs on guitar (either the classical *violão* or the folk *viola*) remains to this day. The lundu and the maxixe contributed the characteristic syncopation and strong rhythmic drive to the choro genre, and we suggested that the maxixe might have arisen from the performance practice of choro musicians who assimilated and adapted the polka according to local taste. Long before the choro genre arose, groups of choro musicians, the "orchestras of the poor," interpreted European salon music as well as popular music of immigrants and African slaves, often blending them to such a degree that the original genres were obscured and overshadowed by new ones.

Social perceptions of the modinha, the lundu, and the maxixe were governed by mores and values of the upper classes, who sought to preserve their elevated status by overtly rejecting manifestations of popular culture. Racism and prejudice against blacks and poor white immigrants was deeply ingrained in Brazilian elites, who looked abroad to France for their cultural models. Despite these attitudes, intellectuals, critics, and artists began to feel the need to develop a Brazilian culture free from reliance on Europe. The basis for this nascent national sentiment was miscegenation, or the particular blending of African, European, and Indian races that characterized Brazilian society. The aspect that made miscegenation palatable to the otherwise racist and classist elites was the concept of branqueamento, or "whitening," which was based on the dubious theory that European blood would dilute and civilize the other races to produce a light-skinned Brazilian race. By the

1880s, branqueamento was endorsed by Brazilian intellectuals and foreigners alike, allowing miscegenation to be accepted on a broad scale as a basis for a distinct national identity. As we shall see in upcoming chapters, the changing tide in intellectual thought had a profound impact on choro, facilitating the formation of professional choro ensembles as cultural ambassadors of Brazil.

Although we have emphasized the negative reactions of elites to popular musics of the nineteenth century and earlier, the lines between popular culture and high culture were often ambiguous and fluid, allowing for a high degree of exchange. The development of an urban middle class and the rise of choro groups adept at performing in a variety of social contexts in a variety of styles encouraged this exchange. Even earlier, elite versions of the modinha and the lundu allowed these genres to flourish in the salon as songs accompanied by piano, and even the infamous maxixe was made suitable for the salon under the guise of *tango brasileiro*. Brazilian composers have long been influenced by popular musics, and some, such as Heitor Villa-Lobos, actively participated in it. As we discuss in chapter 9, many of Brazil's composers are comfortable in both popular and erudite idioms, and choro is often seen as a genre that straddles the popular-erudite divide.

The Roda de Choro

Heart and Soul of Choro

From the journal of F. C., March 19, 1893, 8:00 in the evening, at a small café in Laranjeiras, a neighborhood in Rio de Janeiro.

I arrived at the Café Laranjeiras soaking wet. I had begun my adventure in Rio de Janeiro during the rainy season, and I took this in stride. The café was a dark, dank room with low ceilings and many tables of various shapes and sizes haphazardly placed throughout the room, with chairs that matched neither the tables nor each other. The waiter, a large dark man with vibrant green eyes, realizing I was alone and not a regular, indicated that I could sit anywhere. I decided on an empty table in the corner where I would be unobtrusive yet could easily observe the other patrons.

The place filled rapidly; the only empty table was in the middle of the room. More people arrived, and the waiter directed them to my table. Apparently I would not be alone this evening. The arriving party introduced themselves—two couples out for a night on the town. José, a tall man dressed in a white linen suit (indicating his status as perhaps a high-ranking government official) flashed a toothy smile and apologized for the intrusion, stating loudly that a crowded table was the sign of a good time. He ordered drinks and food for everybody, myself included, announced to nobody in particular that I was his guest for the evening, and told me to ask for anything I wanted. Knowing that refusal of his hospitality—even at what moments before had been my table—was an insult, I graciously accepted after the obligatory protests and counterprotests.

The musicians started to arrive at 9:00, an hour late already according to what I had been told but on time by local standards. They were an odd mix: a well-dressed man in an immaculately tailored business suit (perhaps a banker by day), another in a suit two sizes too small for his ample girth and ten years out of fashion holding a guitar, yet another in a threadbare suit of mismatched trousers and waistcoat, carrying his guitar in a stained, well-worn cloth sack. I finally realized that the one empty table in the middle of the room was reserved for them. One of the guitar players tuned his instrument and began to play passages that were astonishing in their velocity and invention, all the while chatting with his fellow musicians. The banker-flautist seemed more concerned with devouring a plate of rice and beans than with preparing to play, so the other guitar player began to play a melody by himself. The hum of the crowd quickly subsided as the people in the café took notice and awaited the musical delights that were sure to begin. The guitar player, however, stopped in the middle of a phrase, to the great disappointment of the crowd, which protested vociferously. At long last, the flute player, his hunger and thirst satisfied for the moment, took out his instrument, an apparently new silver one with many fancy keys, of which he was obviously proud.

I was struck by the casual air of the musicians gathered around the table in the middle of the room. Were they going to play just like that? Sitting around a table, drinking beer, and eating *salgadinhos,* those salty little tasty treats? The expectant noise of the crowd began to increase, but the musicians took no notice. Someone was missing from the group—the cavaquinho player. The headwaiter, a large dark man in a dirty apron, announced, "He's always late, but he's worth waiting for."

Everyone in the café seemed to know the musicians. They were not shy about talking to them, even from across the room. My newfound friend and uninvited host, José, became restless and shouted across the room for the group to start playing. The musicians responded by shouting back, telling him to relax, and the crowd echoed their sentiments. It was clear that he wasn't a regular, and the rest of his party, embarrassed by his outburst, found something interesting to look at on the other side of the room. I found myself searching the room with his friends. The musicians continued to eat and drink, not in the least concerned about their missing colleague.

Finally, the cavaquinho player arrived, spouting excuses having to do with closing his shop, the vagaries of customers, and the problems of finding good help, all the while hurriedly taking out his instrument. He gulped down a beer and swallowed three codfish cakes (for strength, he said) and tuned up. Finally ready, the musicians looked to the flautist, who began by playing a brilliant polka. The noisy crowd suddenly quieted as they focused their attention on the musicians. After a few notes of the melody, just enough for the other musicians to recognize the tune, the rest of the group joined in. It was "Flôr amorosa" by the great flute master Calado, who had died just a few years earlier. The familiar melody filled the room, and the soloist added graceful melodic twists and turns to the vigorous accompaniment of the stringed instruments. One of the guitarists played an aggressive bass line, almost a melody in itself, filled with diabolical twists and turns, while the other guitarist and cavaquinho filled in with delightful chords struck at just the right moments. It was unlike any polka I'd ever heard played in the salons of my well-to-do acquaintances. A few minutes later, the piece came to an end and the crowd enthusiastically voiced their approval.

They played liked this for hours. After a while some people, my hosts included, began to dance, right there between the tables, undulating to the rhythm in an impossibly small space. Other patrons were satisfied to listen and eat, but all appeared to enjoy themselves. After a while a man joined the musicians' table and bought them all a round of drinks. The appreciative musicians then accompanied him as he started to sing a sentimental love song, a modinha. Before long, the audience joined in. Later, another patron replaced the guitarist in the too-small suit, who seemed happy to move to another table, which was laden with food and bottles of beer. The musicians played on tirelessly.

Later still, another flute player arrived, explaining that it had stopped raining but that the streetcars were still not running so he had walked and that the opera he was playing had run late, but then again Italian operas always ran late. As soon as the new arrival had refreshed himself with food, drink, and banter, the strains of a delicate waltz filled the air. He picked up his instrument and improvised an impossibly lovely countermelody that left the audience breathless. Not to be left behind, the cavaquinho player took up the haunting melody and the flute players accompanied him. Finally one of the guitarists took the lead and the waltz ended quietly, the room seemingly touched by the melody played so tastefully.

As the night wore on, other patrons joined in the festivities, singing and playing, dancing and talking, eating and drinking until dawn began to break. My host asked for the bill for our table and was disturbed by the tally presented to him. I offered to contribute, but he steadfastly refused. Reluctantly, he paid the bill, and my colleagues for the evening bade their farewells, having invited me for lunches and dinners I knew would never take place but having fulfilled their obligation to make the offer. The weary crowd finally headed for home, ready for a few hours of sleep, work, and then, perhaps, another glorious evening of choro.[1]

The above story is a fictionalized account of a turn-of-the-century roda de choro, a social and musical gathering of amateur choro musicians and fans. The account incorporates historical evidence gathered from a variety of sources and includes the many social and musical characteristics that distinguish the roda as a unique event within the choro tradition. The choro roda (literally circle or ring) provides a specific arena for certain sets of expectations, behaviors, and conventions, bound together and given meaning by the act of playing and listening to music. For example, unlike classical concerts, rodas de choro are usually informal gatherings with no set time to begin or end. This flexibility is an important component of an atmosphere conducive to the business at hand: musical expression. Players are expected to play together in a spirit of camaraderie in which every player, regardless of individual talent or status, is treated equally and given a musical space in which to participate. In the story, the different social classes of the musicians, which are indicated by their clothing and their professions, do not govern how the musicians interact musically and socially in the roda. Fluid boundaries allow listeners to become active participants; at certain points, which typically occur after the instrumentalists have played for a while, members of the audience will sing or take up instruments and play to the accompaniment of the group. These and other behaviors and expectations characterize a particular musical experience that forms the core of the sensibility and ethos of choro. These values are implicitly understood by choro musicians and fans that assert that "real" choro is found only in the roda.

In this chapter, we discuss the social and musical components of the roda and its central role in the tight-knit community of choro musicians and fans. We follow this with a consideration of the roda ethos, or the attitudes and beliefs embodied in

民族精神
社会思潮
風潮

behaviors in the roda and articulated in talk about choro. To players and fans, the roda is about musical expression without regard for money, status, or getting ahead. In order to create an environment for the music to flourish, players and fans are expected to be respectful of each other with a certain modicum of deference and humility. The best choro is said to arise out of musical conversations (*conversa dos instrumentos*), not lectures dominated by a single player. The quality of a roda is often judged not only by the level of musical expression but also by the degree of participation; a roda in which only a few people play, regardless of their level of ability, is not considered to be "the real thing." We conclude with a consideration of the roda in today's world of synthesizers and digitized perfection and the tension that arises when the participatory ethos comes into conflict with the slick rehearsed presentational style of playing required of professional musicians.[2]

Before we begin, we feel it necessary to comment on the only printed source for ethnographic information on choro musicians before the 1930s: *O choro: reminiscencias dos chorões antigos* (*The Choro: Reminiscences of Past Choro Musicians*), by Alexandre Gonçalves Pinto, first published in 1936 and republished in facsimile in 1978.[3] The lack of primary sources is always problematic for those studying the history of popular musics. Firsthand accounts of popular traditions are either hard to find or nonexistent. Even the commercial recordings that were made of the music in question give us only a glimpse of what the tradition might have been; they might even mislead us entirely by representing only that form of music deemed commercially acceptable and valuable at the time. Although we can hear choro musicians serving as accompanists to singers on the very first recordings of popular music ever made in Brazil, we can only imagine the sights, the sounds, and the personalities involved in the numerous rodas held in homes, bars, and music stores in late-nineteenth- and early-twentieth-century Rio de Janeiro. The only source that gives extensive, albeit anecdotal, information on a large number of choro musicians before the 1930s is Pinto's book, which he describes as a "profile of all the *chorões* of the old guard, and a large number of *chorões* of today, facts, and customs of the old music parties" that is intended to "revive the great musicians who have fallen into obscurity." Pinto traces the second generation of chorões from the turn of the century until approximately 1930. Although his book contains a great deal of information, it is by no means a literary or scholarly masterpiece. Archaic Portuguese fraught with mistakes makes translation of the work difficult. Unfortunately for the music scholar, Pinto offers little detail about the music in which he and his friends engaged, although he does give information about instruments and performing groups (as well as the abilities of individual players). He offers definitions and descriptions of certain dances, but from the point of view of social function rather than musical form or style. His book is, however, quite valuable as a social history: We are told about the occupations (or lack thereof) of Pinto's choro friends and acquaintances, their places of residence, their musical preferences, their family histories, and their personalities and stories and descriptions of specific gatherings.

Roda Contexts

Most choro musicians make music in two different yet related contexts: as hired professionals, they provide music for parties, dances, and other social functions and at bars, private residences, hotels, and concert halls, and as specialist amateurs, they attend voluntary roda gatherings held in a variety of spaces, including bars, private residences, and music stores. The performance context has a strong effect on the repertoire played, the length of the performance, and the style of performance. Rodas can occur regularly at a given place and time or be arranged for special occasions by a patron or host. Both authors have had the immense pleasure of experiencing rodas arranged for the occasion of our visits and have attended numerous others that took place for a variety of reasons. In São Paulo, the music store Contemporânia has regular rodas each week; in the past, illustrious rodas were held at two competing music stores in Rio de Janeiro, A Guitarra de Prata (The Silver Guitar) and O Cavaquinho de Ouro (The Golden Cavaquinho).

In the late nineteenth and early twentieth centuries, rodas were most often formed on the basis of neighborhood. The southern zone of the city was still undeveloped at this time and was isolated from the rest of the city by steep hills. Transportation around these hills was limited and communication between one section of the city and another was difficult. Musicians from the far end of the northern zone had little, if any, contact with musicians from the southern zone. Most rodas were held in the densely populated center and northern parts of the city. According to Pinto, regularly occurring rodas were held in the Cidade Nova, or the northern zone of Rio de Janeiro: at the house of Maria Prata in São Cristóvão, on Rua do Bom Jardim at the house of Durvalina, in the neighborhood of Catete at the Botequim de Cançela, in Matadouro, at Estácio de Sá in Tijuca, in Engenho Velho, and at the Botequim Braço de Ouro.[4] Sometimes rodas were held at the homes of Afro-Brazilian *tias* such as Tia Ciata, who was famous for her samba gatherings.[5] Composer Heitor Villa-Lobos belonged to the roda de choro of the music store O Cavaquinho de Ouro on Rua Carioca in central Rio de Janeiro. Other members of this roda included Quincas Laranjeiras on guitar, two players of the bass-trumpet, composer and bandleader Anacleto de Medeiros on saxophone and clarinet, two players of the now-obsolete *ophicleide*,[6] a cavaquinho player, and several flautists.

Sessions generally took place in the evenings after work or on Sunday afternoons at bars, restaurants, and yards—anywhere there was good food and drink

Figure 3.1. 1901 photo of a roda de choro gathering. Photo in the collection of the Biblioteca Nacional, Rio de Janeiro.

and room to play. These improvisatory jam sessions were known to last all night as the group moved from bar to bar or house to house. Pinto describes a typical roda after a dance gig:

> The dance drawing to an end late at night, the [chorões] would leave playing a dainty polka and dive into the first bar that they found open. The hefty Portuguese owner of the establishment already knew to ask: "So, what'll it be? Egg-nog with port wine or a mixed drink?" Each one would choose his favorite drink, perhaps a *rabo-de-galo* [cock-tail],[7] which was a mixture of *paratí*,[7] honey, and cinnamon. And the choro would continue. The sun would soon invade the bar to the sounds of the flute accompanied by the cavaquinho and the guitar. The bar would fill up with *seresteiros* coming from other *forrobodós* [parties] and the choro would continue until 9, 10, 11:00 in the morning.[8]

In the 1920s and earlier, rodas were often spontaneous gatherings at locations chosen for the quality and quantity of their libations:

> Most musicians hung out at the musical *chas* [literally teas, referring to rodas] of Rua de Ourives 50, owned by Bushman Guimarães and Bevilacqua, and Moreira's on Rua Gonçalves Dias, as well as [at] the [music stores] Cavaquinho de Ouro on Rua Carioca, and Rabéca de Ouro on the same street. At the taverns one encountered the wise-guy chorões, who were singing modinhas and whistling to the others and playing their favorite choros. Inclined toward choro, they composed music full of inspirations and melodies, which satisfied those who appreciated the splendid serenades in the moonlight, in which the arpeggios of the guitars and

the sonorous notes of the flute were joined by the vibrations of the cavaquinho. They would awaken the residents of the entire block, who opened their windows and doors of their dwellings, welcoming the choro conjuntos (including the riff-raff gate-crashers, who never miss a gathering), improvising dances, and serving food that was prepared in a hurry.[9]

Before the 1930s, it was common for chorões to play at parties called *pagodes,* a name that is still used in Brazil to signify a party with music, often spontaneous, that generally occurred among the lower classes (today it refers to a popular, often commercial, form of samba and any gathering with live samba music). Music, of course, was the most important part of the pagode, and it was a point of honor for the homeowner to present his guests with good music and good food. Choro musicians were often invited to play at such gatherings, and those that participated often expected little in return except for food and drink. Since a party with choro was held in higher esteem than a party without, choro musicians were frequently asked to play at a variety of functions outside of the roda context.

Pinto is careful to list the professions of most of the chorões of the period from 1880 to 1936. His inventory indicates that they were, among other things, professional musicians, civil servants, mailmen, soldiers and sailors, actors, journalists, bank tellers, circus clowns, and janitors. The variety of occupations choro musicians held is surprising. Of 365 choro musicians, 106 are listed as civil servants in some capacity, a great number of whom were employed by the post office.[10] It is difficult to tell with any certainty the degree to which Pinto's inventory can be taken as a representative cross-section of choro musicians in Rio de Janeiro. The book more likely represents Pinto's own social circle of fellow civil servants, since Pinto himself was a postal worker as well as a being a self-described bohemian.

In addition to highly skilled amateur musicians, professional musicians were also inclined toward choro. First-hand accounts describe professional musicians who would gather together to play choro through the night after finishing a paid performance in the theater or salon. Composer Heitor Villa-Lobos describes such a gathering:

A roda might consist of musicians of the orchestra who after playing a concert or an opera that ended at midnight, or eleven, meet up again and say, "Let's play a serenade, or a *'seresta'* or a *choro.*" There it is! When we are in agreement, we take the train, very far, to the neighborhoods, in search of something to eat, to drink *cachaça.* We go knock on the door of a man we know who likes [music]. Before we knock on the door, we all play spontaneous improvisations; everybody plays. So this is it, the *Choros* [sic]. It is always very passionate.[11]

In the roda, the lines between audience and performer are often indistinct. Sometimes listeners will participate by singing a song, adding impromptu percussion, or playing a little on an instrument at certain points during a roda. Participation need not be purely musical: Having a few appreciative and dedicated choro followers show their enjoyment of the music in an intimate setting is something that musicians say adds a great deal to the roda experience. They may participate in the capacity of host of a party or simply faithfully show up at rodas, perhaps purchasing food and drink for the group. Musicians may count on them to attend rodas regularly and share in the joy of music-making. Those who are accepted by the group as "one of them" are often referred to as chorões, just as if they were accomplished musicians. In this way, the roda is a social as much as a musical entity. Pinto describes one such social chorão, illustrating some important aspects of social interaction in the roda:

> I'll describe here the old parties [rodas] of that unforgettable time. . . . This is how the parties at Machado Breguedim's were, in the Rocha Station neighborhood. "Machadinho," as he was known, was a respected flautist. The choros held at his home had plenty of excellent food and fine beverages; being an upper level manager at the Customs was lucrative and for this reason he saved huge amounts of money to be spent on his parties, where he and his musician friends got together. The parties at Machadinho's lasted several days, always with the utmost harmony, intimacy, and enthusiasm. Greatly admired choro groups would play there, each followed in turn by another. Everyone wanted to show his compositions, his masterful phrasing, and his technical agility. Thus were the parties at the unforgettable Machado Breguedim's.[12]

Machado was a chorão of atypical financial resources. Pinto called him a "respected" flautist, which in Pinto's flowery style (which was typical of Brazilian discourse about art and music) might indicate that he was in reality a mediocre player who compensated for his lack of musical gifts by spending lavishly so that he would enjoy the company of more-accomplished musicians. The best and brightest showed up at his rodas, drawn there by the excellence of the musicians present, the social interaction with their peers and admirers, and the quality of the food and drink. All were integral parts of the choro tradition; without all three elements, one could not have a successful roda. Social chorões like Machadinho continue to play an important role as valued members of the roda to this day.

        Historically, the roda de choro was almost exclusively the domain of male musicians. Women who participated upon occasion did so on a social level, rarely participating as musicians. Indeed, Pinto's book refers to only three women. One of these was Chiquinha Gonzaga, a famous composer and performer whose music continues to be a part of the choro repertoire.[13] The other two were Placida dos Santos, a professional singer of modinhas and lundus who performed with well-

known chorões such as Quincas Laranjeiras, Sátiro Bilhar, and Catulo Cearense da **47**
Paixão, and a social *chorona* (a female chorão) named Durvalina, a friend about
whom Pinto fondly reminisces:

> Durvalina's house on Rua do Bom Jardim was where the youth of the choro
> would meet. She was a mulatta, young, beautiful, respected, and very much a
> friend to those who knew her attributes. . . . Rare was the day when she did not
> have there a good musical gathering, according to our good old friends João
> Thomaz, Luiz Pinto, Brandão and Néco, not to mention Bilhar, Horacio Theberge,
> Côrte Real, Quincas, Henrique Rosa, João de Britto, Lulú Bastos, José Maria and
> many others who have already passed away. Durvalina . . . gave equally to all
> of the good *chorões* of that time good dinners and dances which most times
> lasted a week. . . . [T]hese hours, moments, days, months, were full of happi-
> ness.[14]

With these exceptions, it was not until the choro revival in the 1970s and 1980s
that women began to participate as musicians in choro. Only in the last decade,
however, have women felt free to pursue instruments such as the guitar and pandeiro, which historically were viewed as "male" instruments.

Choro Style and the Ethos of the Roda

The primary concern of chorões during Pinto's time was for the music they played
and the freedom of musical expression they enjoyed. Members of choro rodas were
typically good friends bound together by a passionate devotion to choro, which facilitated a high degree of musical intimacy. According to Mariz:

> The chorão had a deep feeling for spontaneous improvisation. He would put his
> entire soul into playing. He had a true religious feeling for the cult of choro, in
> which one lives to play, compose and sing.[15]

Choro musicians still say very much the same thing about their art—it requires
dedication and study but also serves as the path or vehicle for the ultimate in un-
bounded musical expression.

From interviews and observation of numerous rodas de choro, we found that
participants subject themselves and each other to a set of tacit codes of behavior
and attitudes that help maintain the roda as a site conducive to group music-
making in the manner expressed by Pinto's friends and acquaintances. In the roda,
musical behavior is social behavior. As one veteran choro musician observed,

> In order to be well played, choro demands technical mastery of the instrument as
> well as an emotional atmosphere of the music and its players at the moment of
> interpretation. It asks for a permanent and sensitive dialogue between the

The Roda de Choro

soloists and his accompanists. . . . In order to be a chorão, one must absorb the atmosphere of choro and identify oneself with the music and with the group.[16]

This means that regardless of their level of technical expertise, participants are expected not to dominate the session or intimidate other players. When they violate these unwritten rules, they are rarely confronted openly; instead, members of the roda may try to avoid that person in the future or even stop attending that roda. What participants strive for is an atmosphere of camaraderie conducive to making music together. The importance of deference and of fitting in to the whole is evident in a remark made by a veteran member of choro group Época de Ouro. Livingston-Isenhour asked Horondino da Silva ("Dino Sete Cordas") if musicians plan ahead of time what they are going to play at a roda. He replied:

> In general a chorão doesn't rehearse what he's going to play. He arrives, decides to play something and he sees if that guy over there can accompany him well or not. You want an accompanist that doesn't distract, that knows how to accompany well, and sometimes there is controversy over that. So you look for someone who accompanies better. . . . The soloist, who can be a clarinet, or trombone, or bandolim, or [even] cavaquinho, begins playing and from there everyone else fills in; this is a roda de choro. If more people show up to play, they look around to see who's playing and where they can fit in, and they start playing too. . . . [T]he player does something over there and I see where I can come in, a small empty space that is there for me, and I squeeze in my guitar.[17]

The image of fitting one's part into the whole occurs repeatedly in discourse about choro and shows how deeply the notion of social and musical interlock is ingrained in choro musicians. This image serves as a primary metaphor governing all musical and social interaction in a roda.

In their respective studies of jazz improvisation, Monson and Berliner note that it is important for jazz musicians to be able to respond in the moment to what the other players are doing; in other words, they must interact musically without having planned ahead what they will play. Those who do not respond to the group in this way are accused of "not listening," even though they may play the right notes in the correct rhythm.[18] This type of spontaneous musical interaction, of listening and responding musically, is highly valued in the roda de choro, where musical roles are not verbally assigned and there is no prearranged playlist of pieces. Instead, musicians use their past experiences and their ears to guide them; more experienced players tend to be sensitive to "stepping on other people's toes" and naturally gravitate toward filling in the musical role that creates a balanced sound. At a roda in 1994, Livingston-Isenhour noticed that pieces were usually initiated by someone playing a bit of the melody on their instrument. The opening measures of a choro tend to be distinctive and function as an aural tag; this is fortunate, since even experienced choro musicians often forget the names of specific choros. If the others were familiar with it, the music would seem to spontaneously emerge. At other times, a piece was begun and left unfinished if the others couldn't jump in. She noticed a definite need to continue the groove of playing together and heard some pieces repeated several times rather than a reversion to silence while the musicians figured out what to play next. The texture of roda music tends to be very dense; there are many levels of activity and different players enter and drop out as the piece progresses. At times, those who are not playing instruments interject comments about a well-played passage (for example, *beleza!,* meaning "beautiful"), sing the melody, or clap their hands. At times several musical conversations among various instruments may be occurring at once, reflecting the cacophony of the verbal conversations of other participants at the party.

Rodas are an important site for the transmission of Mariz's "cult of choro." Although studying with a master of the instrument is still important in the formation of many musicians, *chorões* expect them to combine this knowledge with the experience of playing with other musicians in the roda. Musicians who play plucked-string instruments (i.e., guitar, cavaquinho, or bandolim) who are relatively new to the tradition usually start out in the roda participating as a center instrument. This role is relatively flexible and allows for any number of rhythmic variations on the basic beat. If the basic rhythmic foundation is solidly established, the contributions of novices will be integrated into the total sound. How a novice participates in a roda is determined by several factors, including what instrument he or she plays, the level of skill of the group, and the balance of the group. Apprentices to one of the core musicians will be given special attention and will be strongly encouraged to play in a solo capacity. Those who simply show up with guitars, cavaquinhos, percussion instruments, or melody instruments may join in or, if the number of instruments is already high, core players may alternate with them.

The line between audience member and performer in a roda is often fluid. Usually after the regular members of a roda have played for a while, they "open the floor" to others who may want to sing a song or play a tune accompanied by the group. The phrase *dê uma canja* is sometimes used to invite others in to play. "Canja," literally "chicken soup," colloquially means "give it a whirl." Garcia gave a canja on guitar at a roda in 2003 attended by seven-string guitarist Marco Guida, bandolinist Marco de Pinna, Nestor de Pandeiro, American clarinetist and ethnomusicologist Andy Connell, and singer Didi:

> My arrival was greeted by hearty welcomes, and with offers of food and drink. My host gave me a guitar and said, simply, "Play." I started with Pernambuco's choro "Brasileirinho," and was instantly accompanied by the group. Marco de Pinna, who generally played the lead part in the group, adjusted to the accompaniment role fluidly, assuming the role usually played by the cavaquinho, which was missing from the roda. Everyone in the roda was familiar with the tune, but it was equally apparent that the guitar was seldom used as a lead instrument in this

roda. The seven-string guitar player asked me to play Pernambuco's "Interrogando," stating that he would fill in the second guitar part the way it was done in Pernambuco's time. Everyone's focus was on me (the gringo) and what I was doing on solo guitar. They listened intently and provided a seamless accompaniment, to which I was not accustomed. On finishing the piece, we played several others by Pernambuco, at which time Marco Guida, the host, asked me to play "Charará" by Baden Powell, which he had heard me play at a *canja* several days before. It was the only tune of the afternoon with which the group was not familiar. The pandeiro joined in, followed by the seven-string guitar; before I knew it, everyone was negotiating the musical swirls of Baden Powell's choro. Although this was a social gathering, the concentration and effort shown by all present belied an intensity not seen in casual music-making.

We continued in this manner for several more pieces, at which time Marco de Pinna announced to the rest of the group that I was a Villa-Lobos scholar, and asked me if I would play Villa-Lobos's "Choro Típico." I began the piece, and Nestor de Pandeiro was encouraged to join me. This piece is atypical of roda repertoire: Villa-Lobos's idea was to compose a piece that demonstrated the characteristics of the choro but in a tightly organized form and with a virtuosic solo guitar part. Rather than have a steady rhythm, it calls for extreme rubato, making it difficult for the pandeiro player unfamiliar with the work's idiosyncrasies. By the second time through the A section (the piece is in typical ABACA form), however, he had caught the tempo changes and was in the groove. Marco, the host, admitted that although he had not heard that particular piece outside of the classical context, it fit perfectly well in the roda setting.

Despite the unusual beginning to the roda, the rest of the afternoon was spent playing the usual standards of the choro repertory: Pixinguinha, Zequinha de Abreu, Garoto, Nazaré, Jacó do Bandolim, Waldir Azevedo, and others. Nevertheless, Garcia remembers that he learned some interesting things about musical and social dynamics in the roda:

During a lull in the roda, most of the participants got up to refill their glasses and started talking. Wanting to keep the music going, I started to play a choro standard that I had learned long ago in a version for solo guitar. After only an instant, the others joined in, forgetting their beverages and hastily putting down their plates. As I was playing I suddenly realized that I had started at too fast a tempo and that I wasn't going to be able to play the piece to the end. Although everyone was polite, I realized that I had made a faux pas. In a roda, you finish what you start, and you do not start what you cannot finish! Although this seemed minor at the time, in retrospect it was an important point: I was the new guy, and I had to prove myself. Although my solo playing was well received, I had not proved myself as an accompanist yet, and my false starts did not do much to build my stock. To be accepted as a member of the roda, one must be extremely proficient in all aspects of choro. Although guitar soloists are rare these days, it is not enough to be the leader; one must also fit into the group.

We have considered points of commonality among the attitudes and behaviors that govern most rodas de choro today and in the past. Beyond these similarities however, each roda takes on distinctive characteristics measured by several variables, including the level of ability of each of the players, the occasion for the roda, the musical familiarity members have with playing with each other, and the interests and desires of other members of the roda. The rodas that took place at the home of musician and composer Jacó do Bandolim in the 1950s were renowned not only for the high level of musicians that played there but also for the strict rules of behavior demanded by Jacó. The music was played in silence, and the consumption of alcoholic beverages was strongly discouraged.

We have experienced a variety of rodas that could be placed along a continuum according to the level of proficiency of the players, from highly skilled (often including professional musicians) to moderately skilled (often with amateur musicians and/or beginner players). Livingston-Isenhour recalls a roda of the former category that occurred shortly after her arrival on her first field trip to Brazil in 1994:

> My host called an acquaintance of his, cardiologist Paulo Alves. Paulo used to play bandolim in a choro group, and he called together his old friends Maurício (guitar), Luciana (cavaquinho), and Joel (bandolim). Shigeharu Sasago, the Japanese guitarist and an old friend of Maurício, also attended. Later I was to discover that all of the musicians had played important roles in the choro revival some twenty years earlier: Joel Nascimento had been a regular at the Sovaco de Cobra and was soloist with the chamber group Camerata Carioca, organized by composer Radamés Gnattali; Maurício Carrilho is the nephew of choro flautist Altamiro Carrilho and was also a member of Camerata Carioca. Paulo Alves and Luciana Rabello (sister of the late guitarist Raphael Rabello) were members together with Maurício of the celebrated revivalist youth group Os Carioquinhas. Since 1987, Shigeharu Sasago had traveled a number of times to Brazil to study choro guitar; he is the founder of the Japanese choro group Choro Club.
>
> We gathered in the evening, and the host provided snacks and beer. The music began in a manner typical of the roda: one person (in this case, usually Joel) would play a phrase of a piece to see if the others knew it. If they did, the other members would all join in and the piece would continue for as long as the soloist felt like playing. During the course of the evening, they played more than twenty-two pieces. Joel played the lead most of the time, although Paulo played a few pieces, and Maurício and Luciana also took some solos. At times Paulo played an accompanying line to Joel's solos. Because the soloists were bandolinists, the repertoire was heavily weighted towards the works of Jacó do Bandolim. As is typical in many rodas, the players knew the tunes but often couldn't remember the composer or title of the piece. Instead, pieces were identified by their theme, which the musician either played or sang. I was impressed with the tightness of the group; there were very few times when one member stumbled or couldn't follow the piece. I also noticed that the group worked together well as an ensemble; they executed a range of dynamics that only experienced musicians that know each other well are able to achieve. After the players had gone through all the pieces they knew together, the guitarists took out musical scores (lead sheets with melody and accompanying chords) to refer to. This was towards the end of the roda, and Shigeharu finally joined in for a few pieces. He confided to me that he felt his role was as a student of choro and that he didn't feel comfortable joining

in much of the time; he was there to learn as much as he could to teach his group back in Japan.

In comparison to other rodas we attended, this one was atypical in a number of ways. First, the combination of the high level of skill of the musicians and their long experience playing together is rare. All except Paulo played choro since the revival almost twenty years earlier, and their experience showed in the tightness and musicality of their executions. Second, the repertoire consisted mostly of lesser-known choros—not once did they play any roda standards such as "Noites cariocas" (Jacó do Bandolim), "Tico-Tico no fubá" (Zequinha de Abreu), or "Carinhoso" (Pixinguinha). Garcia noted similar characteristics in the roda he participated in as a guitarist in 2003 (described above). In that roda, several of the participants were full-time professional musicians and the others had attained a high level of performing ability and played occasional gigs but made their primary income elsewhere.

Contrasting with these small intimate rodas in which all the players are at about the same high level of ability are larger, open-invitation rodas to which people of varying ability show up. In these cases, musicians make concessions in order to enhance participation for all; they may choose to play more familiar pieces and there may be more repetitions of a given piece to give everyone a chance to figure out the chords and melody. Although pieces may be played more than once during a session, it is unlikely that they will be played in the exact same way each time. This brings up an important point in the discussion of performance goals and social integration that is often missed by nonplayers and observers of choro: that of using common repertoire and repeating pieces many times as a means of attaining maximum playing pleasure for the most amount of players. In these situations, music is performed not for the benefit of an audience but for the enjoyment of the players, as was made clear to Livingston-Isenhour during the course of a particularly lengthy roda:

> In the spring of 1994, I attended a roda de choro in Brasília that lasted three days. It was ostensibly held in honor of a civic holiday that had brought a variety of musicians to the capital city for the weekend, including the famous pianist Artur Moreira Lima. The party was held at the spacious house of Dr. Assis, which had ample indoor and outdoor space for music-making. During the party, different kinds of music-making took place. In the afternoon there was a "concert" of choro and other music played by musicians in the salon. Artur Moreira Lima, known for his recording of the works of Ernesto Nazaré, played some solo works and accompanied choro flautist Carlos Poyares, the cavaquinho player from Época de Ouro Jonas Pereira, and various bandolinists. People gathered around, remained silent, and applauded after each selection. Although the pieces were not rehearsed ahead of time, the goal was clearly a performance for an audience. Pieces were not repeated, improvisation was limited, and it was implicitly understood that it was not appropriate for audience members to suddenly join in and play percussion, for example.

In the evenings however, the same people acted in very different ways. The party moved outside and people gathered in groups around circular party tables. Snacks were plentiful and alcohol flowed freely. Guests arrived throughout the evening; many brought instruments, including flute, bandolim, six- and seven-string guitars, pandeiro, and surdo. Levels of ability and specialization ranged from professional musicians to weekend amateurs; young players, including adolescents (sons of musicians, for the most part); and nonspecialists. Levels of acquaintance varied as well; some were old friends, others had just been introduced to each other. All of these differences were set aside once the music started. Unlike the roda at Paulo's house, I recognized many of the choros as standards; many were played several times during the course of the evening. Late in the evening of one of the rodas, I was standing off to the side watching the musicians play. I was approached by the wife of one of the musicians who was clearly unhappy at having to remain in Brasília for three days. She turned to me and said in a weary voice, "How can they stand to play those same pieces over and over again?" I remembered that I had read this very same criticism in several reviews of choro recordings. The critics complained that the same pieces were recorded and released over and over again and that they all "sounded the same." It struck me then how different choro is for musicians playing in a roda than for a passive listening audience. In the roda, the "piece" is more important as a vehicle for musical participation than as an end in itself.

This is a point that is difficult for outsiders to the tradition to understand. The joy of playing old choro standards even entered the high-level roda Garcia attended in which mostly music professionals and semi-professionals participated. Garcia recalls:

> At one point we played "1 × 0" by Pixinguinha ["Um a zero," a choro standard] at a slow pace. When we finished, someone complained that it was not satisfying, so we repeated the entire tune, this time at a blistering speed. There were smiles all around; this was much better. This points out one of the principal characteristics of the roda de choro: the overwhelming tendency is to play standard tunes by accepted composers. Although many chorões compose, it seems they rarely play their own compositions in the roda.

Although principles of maximizing participation and minimizing social differences are emphasized in the roda context, we do not want to give the impression that the roda is completely immune from conflict. Although most musicians would prefer to play rather than not, even if it means temporarily setting aside personal differences, sometimes conflict enters the roda. One source of conflict that is rarely acknowledged yet seems to exist concerns gender exclusion. In the mid-1990s, few women participated as musicians in the majority of choro events we attended. The opinions of many men about women players were usually restricted to generalities—few were willing to name specific players. Nevertheless, Livingston-Isenhour heard comments that implied that women just aren't adept at playing choro or that if they insist on playing, certain instruments were more appropriate for women than others. Women could play flute, piano, bandolim, or perhaps even cavaquinho, but it was not "ladylike" to play guitar (six- or especially seven-string guitar), pandeiro, or large percussion instruments such as the surdo drum. Livingston-Isenhour worked closely with two female choro players, a flautist and a pandeiro player, and both expressed frustration at not being accepted as equals by their male colleagues. Although she did not witness any outward signs of prejudice at rodas, she suggests that women tend to play in groups in which they know they will be accepted rather than overtly challenge male players in a public musical arena. In this way, the ethos of maximum participation and the creation of an atmosphere conducive to music-making so typical of the roda is maintained, even at the expense of gender equality.[19]

Presentational Rodas

Contrasting strongly in style and sound with choro played in the roda are the presentational forms of choro most visible to the general public. These include large events such as competitions and festivals, concerts, and even "hired rodas." Presentational forms of music are characterized by a separation between the audience and the musicians. This separation may be physical (a stage, for example) or technological (as in the recording of music for purchase and consumption). Because the emphasis is on sound as a product, there is generally a premium on precision of playing, and pieces and their order of performance tend to be arranged ahead of time. Choice of repertoire is affected by the presence of a passive listening audience that desires to be entertained.[20]

The gathering called Choro na Feira is an example of a roda with characteristics of presentational choro. Although it gives the appearance of being a spontaneous roda, it actually consists of a core of regular, albeit flexible, group of musicians who meet every Saturday at the street fair in Laranjeiras, in the southern zone of Rio de Janeiro. It is advertised in the local newspapers and has a loyal following. The musicians are not paid, yet they have agreed to play at a regular time and place. Musicians may join in, but there is a feeling that novices are not particularly encouraged to join. Most who attend the roda do so to be entertained while they enjoy the other attractions of the fair, such as the stalls that sell beverages, food, and choro CDs.

In this chapter we have considered the roda as a social and musical space where quality is measured by maximum participation in terms of musical engagement. There are situations, however, when the rules of the roda shift somewhat, sometimes with unforeseen consequences. One of these situations is the phenomenon of the "hired roda" where the musicians are paid to act as if they were presenting a spontaneous event. Sometimes conflict is brought about by a confusion

Figure 3.2. "Choro na Feira," May 2003. Photo by Thomas Garcia.

of contexts, for example when an ensemble is hired to play in a bar yet it is made to appear as if the event were spontaneous. Livingston-Isenhour witnessed a roda of this type that took place in a bar located on the second floor of an old building in the historic Lapa district in downtown Rio de Janeiro. A particular choro group was contracted to play weekly at the bar. There was no stage; musicians chose a central table and the establishment provided beverages and food. The group could wear what they wanted and play what they wanted. The only obligation was that they were to play for a certain minimum time; on many occasions, the musicians continued to play beyond the designated time.

Sometimes the appearance of spontaneity confused the boundaries between players and audience members, who thought that it was a roda and who wanted to join in. Although the group welcomed audience members to join in and play small auxiliary percussion (i.e., anything except pandeiro or surdo), it was generally understood that this was not an open roda. When this set of expectations was transgressed, however, it was interesting to note the reaction of the musicians. On one occasion an enthusiastic young man showed up with a guitar. None of the musicians knew him, but he was treated courteously. He managed to wedge himself into the circle and he started to play. Even though he was clearly outranked in terms of ability, no one objected when he started to play; no one encouraged him, either. The group simply played a little louder, and every now and then they exchanged glances as if to say, "Well, what can we do?" Had the young man played more aggressively or played an obtrusive instrument such as trombone, the group might have objected. As it stood, however, the group chose to act as if they were in a roda and tolerated the outsider with courtesy and respect.

On another occasion, Livingston-Isenhour witnessed a confrontation that challenged the idea of "hired" spontaneity. The timbre of the seven-string guitar is such that it is frequently overpowered by flute, pandeiro, and cavaquinho. In this instance, the guitarist protested against playing elaborate bass lines that "no one can hear." Because he would be playing not just for the group but also for the patrons of the bar in general, he was concerned about his sound being drowned out. He asked the bar owner if he could use a pickup for his instrument. The owner reacted strongly against it, saying that he didn't want any technological equipment in the room at all when the choro group was playing—no amps, no monitors, no speakers. He said that if you wanted to amplify yourself, you might as well be playing electric guitars on a stage. The guitarist rejoined that he would be the only one with amplification and that the equipment would be unobtrusive. The owner held firm, and the guitarist subsequently refused to play there again. The issue of amplification has not been raised in any of the rodas in which we have participated, most likely because the aesthetic requirements of a roda are substantially different from those of a concert performance.

Nevertheless, there is a growing concern for the "sound product" even in the roda context. There are several possible reasons why this may be so. Recordings play a strong role in affecting stylistic trends and values that sometimes carry over into the roda. The music industry has undergone rapid expansion, from a negligible presence in the Brazilian economy before the 1960s to an important economic sector with strong ties to transnational companies in the 1980s and 1990s. Accompanying the increase in economic value is the idea that musical value is strongly dependent on media exposure and record sales. Many musicians have argued that there is no space in the media for them, that they are forced to fight a losing battle against artists such as Michael Jackson and rap singers. The presence these popular artists have in record stores, on the radio, and on television directly and negatively affects the value placed on their music, what many have called the *desvalorização* ("devaluation") of Brazilian music by Brazilians. This was of great concern in the 1990s, when Livingston-Isenhour and Garcia did most of their fieldwork. At that time there was a feeling among professionals and nonprofessionals alike that the legitimation of choro was necessary and important and was possible only through performances appreciated by a general public in the form of concerts and recordings. Even the appearance of musicians was held by some as necessary for the public to "value" choro. Livingston-Isenhour recalls that at the roda in Brasília, the host pointed to a photograph on the wall of a professional group of choro musicians from perhaps the 1940s posing in tuxedos. He commented, "Chorões these days don't dress like that; of course no one takes them seriously."

Another reason why participatory and presentational values of music may clash is simply the sheer number of professional musicians that take part in rodas. These musicians are accustomed to the concert stage and the recording studio, where quality of sound is of the utmost importance. Their value judgments about sound are those characteristic of presentational contexts, including technical precision, tonal accuracy, and tight arrangements. Complaints of sloppiness and loose playing styles are sometimes indicative of this viewpoint, and they tend to clash with participatory values in the roda context. It is practically impossible for musicians to play within completely different sets of aesthetic standards according to the context of performance.

We suggest that there has been a fundamental shift in the last twenty years in the practice and perception of choro: It has moved from an essentially participatory tradition based on the roda to a largely presentational and recorded tradition as represented by the younger generations of choro musicians. As we discuss in chapter 8, the revival introduced choro to a new social sector—middle- and upper-middle-class youth with university educations. In the process, choro was adapted to the preferences and musical sensibilities of the new chorões. Besides being able to read and compose music, these musicians generally exhibited a cosmopolitan orientation that distinguished them from older generations of choro musicians.

Although the roda de choro is still considered by many to be the site of "real" or "authentic" choro, by the 1980s and 1990s it had become less important to professional choro musicians concerned with composition and arranging. Nevertheless, the roda still serves a very important function in passing on the choro tradition. Many, regardless of age, have cited the spontaneity and socio-musical interaction found in the roda as important qualities that help make choro what it is. Having observed many choro musicians in the roda, we can only conclude that the experience of playing together in such an environment provides a contrast from the careful work that characterizes the work environment where professional musicians spend much of their time; it is a chance for them to enjoy a bit of spontaneity free from the rigors of performance and recording and to enjoy each other's company through music.

From the Plantation to the City

The Rise and Development of Early Choro in Rio de Janeiro (1870–1920)

The emergence of choro in Rio de Janeiro in the latter part of the nineteenth century represents both a continuation and a departure from earlier ensembles, styles, and genres. The modinha and the lundu were still a part of popular culture at this time but represented only a fraction of the diverse musics found in the rapidly expanding urban context. In this new environment, the terno ensemble became indelibly linked to a new style of playing and, by the 1890s, to the new genre of choro. In this chapter we explore the antecedents of the terno by looking at the history of the word "choro." This investigation leads to several important Afro-Brazilian instrumental groups from which the choro terno developed, including the *choromeleiro, música de barbeiros* (barbers' groups), and *fazenda* (plantation) bands, all of which relied on the terno as their core instrumentation. Afro-Brazilians who gravitated toward the cities brought their musical skills with them. In the capital city of Rio de Janeiro, a vital port city where immigrants, slaves, and former slaves mingled in an environment rich with imported and local popular musics, the terno became more than an ensemble type; it give rise to a new musical style and ethos that defined and distinguished choro. Sometime in the twenty years since the founding of Joaquim Antônio Calado's terno called Choro Carioca in 1870, certain defining elements of the choro style coalesced and were stylized in composed pieces known as choros.

As a window into the practice and social milieus that constituted the choro world before the turn of the century, we examine the lives and works of four musicians and composers, each of which represents major trends within the choro tra-

Joaquim Antônio da Silva Calado (1848–1880) and Anacleto de Medeiros
(1866–1907) represent the stylistic extremes of early choros. Calado was a professional flautist who wrote much of his music to exhibit his talent. Medeiros was a
bandleader who relied upon straightforward pieces composed for the limited abilities of his band members. Whereas Calado wrote all his compositions with the
choro terno in mind, Medeiros made the new choro style a part of the performance
practice of his bands. In doing so, he became one of the first to compose and
arrange pieces with formal scoring that would have been unnecessary in the orally
transmitted choro of the roda. Choro composers Chiquinha Gonzaga (1847–1935)
and Ernesto Nazaré (1863–1934) both played the piano, an instrument that straddles the divide between popular and elite cultures; Gonzaga and Nazaré worked
within the realm of popular music. Gonzaga embraced the middle and lower sectors of society that produced the music she loved, and she was one of the few
women to regularly attend rodas de choro. Besides being a prolific composer of
music for the roda, the salon, and the stage, Gonzaga was a political activist; all of
these activities were unheard of for upper-class women in turn-of-the-century Rio
de Janeiro. In contrast, Nazaré took great pains to distinguish himself and his music
from the lower classes, even going so far as to claim that his maxixes were Brazilian tangos. As a classically trained pianist with a great love and respect for Chopin,
Nazaré's music is the most sophisticated in terms of melody and harmony of the
composers discussed in this chapter.

The Choromeleiro and Origins of Choro

The etymology of the word "choro" provides a fascinating window into the origins
of the musical style and genre and illustrates the powerful interplay of words, associations, and music. To Portuguese speakers, "choro" (present tense of the verb
chorar) immediately evokes an emotional response, for "chorar" literally means "to
cry or weep." Therefore, some have supposed that choro music is so moving that it
brings one to tears. Musicologist David Appleby subscribes to this line of thought;
he suggests that "choro" be translated literally into English as "lament" and
"chorões" as "weepers."[1] Although some modinhas and serestas performed by
chorões could be characterized as melancholy, extant early choros are for the most
part quick and lively in tempo and in predominantly major keys. Appleby argues
that over time the melancholy associations with the term were lost as the choro
style developed and as fast, lively choros became the norm. Brazilian musicologist
Baptista Siqueira also believes the term came from the verb "chorar" but was not
used literally. He suggests that the term was derived from phrases that refer to
salon genres popular in Portugal, specifically the *doce lundu chorado* ("sweetly
cried lundu") and the *chorar no pinho* ("to cry on the guitar").[2] A contemporary

60   chorão advances an interesting idea that the term does indeed come from the verb "to cry," but that "cry" is meant in a humorous way and should be understood within the social context of the day:

> The musicians who originally played choro were not [just] of the highest class, but of all classes. In the salon of the period, the musicians of the [higher social] status would play the lundus and modinhas of the day, to the appreciation of the audience. The other musicians [of the lower classes] would engage in their own parties, but without a patron and with very little money, each made a contribution towards the expenses, either by giving money to the host or, more commonly, bringing something to eat or drink. Because it was often a sacrifice to make such a contribution, the donor was said to "cry" [*chorar*] while handing over his morsels or bottle. The donation came to be known as a "choro," and the name became associated with the party in which this kind of music was played. The music took its name from the party: the choro.[3]

That "choro" was used in a playful, hyperbolic way in such a context is fully in keeping with the attitude of malícia held by choro musicians, in which verbal and musical jests and banter are part of being a chorão.

In the 1960s and 1970s, ethnomusicologists became interested in establishing historical links between African precedents and New World musics. From this perspective, musicologist Gérard Béhague suggests a connection between choro and the Afro-Brazilian dances known as *xolo*.[4] Brazilian musicologist Renato Almeida shares Béhague's view and asserts that Afro-Brazilian festivals and saint days were originally called "(t)xolo," then "xoro," and finally "choro" when the term arrived in the cities with migrating blacks.[5] The Afro-Brazilian celebration of xolo, however, was primarily sung, and no evidence supports this connection other than orthographic mutation, a common occurrence in Brazil, where oral culture predominates over written culture.

Ary Vasconcelos provides the most convincing and logical explanation for the origins of the term "choro," explaining it as a derivation of "choromeleiro." Some Brazilians interpret "choromeleiro" literally as "sweet music" ("chorus" = voices in harmony, "melliseus" = honey [sweet]), but the term actually refers to a colonial wind instrument, the *charamela*, a folk oboe from Spain and Portugal. Known also as *choromela, charamel, charamelinha, charamita,* and *charumbela,* the instrument was found in wind bands in both Brazil and the Iberian peninsula. Vasconcelos explains that there is a clear connection between "choro" and "choromeleiro":

> [The] relationship of choro as a style and musical genre to choro [meaning] melancholy is seductive, but does not seem correct to me. It appears . . . that the designation is derived from *choromeleiros,* a musical fraternity of some importance during the colonial period in Brazil. The choromeleiros not only played the charamela, but other wind instruments as well. For the people, naturally, all instrumental ensembles would end up being called choromeleiros, an expression that, for simplification, ended up being shortened to choro.[6]

CHORO

Vasconcelos's interpretation is supported by substantial historical evidence documenting the musical instrumentation employed in the choromeleiro, its development in the interior state of Minas Gerais during the period when the state was an important mining area, and its importance as part of the cultural capital of wealthy mine owners. The choromeleiro came to Rio de Janeiro and became a part of its cultural life in the 1830s, brought by rich mine owners who had abandoned provincial Minas Gerais for the glamour of court life in the capital city. Like choro, it was exclusively instrumental in its earliest form, although these ensembles also accompanied vocal modinhas, serestas, and serenatas (as did later choro ensembles). Choromeleiro came to mean a group with charamelas as well as the musicians who played the instrument. Over time, the term came to designate any musician, regardless of instrument, who played in an ensemble that included charamelas. Eventually, the flute supplanted the charamela as the wind instrument of choice; because the charamela was loud and suitable only for playing outdoors, the versatility of the ensemble increased with the permanent addition of the flute. Even after the charamela had become obsolete, any instrumental ensemble with a wind instrument was called choromeleiro, including the choro terno of flute, cavaquinho, and guitar.[7]

The guitar had been a part of the choromeleiro since its introduction to Brazil during colonization. African slaves were frequently trained as musicians and taught to play the charamela and guitar. These skills were prized by wealthy slave owners who took pride in their slave bands. The guitar's portability and ability to provide harmony made it an excellent addition to the choromeleiro, and there is substantial documentary evidence of its use in this context. In 1748, a French traveler observed that "there were many guitars and one also hears many charamelas which made pleasant chords. . . . [The blacks] played this instrument with good taste."[8] The cavaquinho was also used in choromeleiro ensembles for rhythmic and harmonic accompaniment as well as melodic counterpoint, allowing the guitarist to play solo parts. Because the guitar and cavaquinho also form the core of the choro ensemble, it seems likely that the two ensemble types are related. Although it is difficult to pinpoint why musical trends and practices come in and fall out of fashion, it is probable that the choromeleiro fell out of favor when it was transplanted in Rio de Janeiro due to the change in social and cultural contexts. Nevertheless, aspects of choromeleiro performance practice survived and were applied to the newly arrived European waltz (approximately 1837) and the polka (1840s).

Despite the overwhelming evidence to support the derivation of the term "choro" from "choromeleiro," it is interesting to note that this relationship is virtually unknown by most choro musicians. Of the more than fifty chorões we interviewed, only one had heard of the choromeleiro connection. When presented with the evidence cited here, many listened patiently, agreed that the argument is strongly supported by historical data, but nevertheless maintained that the historical origins of the word are unimportant. Most chorões prefer to stress the relationship between choro and the verb "chorar" because emotion is such a large part of the expected musical effect. What almost all choro musicians emphasize is that choro is above all an emotion, a means of musical expression that can be personal or communal. In this way, choro has come to mean something much more than the historical details that interest musicologists and historians.

Música de Barbeiros and Fazenda Bands

In addition to the choromeleiro, the roots of choro ensembles can also be traced to another black musical tradition in Rio de Janeiro popular since the late eighteenth century: música de barbeiros, or "barbers' music." According to Freyer, "Barbers' customers expected to be entertained with music, and the barbers, who also worked as surgeons, dentists, blood-letters and musicians, were often black slaves or freedmen."[9] These barbers' groups were based on the terno of guitar, cavaquinho and flute, although other instruments, such as French horns, trumpets, and kettle drums, were sometimes used depending upon the performance context and availability of instruments and players. Barbers' groups were hired to play in a variety of contexts, from middle-class parties to church festivities, and they entertained audiences with a variety of songs, such as modinhas, lundus, and *fados* and dances, such as the quadrille, the *dobrado* march, and Brazilian versions of the Iberian dances *tirana* and fandango.[10] These songs and dances were modified to local tastes, which included topical lyrics and African rhythmic elements. These ensembles were also among the first to play the lundu—a genre with strong African associations—for white middle-class audiences. In the barbeiros ensemble, the musical division of labor was similar to later choro formations; the flute played the melody, the guitar was responsible for the bass and harmony, and the cavaquinho provided rhythmic/harmonic accompaniment in the middle register.

The choro tradition has roots in yet another early musical ensemble dominated by blacks: the fazenda band. Although fazendas—large self-sufficient farms, resembling the plantations of the American South, that relied on slave labor until universal emancipation—were rural, their owners were influenced by urban trends. Most kept houses in the city and spent much of their time away from their plantations. They adopted fashions of the city, including music, and their bands were expected to play the latest urban songs and dance music at rural parties. *Fazendeiros*, or fazenda owners, demonstrated their wealth in many ways: the size of the main house, the number of buildings on the property, the numbers of slaves, the opulence of furnishings, the grandness of parties, and the size and ability of their bands. The demand for accomplished slave musicians led to the establishment of music schools, which were often run by Jesuit priests. Because service as musicians often exempted slaves from other more strenuous duties, it was a skill well worth acquiring.

Although choro ensembles were directly influenced by choromeleiros, barbeiros, and fazenda bands in terms of instrumentation, repertoire, and playing style, one important difference separates them. Choro arose as a tradition based on the ethos of the roda, a communal voluntary musical gathering. In contrast, fazenda bands were organized by all-powerful plantation owners and barbeiros and choromeleiros were professional groups that played to make money. It was not until the rise of recording in the early twentieth century and radio some decades later that professional choro ensembles, called *regionais*, began to proliferate. These ensembles were direct descendants of the historic *ternos de barbeiros*, one of the few professional urban instrumental ensembles that performed popular music for much of the colonial and imperial periods. Tinhorão suggests that the legacy of the barbeiros continued into the late 1950s with the advent of the popular-music style and genre of bossa nova:

> In the city of Rio de Janeiro the música de barbeiros was the mother of the choro, the grandmother of the professional *regional* of the radio and the great-grandmother of the bossa nova groups. [It] appears to constitute all that is known about the instrumental popular groups that, in a direct line, since the 18th century had contributed to an urban musical tradition founded in the *chorada maneira* [emotional style] of interpreting compositions of the time. All through a curious evolution which, beginning with the poor black barbers, passed successively to the mulattoes of the lower middle class of the end of the nineteenth century, known as chorões, and the professional musicians of the radio of the first three decades of the present century, to arrive at what the *rapazes bem* [white upper-class university youth] of the current time called the bossa nova.[11]

Barbeiros, choromeleiros, and fazenda bands all occupied the same functional niche in popular-music culture: They were professional ensembles formed for the purpose of providing popular songs and dance music of the day. This meant that musicians were required to be versatile in order to be able to play whatever genres were appropriate for the occasion. The heart of these ensembles was the terno of guitar, cavaquinho, and wind instrument; other instruments were added depending upon the ensemble type, the performing context, the location (indoors or outdoors), and the availability of players and instruments. Some of the most notable musicians of the day came from these black professional ensembles, and, as Pinto notes, so many identified themselves with their instrument that they assumed it as part of their name. For example, a cavaquinho player named João might be known as João Cavaquinho. Early choro musicians also adopted this practice, and many carry on with the same tradition even today, with the result that a musician's given name may be known only to close friends and family.[12]

In the second half of the nineteenth century, a great number of well-trained black musicians left the fazendas for the cities. Some were accomplished slave musicians who had won their freedom upon the death of their master or as a reward for years of good service. Others gained their freedom with the Golden Law of 1888, which permanently abolished slavery. It was only natural that these men would seek out kindred musical spirits, and many joined forces with the urban música de barbeiros and nascent choro groups.

The Emergence of Choro in Rio de Janeiro

The choro tradition is firmly embedded in the cultural and social conditions of Rio de Janeiro in the late nineteenth and early twentieth centuries. Situated on Guanabara Bay, Rio de Janeiro was historically an important port city and coffee producer. In 1763, the capital of the Brazilian colony was moved there from Salvador, a move that permanently shifted political and economic power and influence from the northeast to the southeast. Although no longer the capital of Brazil today,[13] Rio de Janeiro is still considered to be the cultural center of the nation as well as a major tourist attraction. In the 1870s, the decade when choro arose, the *cidade maravilhosa,* or marvelous city, as Rio de Janeiro was often called, bore little resemblance to the glitzy cosmopolitan city later portrayed in Hollywood films. At this time, the city had not yet been modernized: Streets in the city's center were narrow and dirty, sanitation was rudimentary, and electric lights were nonexistent. The various neighborhoods, or *bairros,* that today are world famous (e.g., Copacabana, Ipanema, Leme, Gloria) were scarcely settlements, and they were divided by impenetrable hills. Nevertheless, an elite class had already settled in the city, and European fashions, theaters, and opera houses were available for their entertainment.

Supporting this relatively small group of people was a large and diverse population of slaves, poor foreign immigrants (mostly Portuguese and Italians) in search of a better life, and indigent settlers from the northeast fleeing the incessant droughts and hardships of life in the *sertão,* the arid backlands of northeast Brazil. Arriving in Rio de Janeiro with high hopes for a better future, they found instead cramped tenements called *cortiços,* or "beehives"; diseases such as yellow fever; and meager salaries for difficult, sporadic, and often dangerous work. The population tended to settle into ethnic communities: Afro-Brazilians from Bahia (northeastern Brazil) gravitated toward the center of the city, and Portuguese and Italians formed their own districts. Within these communities, many cultural practices brought by the immigrants were maintained. There are numerous reports of Afro-Brazilian religious candomblé ceremonies, accompanied by drums, singing, and dancing, taking place in the parts of Rio de Janeiro known as "Little Africa." Serenaders from the Portuguese communities were known to sing Portuguese fados accompanied by mandolins and guitars, and northeastern Brazilians sang their *embo-ladas* and *toadas* from the sertão.[14]

Between 1870 and 1920, Rio de Janeiro underwent intense, dramatic, and sometimes violent change as it grew from a provincial town into an industrialized city. Realizing that population pressures necessitated citywide sanitation systems to control disease, city officials took the opportunity to transform Rio de Janeiro into a modern European-style city. Using Paris as their ideal, they swiftly replaced the city's narrow winding streets with broad and stately avenues. The social conse-quences of the city's beautification were drastic, however; in order to obtain the space needed for the avenues, most of the *cortiços* (lit. "beehives," but the term came to mean "slums") were torn down, and many of their inhabitants were forced to move to the surrounding hillsides where they constructed flimsy dwellings in makeshift neighborhoods called *favelas*.[15]

During the course of the nineteenth century, an urban middle class (or, more accurately, classes) arose that was made up of inhabitants of Rio de Janeiro who were neither rich plantation owners nor slaves. Immigrants and former slaves took advantage of the jobs opened up by rapid industrialization and others attained petty government jobs. E. Bradford Burns argues that the great disparity among the middle classes in terms of income, education, and family background precludes the grouping of these sectors into a single social class.[16] Nevertheless, they played a critical role in the development of new popular musics, unabashedly blending the erudite with the common and the African with the European.

Choro was one of the first musical expressions of the middle sectors of cario-can society, and it occupied a social position squarely between the European-based music of the elite classes and the music brought to the city by immigrants, freed slaves, and peasants. The middle-class aspects of choro practice were several: Firstly, in order to be able to buy an instrument, whether flute, cavaquinho, or gui-tar, one had to have at least a modicum of disposable income. Secondly, the loca-tions where choro gatherings took place were characteristic of middle-class dwellings and venues; for the most part, they occurred in homes equipped with a yard, or *quintal*, not in the cramped quarters where the lowest classes lived.

From Style to Genre

Between the 1870s and the 1890s, the style of playing waltzes, polkas, lundus, schottisches, and other dances by ensembles of flute, cavaquinho, and one or two guitars known as choro (or the diminutive "chorinho"[17]) gave rise to an entirely new genre of popular instrumental music based on the formal structure of the polka. When the choro first emerged, it was called *polca serenata* (serenade polka) or *polca ligeira* (fast polka) in published sheet music to distinguish it from the danceable variety of polka. The first use of the word "choro" to designate a genre dates from 1889, with the publication of the piece entitled "Só no choro" ["Only in Choro"] by pianist and popular-music composer Chiquinha Gonzaga. Because of lower-class associations however, the appellation "choro" was rarely used on published sheet music until the 1920s. The generic term "polka" was preferred for record labels and sheet music. In much the same way that pianist and composer Ernesto Nazaré insisted on calling his maxixes "tangos brasileiros," the great flautist and choro musician Pixinguinha called his choros "polkas" until "choro" lost its stigma.

In terms of structure, the choro genre shares many characteristics with its European predecessor: It is in duple time and in simple form. The choro generally relies on standard European harmonic progressions (I-IV-V7-I or i-III-VI-ii°-V7-i). Because the genre emerged from the improvisatory style of choro musicians, however, it is also characterized by the stylistic tendencies of highly skilled musicians. The flute was the most common solo instrument until the rise of the professional *regionais* in the 1930s and 1940s. Choro melodies illustrate the most common ways that flautists improvised, including wide leaps, fast chromatic scalar passages, and fast repeated notes. As showpieces for the soloist rather than accompaniment for dancing, choros were intended to be played at a lively tempo with special emphasis on syncopated melodies and/or accompaniments. Many choros start with a three-sixteenth–note pickup played by the soloist, another stylistic device used in practice that became stylized and incorporated into the choro genre. The value of malícia is evoked in the titles of many choros, such as "Apanhei-te cavaquinho" ("I Got You, Cavaquinho"), "Segura ele" ("Catch Him"), and "Cuidado, colega" ("Careful, My Friend"). Other choro titles recall the tender sentiment and longing (*saudade*) of modinhas of the past: Examples are "Relembrando o passado" ("Remembering the Past") and "Velhos tempos" ("Old Times").

Even though a distinctive genre had evolved from choro performance style in the late 1880s, musicians continued to play the earlier repertory as transmitted orally; much in the way that American ragtime musicians would "rag," or play a piece that was not composed as a ragtime in ragtime style, chorões could play any piece from any genre in the choro style. A mazurka, for example, could be played in this way, becoming a mazurka-choro. As Charles Hamm points out, "Flexibility of genre in popular music extends beyond the fact that a given piece can belong to two or more genres, or fall in the intersection of several of them; genre can change from performance to performance."[18]

Joaquim Antônio da Silva Calado (1848–1880)

One of the most important figures in early choro was flautist and composer Joaquim Antônio da Silva Calado (also spelled Callado). Calado was one of the first musicians to embrace the new choro style and the first great choro flautist. In the 1870s, he formed a group consisting of flute, cavaquinho, and two guitars. The group was called Choro Carioca, the first reference to the new ensemble type and musical style. Calado's terno grouping was not new; it was already the core of the black choromeleiro and barbeiros groups found on plantations and, more recently, in the cities. In the choro ensemble, however, the terno came to be more than a convenient grouping of instruments; it affected both the style of the music and the social and musical interaction associated with choro. Calado was one of the first well-known musicians to play polkas in the new choro style, over which he exerted considerable influence. Not only did he provide the musicians in his group with the harmonic progressions for the pieces they performed, but he also demanded that his guitarist provide a baixaria when they played.

The son of a musician, he began his musical studies early; at 8 years of age, he began studying composition and conducting with Henrique Alves de Mesquita, one of Brazil's most respected composers (see chapter 9). Although he was composing actively by 1863, his first major success came with the quadrille "Carnaval de 1867." In 1866, he performed for the imperial family. This was his first performance in a concert hall, and it launched his career as a concert musician. Calado married very young and supported his growing family for years by playing dance music and salon concerts, an activity that exposed him to the new style of playing.

By 1871, Calado was considered the greatest flautist in Brazil and was appointed to the Conservatório de Música. Although he was recognized for his abilities as a classical flautist, he preferred the new popular music that came naturally to him. Like many chorões of later generations, he earned a living performing classical music and played choro for sheer enjoyment in his spare time. He frequented rodas de choro with some of the biggest names in popular music in Rio de Janeiro, such as pianist and composer Chiquinha Gonzaga and the guitarist Saturnino, Calado's favorite accompanist and a great improviser in his own right.[19] Calado contracted meningitis and died in 1880.

The flute that Calado played already had a long history in Brazil, having been introduced by Jesuit missionaries in the sixteenth century as a means of converting the heathens through music education. By the 1870s, the flute had become the favorite melody instrument of the terno formation. Its range, portability, and capacity for dynamic contrast helped the flute survive while other winds, such as the charamela, fell into obscurity. In the terno, it was not uncommon for the flautist to assume the position of group leader. Before the rise of the professional *regionais,* the flute player was typically the only one in a choro group who could read or write music. Players of percussion and plucked-string instruments for the most part learned to play by ear, imitating other players.[20] Unfortunately, there is little data concerning the performing style of early terno flautists such as Calado. From extant recordings, it seems that choro flautists varied articulations, tending to use soft attacks and slurs. Legato seems to have been the preferred articulation, a logical choice considering the sweeping lines of choro melodies, but long notes were rarely sustained. Leaps often included portamento, a common characteristic of choro performance practice.[21] Tadeo Coelho, a flautist and expert on historical Brazilian flute-playing, believes that choro flute players often played very fast but were not concerned with keeping strict and constant time. This flexibility is entirely consistent with the ideal of emotional interpretation and suggests that players were more concerned with the participatory values of the roda than with a technically correct performance.[22]

In addition to his flute-playing, which was by all accounts exceptional, Calado was known for his compositions. He was famous for composing choros on command:

> Calado was not just a musician who could perform at sight, [he] could also compose any improvised choro. Many times he found himself playing at a wedding party, a baptism party, birthday or any other meeting and on these occasions if a lady or gentleman asked him to compose a choro dedicated to the guest of honor, he did not say no, grabbed whatever piece of paper if he had no manuscript, took a pencil and *zaz!* He would start to write [and] in a moment [would] give it to a chorão who played it, becoming a dream for all of the guests because of its clarity and beautiful inspiration.[23]

Calado's compositions, which were mostly polkas and quadrilles, were considered by many to be the best choros of the period, and they have endured the longest of the compositions of any choro composer. His most famous composition, "Flôr amorosa," foreshadows the characteristics of the later mature choro, such as a fast melody with chromaticism, embellishment, wide leaps, rhythmic interest and syncopation, and emphasis on the beat. The most notable difference between other early choros and Calado's music as exemplified in "Flôr amorosa" is the rhythmic component: The melody is dominated by sixteenth-note runs and the accompaniment is dominated by the Afro-Brazilian rhythm and variants on that pattern (see Examples 1.4 and 1.5 in chapter 1).

Calado's legacy in Brazil is profound, both as an instrumentalist and composer. He is considered to be one of the first composers to consciously cultivate choro as a Brazilian genre in opposition to European dominance of the popular arts. He raised the level of flute-playing in Brazil to new heights and is considered to be the first in a long line of choro flute virtuosi that includes Pixinguinha, Benedito Lacerda, and Altamiro Carrilho. Calado is remembered today as one of the first great chorões to establish the new genre as the most popular in Rio de Janeiro at the end of the nineteenth century. Alexandre Gonçalves Pinto placed Calado's biography first in his book, saying, "Calado was a flautist of the first magnitude, and even today he is remembered and missed by the musicians of this time [1935], because his musical compositions have never lost their value. . . . Calado became a god to all who had the pleasure of hearing him."[24]

Anacleto de Medeiros, the son of a freed slave, demonstrated musical ability at an early age. He began his formal music training at age 9 at the Companhia de Menores do Arsenal de Guerra band of Rio de Janeiro. In 1884, he became a type-setting apprentice at the Imprensa Nacional (National Press), and that same year he enrolled at the Conservatório de Música, where he was a classmate of classical composer, conductor, and professor Francisco Braga. Medeiros concentrated on flute and clarinet. Although he graduated from the Conservatório in 1886 with a certificate as professor of clarinet, he later chose the soprano saxophone as his instrument.[25] By 1887, he was recognized as a gifted composer of polkas, waltzes, and schottisches, all genres in the repertory of choro ensembles. His most famous piece is a schottis-che (a salon dance in duple meter similar to the polka) called "Yara" (or "Iara"), which was later used by Villa-Lobos as the theme for his *Choros #10*.[26]

In the late 1890s, choro could be heard at outdoor gatherings played by wind bands. As the founder of several important wind bands in Rio de Janeiro, Medeiros was an important link between the terno and this ensemble. His first band, Recreio Musical Paquetaense, was made up of colleagues from the Arsenal band and local

Example 4.1. "Yara," by Anacleto de Medeiros.

Figure 4.1. Photograph of the Banda do Corpo de Bombeiros. Photo in the collection of the Biblioteca Nacional, Rio de Janeiro.

musicians on his home island of Paquetá (in Guanabara Bay, around which Rio de Janeiro is located, and a short ferry ride from downtown). Later, as a typesetter at the Imprensa Nacional, he organized and conducted the Clube Musical Guttenberg, a small band in Magé, and later he formed a similar band in Bangú (both are neighborhoods in suburban Rio de Janeiro). Most significantly, however, he was the founder of Rio de Janeiro's most respected military band, the Banda do Corpo de Bombeiros (Band of the Fireman Corps),[27] which he conducted until his death in 1907. In these groups, rehearsals were carefully organized, which showed in the quality of the performances.[28]

Medeiros was a regular participant of the roda de choro at the Cavaquinho de Ouro, a music store in downtown Rio de Janeiro, where he played clarinet with young guitarist and composer Heitor Villa-Lobos, choro guitarist Quincas Laranjeiras, modinha enthusiast and "reformer" Catulo da Paixão Cearense, and others. According to Pinto, Medeiros's activities played a significant role in introducing choro style and repertoire to wind players.

Although there is much evidence associating the choro with military and paramilitary bands, little is known about how the bands performed in the choro style. Photographs and early low-quality recordings reveal instrumentation similar to that of military bands in the United States and Europe. These bands performed at various military and civic functions, parties, dances, and annual Carnaval celebrations. Official photographs show band members in uniform holding woodwind and brass instruments, drums, and cymbals. It is possible that in certain circumstances, guitars and cavaquinhos were used as well. Pinto reports that several members of the Banda do Corpo de Bombeiros also played guitar and cavaquinho, himself included, and it would seem logical for this to be true for other bands as well. Jota Efegê confirms the guitar's use in the bands by telling the story of fireman and band member Eduardo das Neves (aka Dudú), who thought that by being a fireman and playing in the band he would not be expected to allow his guitar to gather dust. He was a bohemian before joining the Corpo de Bombeiros and fully intended to remain one after joining. He was devoted to what he had always done—singing and playing guitar—and was in and out of trouble for several years, occasionally ending up in jail for dereliction of duty. Dudú remained in the band because of his ability to play "his magnificent canções (modinhas) and lundus accompanied by his melancholy [choroso] guitar." He ended up a captain in the National Guard band.[29]

Military bands played various styles and genres of music, depending on the occasion. They were expected to maintain a certain level of music proficiency, and some were among the best ensembles in Brazil. Their primary purpose was to provide music for various civil ceremonies and military or paramilitary functions, such as parades. Away from official duties, they provided popular listening and dance music for the members of military organizations and the public at large. Many bands provided recreational music at parties of all varieties, accompanied singers of modinhas, and provided music for Carnaval. In such informal settings, the guitar and cavaquinho were undoubtedly included.

Medeiros and his music are indelibly connected to Carnaval celebrations. By 1895, one year before he founded the Banda do Corpo de Bombeiros, he already had a reputation as an events organizer. That year, the nightclub Phoenix Dramática, which was located on the street where Medeiros lived most of his life, asked him to organize its Carnaval celebration with an Asian theme. To enliven the festivities, he contracted 300 mulatta maxixe dancers as well as a first-rate band that he conducted:

> This large band ("the biggest of all," according to the publicity), executed a varied repertory, very appropriate considering the hip-swaying of 300 maxixe dancers, consisting of polkas with the most exotic and notorious titles: "Queimou a luz!" "Está se coçando!" "Oh! Não me fujas, candongas!" ["I Burned Out the Light!" "You're Scratching Yourself!" "Don't Run Away, Hayseed!"], and other similar ones were some of them. Everything possible [was done] . . . to ensure that the Phoenix Dramática dance would give the public . . . a sleepless night of absolute Carnaval joy.[30]

By 1900, the maxixe had become a mainstay of both the roda de choro and the military band. The minister of war banned the maxixe from military bands in 1907, which confirms that it indeed had been part of military band repertoire before this date. The ban, of course, served only to make the dance even more popular, and many band members reacted by forming other bands to continue performing what they wished or by continuing to play polkas and schottisches but with the feeling and rhythm of a maxixe. Such was the case with Medeiros. Disappointed with the ban affecting Carnaval celebrations for that year, he formed a new Carnaval band, Resedá Ameno, which subverted the ban by playing maxixes disguised as a variety of other genres, including the tango and the polka. Resedá Ameno remained one of the most popular Carnaval organizations for many years after Medeiros's death.

In addition to setting the standard for military bands and for the integration of choro into larger formal ensembles, Medeiros and the Banda do Corpo de Bombeiros were important in another regard in Brazilian music: They were the first ensemble to record music using Edison's new technology. Under Medeiros's baton, the band recorded fifty-five pieces, such as choros and the national anthem, some of which are now available on compact disc.[31]

That Medeiros earned a living as a typesetter made him a true chorão; he played and conducted for the camaraderie and love of the music. He was memorialized as such in Pinto's nostalgic reminiscences:

> Anacleto was a great teacher, and as the maestro of many private bands he left many disciples who did honor to the gifts of the esteemed professor. As the leader of the Banda do Corpo de Bombeiros, he immortalized it with his intelligence, his devotion, and his work, correcting, modeling, and perfecting all of those in his charge with the great magic wand he used in the rehearsals in the guise of a baton, making his students obedient. As a master rehearser, he transformed the Banda do Corpo de Bombeiros into an ensemble of musician-teachers who respected and obeyed him with the all their energy, because Anacleto was a capricious and violent director of music. However, when he did not have the baton in his hand he was as gentle as a lamb. . . . The choros organized by Anacleto made the mute speak and the paralyzed move, made the young crazy and brought youth to the hearts of the old. Anacleto's . . . innumerable compositions . . . are all known by the chorões of the Old Guard.[32]

Medeiros wrote music appropriate for the musicians with whom he worked, who for the most part were amateurs; many of them were marginally trained, if at all. Nevertheless, he was known for the precision of his bands. Piano arrangements of Medeiros's music give clues about the skill level of the ensembles for which they were written; they have clear and predictable melodies and rhythms. Although they are not harmonically sophisticated, they demonstrate some of the hallmarks of choro harmonic motion and accompaniment style.

The Choro Piano: Francisca Edwiges Neves ("Chiquinha") Gonzaga (1847–1935) and Ernesto Nazaré (1863–1934)

Although not a regular instrument in the roda de choro, the piano plays an important role in the choro tradition. Popular piano players, called *pianeiros* to distinguish them from the *pianistas* who played classical music, frequently incorporated the choro style and genre into their performances at theaters and music stores. The most famous pianeiros at the turn of the century were without doubt Chiquinha Gonzaga and Ernesto Nazaré, and their compositions are still favorites in the choro repertoire. Both can be said to have straddled the divide between art and popular music.

As in much of the Western world, owning a piano in Brazil at the turn of the century was considered a mark of social distinction and a must for the aristocratic salon:

The huge grand piano become a symbol of distinction, of taste and social prestige, whether in the aristocratic villas of the suburbs, the upper- or middle-class city homes, or distinguishing, too, the mansions of the more cultivated planters and sugar processors from those more humble or rustic. Contented with a mere guitar or cavaquinho, more rustic plantation homes came to be known disdainfully as "homes without pianos." Thus, the piano became part of the Brazilian social, or socio-cultural, system.[33]

The elite enjoyed the piano sonatas, chanson, and lieder that were popular in Europe as well as the music of Brazilian art-music composers. Some of the more respected pianeiros might be heard in middle-class salons, engaged to entertain at a party where they would play both solo pieces and accompany singers. In the cartoon reproduced in Figure 4.2, three levels of social class are distinguished by the instruments present and the behavior of guests at musical gatherings. The top panel shows the lowest social level—a singer accompanied by guitars and cavaquinhos, the middle shows a singer accompanied by an upright piano in a middle-class salon, and the bottom illustrates richly dressed guests with a singer accompanied by a grand piano in the background. If a home or club happened to have a piano, it was more economical to hire one musician than it was to hire an ensemble; with their versatility, pianeiros filled this niche in the musical market.

Francisca Edwiges Neves Gonzaga, known as "Chiquinha," was a composer, musician, and conductor and the first important female composer and performer of popular music in Brazil. At great personal cost, she broke away from the limited role allowed to women in the Brazilian Republic and defied tradition to establish herself in the musical world.[34] Chiquinha came from humble origins; she was the illegitimate daughter of Field Marshal José Basileu Neves Gonzaga and Rosa Maria, a mulatta. Fortunately, her father decided to recognize her as his own and provided her with an education that included musical training. She began her musical studies at an early age, and by the age of 11 she had composed her first piece, a Christmas song entitled "Canção dos Pastores." She participated in piano recitals throughout her youth and demonstrated exceptional skill. Her desire at a young age to pursue music professionally, however, alarmed her family, as she was ex-

Figure 4.2. The three levels of music. The heading reads "Tell me what
you sing . . . and I will tell you what neighborhood you are from."
Below each panel is a song title, followed by the neighborhoods of
Rio de Janeiro associated with each social class.

pected to conform to the social norms of upper-class society that required women to stay at home. At age 13, she was forced into an arranged marriage but by 18 had already left her husband, who, like her family, insisted that she abandon her musical aspirations. Chiquinha became a single mother who played the piano to support her children. Her family found the situation unacceptable: They took away her daughter, threw her out of the family, and even declared her dead. Over time, Chiquinha succeeded in making a living and a name for herself as a performer and piano teacher.

Gonzaga began attending rodas de choro in the 1870s with the help of Calado, who dedicated "Querida por todas" to her and aided her entry into this musical world. Women were discouraged from participation in rodas, but she nevertheless embraced the bohemian lifestyle and was the first pianist as well as the first woman to regularly participate in the roda. She started composing in the new choro style; her first hit was the polka "Atraente" (1877), originally improvised at a party in homage to the composer Henrique Alves de Mesquita and later published by Artur Napoleão, the publisher and composer with whom Gonzaga studied. The piece was later given lyrics that made references to the composer's lifestyle as a popular musician, which increased her popularity. In 1897, she composed one of the most popular choros of all times, "Corta-jaca" (also known as "O Gaúcho"). In 1899, at the request of the Carnaval group Cordão Rosa de Ouro, Gonzaga composed what is generally considered to be the first Carnaval march, "Abre alas." She performed throughout her career with some of the best-known popular musicians of the time, who would collectively become known as the Velha Guarda, the Old Guard of Brazilian popular music. Flautist and bandleader Pixinguinha used the term "Velha Guarda" for his group in 1932. It is likely the term came into common usage in the 1930s to refer to choro musicians, as by this time choro was viewed as music of an earlier age.

Gonzaga composed much music for the popular theater, a field of musical endeavor usually closed to women at the time. Her work often pushed the limits of good taste according to polite society, thus endearing her to her middle- and lower-class publics. She composed and conducted the music to the one-act play *Festa de São João* in 1883, and two years later she composed and conducted the period opera *A corte na roça*, which premiered at the Teatro Imperial (later São José) in Rio de Janeiro. The opera ended with a maxixe, a genre as popular as it was controversial. Of even greater concern to polite society was her incorporation of lower-class speech in her theatrical productions. In 1885, Gonzaga conducted performances that included the Banda da Polícia Militar, thus becoming the first woman to conduct a major ensemble in Brazil. In 1887, she promoted a concert of 100 guitars at the Teatro São Pedro, giving an air of legitimacy to the guitar, an instrument shunned by the elite. She wrote a number of theater pieces, including the 1895 operetta called *Zizinha maxixe*, through which both she and the maxixe attained a degree of acceptance hitherto unknown. *Zizinha maxixe* featured twenty-three of her pieces, mostly maxixes and her popular choro "Corta-jaca."

Gonzaga was an outspoken activist for a variety of causes. She was a dedicated participant in the abolition movement, perhaps due to her own experiences of being marginalized. For a time she sold her scores door to door to raise money for the Confederação Libertadora (Confederation for Freedom), and she was involved in the campaign for the proclamation of the Republic.[35] She was active in the movement to protect authors' and composers' rights and was one of the organizers of the Sociedade Brasileira de Artistas Teatrais (Brazilian Society of Theater Artists).

By the time Gonzaga reached middle age, she was well established and accepted in musical circles of all classes, and she continued to be active in both popular music and opera. Her work in the theater lent some legitimacy to her other works among the elite and enhanced her overall popularity; between 1885 and 1933, she produced the music for over seventy stage productions. By the time of her death in 1935, her musical works included a great number of theater pieces as well as sacred music, maxixes, marches, serenades, choros, and waltzes.

Chiquinha Gonzaga could have had a comfortable upper-class life as a wife and mother. Instead, she chose to embrace the music and culture of the lower classes and to participate in them to a degree unheard of for any woman. By the time of her death, she had finally been recognized by the upper classes that had for most of her life shunned her both socially and professionally. Eventually her music was even accepted by the elite, and her legacy as an important composer of Brazilian popular music continues today.

Whereas Chiquinha Gonzaga embraced the middle and lower classes in her music and activities, her contemporary Ernesto Nazaré took great pains to try to distinguish himself from the common people. Despite his intentions, Nazaré's works have long been an important part of the choro repertoire and he is considered today to be one of the most important figures in the development of the genre. Nazaré occupies a unique place in the history of choro. As a pianist, he was somewhat outside the choro tradition of the terno and the roda de choro, and, unlike Chiquinha Gonzaga, Nazaré had no desire to mingle with chorões. His preferred audience was the elite of Rio de Janeiro, for whom he played in private homes and as a regular at the prestigious Odeon Cinema in the heart of the city. Although he composed numerous popular works for piano, such as waltzes, choros, and maxixes, he was very careful to avoid using terminology that associated him with the lower classes. For Nazaré, a maxixe was called a *tango brasileiro* and a choro was a polka. It is interesting that Nazaré is considered to be one of the most important nationalist composers of his generation; Villa-Lobos called him "the true incarnation of the Brazilian musical soul."[36] Nazaré openly considered himself a nationalist composer, but believed that he was nonetheless forced to use foreign designations, such as *tango,* for his Brazilian urban popular music: The need to make a living overrode his desire for an openly Brazilian music. The elite would not come to appreciate Brazilian culture for some time, and until it did, musicians such as Nazaré continued to use artificial labels for their music.

Nazaré (also spelled "Nazareth") came from a musical family and began his musical studies with his mother. He quickly developed an ability to improvise and an affinity for Chopin; both of these factors influenced his development as a composer.[37] The music of Chopin has always been very popular in Brazil. Villa-Lobos's first wife, a pianist, undoubtedly played many Chopin pieces, as did many women in her social stratum. Every home from the middle and upper classes had a piano, and young ladies and gentlemen (especially ladies) were expected to become somewhat accomplished pianists.[38]

Nazaré was a classically trained pianist whose technique was based on classical rather than popular sources. Throughout his career he performed both popular and classical music, such as Beethoven, Schumann, Brahms, and, most important, Chopin. His compositions were often more sophisticated in terms of harmony and melody than other popular pieces of his time, and they did not become a standard part of the choro repertoire until many years after his death. Nazaré's music was beyond the technical capabilities of most choro musicians. In fact, his music was little known in his lifetime outside elite social and musical circles.

Nazaré was well thought of by classical musicians of his time, but he performed almost exclusively in salons and theaters. Villa-Lobos admired Nazaré, and for a time they both played at the same theater. Nazaré dedicated music to Villa-Lobos, and Villa-Lobos dedicated the first piece in his *Choros* series to Nazaré. In December 1922, Luciano Gallet promoted a concert of Nazaré's music at the Instituto Nacional de Música, at which Nazaré performed his own compositions in a concert hall for the first time.[39] This concert took place after the Semana de Arte Moderna,[40] when nationalistic fervor had reached a new height in Brazil, particularly in the capital. Audiences finally embraced Nazaré's music as quintessentially Brazilian, no longer needing the disguise of "polka" or "tango."

Nazaré's music has remained popular with Brazilian pianists and classical audiences since his death in 1937. In the 1950s, his works made their way into the rodas de choro, played by terno and other instrumental combinations, and arranged for solo guitar. It is significant that chorões today assume that Nazaré's music has always been performed in this manner; they claim the composer as one of their own.

The origins of choro lie in several Afro-Brazilian ensembles formed on rural plantations and in urban areas. The colonial choromeleiro ensemble from the rural mountain state of Minas Gerais was based on instrumentation reminiscent of the later choro terno and is the most likely origin of the term "choro." In urban areas, many slaves and former slaves were barbers as well as musicians. Barbeiros bands

Figure 4.3. "Ouro sobre azul" ("Gold over Blue"), a maxixe by
Ernesto Nazaré (São Paulo: Editora Bevilacqua, 1910).

were highly versatile ensembles based on guitar, cavaquinho, and flute. These
groups were hired to provide music for a number of different occasions and were
among the first to perform popular lundus for white audiences. Bands of highly
trained slave musicians were formed on fazendas throughout Brazil as a status
symbol for their owners. These bands were capable of playing the latest dance
music from Europe as well as popular modinhas and other Brazilian favorites. With
the abolition of slavery, blacks gravitated in large numbers to the cities, including
Rio de Janeiro, bringing their instrumental skills and knowledge with them.

As the middle class began to form in cariocan society, choro developed as its quintessential musical expression. In 1889, with the piece "Só no choro" by Chiquinha Gonzaga, the choro style gave rise to a new genre of popular music that was based on the form and harmonic structure of the polka and that incorporated aspects of choro performance practice. That choro appealed to and was practiced by a wide variety of musicians is evident in the life and works of four early choro composers: Joaquim Antônio da Silva Calado, Anacleto de Medeiros, Chiquinha Gonzaga, and Ernesto Nazaré. Their works span the period from 1870 to the 1920s and are written for diverse instrumentation that included terno, wind bands, and piano. Elites often shunned choro music because it emanated from the middle and lower classes. This prejudice would gradually erode in the 1920s, and by the 1930s, choro would be upheld by nationalist critics as a proud example of the blending of the races. This allowed for the rise of the most influential ensemble in the history of choro: the professional *conjunto regional*, which would be heard throughout the nation on recordings and radio.

From the Terno
to the
Regional

The Professionalization
of Choro

In the 1920s, Brazilian culture underwent a quiet revolution. After decades of intellectual debate on the scope and nature of Brazilian national identity, the emphasis of *mestiçagem,* or the blending of the races, shifted from the Indian to the African contribution. The sheer number of Africans brought to Brazil over the centuries made the African presence impossible to ignore. Nevertheless, deeply embedded racism as well as disdain for anything emanating from the lower classes prevented the upper classes from accepting anything Afro-Brazilian as valuable. Over time, as nationalism flourished in Europe, the idea became more palatable to the Brazilian elite, who were also comforted by the flip side of mestiçagem: *branqueamento,* or the "inevitable" disappearance of the African and the Indian after complete assimilation by the European. By the end of the 1910s, intellectuals had begun to locate the source of Brazilian musical identity in African-influenced popular music, a position that would have been untenable just a few years earlier.

A revelatory moment in the "discovery" of authentic popular music is captured by sociologist Gilberto Freyre in a diary entry from 1926. The event he describes is an informal musical evening attended by Freyre, journalist Prudente de Morães Neto, historian Sérgio Buarque de Holanda, composer Heitor Villa-Lobos, composer and pianist Luciano Gallet, sambista Patrício Teixeira, and choro musicians Pixinguinha and Donga. Villa-Lobos was already known at the rodas de choro held at the Cavaquinho de Ouro music store and Pixinguinha had by that time established his reputation as a bandleader and virtuoso choro flautist. Freyre had recently investigated the nightlife of Rio de Janeiro outside of the theater and salon, and he enthusiastically described the evening as the most authentic expression of Brazilian culture. He wrote:

> Yesterday, with a few friends—Prudente, Sérgio—I spent a night which almost turned to dawn listening to Pixinguinha, a mulatto, play some of his Carnaval pieces on flute, with Donga, another mulatto, on guitar, and the black, very black Patrício, singing. A great Brazilian night, Rio-style. . . . Hearing the three play we felt the greatness of Brazil which is fettered by the official, false and ridiculous Brazil of mulattos who want to be fair-skinned . . . and of *caboclos* interested in appearing as Europeans or North-Americans.[1]

Freyre felt that this was a prime example of the essence of Brazilian national culture, the blending of the races. He believed popular music to be a unifying force because it had developed "unfettered" by conscious adherence to European models:

> Music, from that of the church to that of the public square, represented by the bands that played at civic functions or the African-derived *sambas* and *maracatús* of Recife or Salvador or Rio de Janeiro, was so important in the life of the Brazilian of the Second Empire in its various and contradictory expressions of life and of culture, in some fashions harmonizing them and in others approximating them, which is realized by the ears better than any other method, as to form the most unifying element in a society of otherwise wide variety in its origins, appearance, and ways of living and thinking. If some types of music suggested different racial or class origins, others acted as a harmonious synthesis of social antagonism and contradictions. The *modinha*, for example, was an important musical agent of Brazilian social unity, sung, as it was during the Second Empire, by some to the piano of a fashionable home or by others to a guitar in the street or the doorway of a humble thatched hut.[2]

Freyre's observations and conclusions are important for the history of Brazilian music, including choro, for they represent a new interest in Afro-Brazilian manifestations of culture. This interest did not go unnoticed by the state, which made use of it for the purposes of gaining popular support during the regime of Getúlio Vargas in the 1930s. Brazilians realized that their nation had an identity and destiny that could be controlled by Brazilians and "for the first time, the mainstream of Brazilian thought learned how to rebel against the framework within which European ideas had straitjacketed it."[3]

The Semana De Arte Moderna

An important event that combined the artistic and intellectual concepts and trends of Freyre's nationalism with European ideas of modernism was the Semana de Arte Moderna (The Week of Modern Art), which took place in São Paulo in February of 1922. It marked a turning point for Brazilian classical composers and continues to serve as a point of reference for artists. The event was intended to be a portentous occasion, as 1922 marked the centenary of Brazil's declaration of independence from Portugal. The modernists who organized the event, led by painter Emiliano Di Cavalcanti, were followers of the artistic modernist movements emanating from Europe including cubism, Italian futurism, German expressionism, and Swiss dada.[4] They believed that Brazilian artists should embrace these trends in their search for an authentic national voice. The goals of the Semana were to shock the public into recognition of the movement, to draw the attention of journalists, and to share the work of Brazilian modernist artists. The Semana consisted of three days of events, including readings from modernist poetry; lectures on modernism in the arts; dance recitals; concerts of classical music by Heitor Villa-Lobos, Ernani Braga, and other composers; and exhibitions of artworks.[5]

The Semana de Arte Moderna was not the beginning of a modernist and nationalist movement in Brazil but rather the culmination of that which had already taken place. It was primarily a literary movement, but many composers and artists shared its goals and aesthetic concerns. Spearheading the intellectual component of the movement was the critic, writer, and musicologist Mario de Andrade, followed by pianist Guimar Novais, writers Oswaldo de Andrade and Graça Aranha, composers Frutuoso Viana and Mozart Camargo Guarnieri, and dozens of other artists. The Semana had important repercussions in Brazilian artistic circles and was responsible for launching the career of composer Heitor Villa-Lobos. It also aided the acceptance of Brazilian popular music as a legitimate national expression and facilitated the rise of the professional choro ensemble, the *conjunto regional*.[6]

Rise of the Choro Regional

During its first fifty years choro was by and large the music of amateurs. Although many were highly skilled musicians who devoted a great deal of time to their art, most held other jobs that supported them and their families. Bandleader Anacleto de Medeiros worked at the Imprensa Nacional, chronicler Alexandre Gonçalves Pinto and many of his choro acquaintances were employed by the postal service, guitarist Quincas Laranjeiras was a civil servant, and Sátiro Bilhar worked at the telegraph office. Pinto's inventory of choro musicians of the Old Guard lists only a few professional musicians in comparison to the number of civil servants; accordingly, early choro was strongly associated with the lower-middle-class sector of society made up of *pequenos funcionários*, petty civil servants.[7]

The changes in attitude toward popular music in the 1920s reflect the profound changes in the city of Rio de Janeiro; the once provincial backwater teeming with yellow fever had become a sophisticated, cosmopolitan metropolis. With the rise of new media and technologies, choro musicians quickly found that their skills were in demand by a large audience. The budding silent film industry began to employ musicians to accompany films, to occupy the audience between reel changes, and to **83** entertain the public in the lobby before showings. Pianeiros were often hired in such capacities, the most famous being Ernesto Nazaré, who was employed by the prestigious Odeon Theater in the fashionable Cinelândia district of Rio de Janeiro. Choro ensembles were also typically hired to play at cinemas and theaters from the turn of the century to the 1920s, and the quality and size of the groups were used as part of their advertising. Olga Prauger de Coelho (b. 1907), a singer, guitarist, and great friend of Villa-Lobos, remembers going to the cinema in her youth:

> On Sundays we would get all dressed up to go downtown to see the pictures. We would get there early, to hear the great Nazaré play in the lobby, or sometimes between the movies. My guitar teacher, Patrício Teixeira, would play the guitar and sing, and the bands would be there too. It was a magnificent sight, these bands, all dressed up and playing those famous maxixes and choros.[8]

Choro ensembles during this transitional period increased steadily in size, incorporating percussion instruments such as the pandeiro and the newly introduced seven-string guitar as regular members. Recordings and radio in the years to come put new demands on the musicians, who were compelled to perform at a consistently high level to satisfy the demand for quality music. The result was greater technical precision and a stylistic change favoring faster, more intricate choros. As professional choro musicians became part of the new media, their primary audience shifted to the middle and upper classes—in effect, those who could afford to participate in the new types of entertainment offered by cinema, the recording industry, and radio. Despite these changes, the old rodas de choro and amateur choro musicians did not disappear, as some historians and musicologists have suggested. Instead, professional musicians augmented the ranks of chorões, when public attention was turned toward the new advances in technology. Rodas de choro became less frequent, and it became cheaper to invest in a record player or rent one for a party than to pay for the food and drink for hosting an ensemble. According to Ary Vasconcelos:

> The choro, between 1919 and 1929, only had a chance to be heard at the popular parties like the Festa da Penha and private parties in the houses and yards of roda members, generally in the suburbs of Rio de Janeiro. In 1927, there was the beginning of the so-called golden age of Brazilian popular music, which, at least for the choro, would be an age, in the best of cases, only of gold-plated tin.[9]

João Pernambuco (1883–1947)

Rio de Janeiro was a common destination for poor migrants from all over the country, especially those fleeing the harsh droughts that plagued the sertão, the arid backlands of the northeast. One such transplant from the northeast was choro guitarist, composer, and teacher João Teixeira de Guimarães, better known as João Pernambuco. His compositions are among the earliest to illustrate the capacity of the guitar to function as a solo instrument. Pernambuco composed a number of solo guitar choros and a series of etudes about which Villa-Lobos said, "Bach would not have been embarrassed to sign his name to them."[10]

Pernambuco arrived in Rio de Janeiro in 1904, where he lived until his death in 1947. During his lifetime he saw the gradual acceptance of the guitar by the upper classes, the birth of the recording industry and radio in Brazil, and the rise of the professional *conjunto regional*. Although he never learned to read or write, Pernambuco nevertheless managed to survive in the city, where he became known in musicians' circles for his skill in accompanying and playing solo, his teaching, and his compositions. His pieces were a direct reflection of his playing style; since he was unable to read or write music, he depended on others to notate his pieces.

Pernambuco was born in the small town of Jatobá in 1883, but the family moved to the coastal city of Recife after the death of his father. One of thirteen children, he was trained as a blacksmith but spent his free time learning guitar and northeastern traditional music from street musicians. In 1904, he decided to try his fortune in Rio de Janeiro; upon his arrival, he found employment at an iron works in Rio Comprido, an outlying region of Rio de Janeiro. Some time later, he earned his keep by shoeing the horses that pulled the city's streetcars. On weekends and whenever he had spare time, Pernambuco frequented rodas de choro. He quickly adopted the choro style and by 1912 was known by some of the best chorões, including Pixinguinha, Donga, and Villa-Lobos. He frequented the rodas at the Cavaquinho de Ouro, where he played with Quincas Laranjeiras, the "grandfather" of the Brazilian guitar tradition, and the Paraguayan guitarist Agustín Barrios. Thus were gathered together the three most important guitarists in the choro tradition until that time. Pernambuco was described as

... the inspired poet of the guitar who makes with this magic instrument a passionate interpreter of his own fantastic artistic imagination, a marvelous instrument which he manages with a naturalness with which the birds sing in the forest in the clear wee hours of the morning or on rainy afternoons or on the moonlight nights in the backlands.[11]

Pernambuco also left his mark on the modinha when he joined Catulo da Paixão Cearense in his efforts to revive the genre. Catulo wrote the lyrics to several of Pernambuco's pieces that became popular contemporary modinhas, including the well-known "Luar do sertão" ("Moonlight on the Sertão"),[12] composed in 1911. By 1914, Pernambuco had abandoned his career as a blacksmith to become a full-time professional, making his living playing in movie theater ensembles. Despite his immersion in cariocan choro, Pernambuco never forgot his northeastern roots. That same year he became a member of the Grupo Caxangá, which was

Figure 5.1. Photo of João Pernambuco (left), Quincas Laranjeiras (right) and Augustín Barrios (seated) at the Cavaquinho de Ouro music store. Photo in the collection of the Biblioteca Nacional, Rio de Janeiro.

named after a town in the northeast and featured música nordestina (traditional music from the northeast). Some of the best-known musicians in choro and samba passed through this group, including Pixinguinha and samba musicians Donga and Nelson Cavaquinho. In 1915, he formed the Troupe Sertaneja, which played both música nordestina and choro. Cariocans had developed a taste for música nordestina in the early twentieth century as an exotic and quaint tradition from a distant land having little to do with them, despite the large number of migrants from that region in Rio de Janeiro.

The renewed interest in Brazilian popular music as a source of national pride meant that by the 1920s, Pernambuco was performing for the upper classes in their salons. Philanthropist Arnaldo Guinle was so taken with Pernambuco's talent that in 1919 he insisted that Pixinguinha's distinguished group, the Oito Batutas, add Pernambuco to its ranks. Pernambuco had already met and played with most of the Batutas (many had been members of Grupo Caxangá) and was immediately accepted by his peers. His last performance with the Batutas was given in 1921.

Choro musicians typically learn to play choro by attending rodas and by listening to and watching more-experienced players. Pernambuco was one of the few chorões who put a great deal of time and effort into pedagogy, and by all accounts he was an excellent guitar teacher. He and fellow choro guitarist Quincas Laranjeiras gave lessons at the Cavaquinho de Ouro music store in the late 1920s. Although he was self-taught, Pernambuco was concerned with what he considered proper use of the instrument, which had nothing to do with accepted "correct" technique:

> His relationship with the instrument was so profound that he gave us the impression that it was an extension of his body and used it as if it were a natural function, such as walking and breathing. Also great was his respect and preoccupation with the use of the guitar, so much so that João became furious when he saw anybody playing the guitar by strumming the strings. He said that the strings were to be played one by one, which is to say, drawing the sound out of each string. This technical understanding was acquired on the corners, in the streets, at fairs. These were his schools. Later it was his great friend Quincas Laranjeiras who passed on to him some understanding of music theory augmented by the frequent gatherings with his friends.[13]

Besides his works for guitar, Pernambuco's greatest contribution to the choro tradition was his guitar technique. He did not feel restricted by existing methodologies, and he used all of the resources available to him. Among the innovative yet practical techniques he developed was the use of the left hand in addition to the right, as described by his brother Joca:

> He often played the guitar only with his left hand, which is to say, he made the sounds only on the neck of the guitar. He did this with the greatest naturalness.

He played whatever piece looking towards the sky, towards a wall, not paying attention to the neck of the guitar. He had a fingering and quality that until today I have not seen.[14]

One cannot fully appreciate Pernambuco's contributions to the guitar without understanding that until approximately the 1920s, his instrument was the object of disdain among the elite. Although cherished in popular culture, the elite saw the guitar as a despised manifestation of low culture. For this reason, popular genres were played on piano in the salon, not the guitar. The police were subject to the whims of powerful individuals whose dislike sometimes turned into active persecution. There are countless reports from the turn of the century of cariocan police arresting guitar players for no reason other than that they were playing a guitar.[15] Even Villa-Lobos had to learn the instrument in secret, having been forbidden to study so vulgar an instrument. Donga recalls:

> Dr. Nair de Teffé told me of interesting cases with respect to the restrictions imposed by the police on guitar players. The bourgeois prejudice against the instrument made for a scandal in society of the time: on this particular occasion it involved Brazil's First Lady, who liked music. One night, at an official reception, she came into the room with her guitar and played no less than "Corta-jaca" by Chiquinha Gonzaga. There were of course tremendous repercussions![16]

Pernambuco's teachings and solo compositions were embraced by choro guitarists, and his legacy was carried on by other musicians such as Paraguayan guitarist Agustín Barrios and Brazilian guitarists Garoto and Dilermando Reis.

Pernambuco was only one of many choro musicians to come from the northeast.[17] With the advent of radio and the rise of the *regional* in the 1930s and 1940s, choro was no longer confined to the urban areas of the southeast, and choro musicians could be found from many different regions of Brazil. Although it was considered important for musicians to journey to the source of choro, Rio de Janeiro, many musical migrants returned home, establishing regional variants of the choro tradition throughout Brazil.[18] In this way, choro truly did become a national style and genre.

Choro, the Recording Industry, and Radio

The birth of the recording industry and the establishment of live radio shows in Brazil were the two most significant factors in the professionalization of choro. With the introduction of recording in Brazil in 1902, popular music came to be influenced by the nascent consumer industry that developed in conjunction with the new communication technologies. The introduction and proliferation of radio in the decades to come would have an enormous impact on the course of popular music; these new technologies not only changed the face of Brazilian music but also allowed American and European musics to flood into Brazil, resulting in an increased diversity of styles.

The first recordings of music produced in Brazil were made available by Czech-born Frederico Figner, who had learned about recording technology in the United States in 1882 at the National Phonograph Company. He went to Brazil in 1891, and by 1901 he had founded one of the first recording companies in Brazil, the Casa Edison Company. Relying on Emile Berliner's technique of recording on discs, Figner produced and sold *chapas* (double-sided discs), cylinders, and "talking machines." An announcement in the newspaper *O Correiro da Manhã* of August 5, 1902, conveys some of the excitement this novelty must have produced and highlights the importance of choro even at this early date:

> The biggest event of the epoch arrived at Casa Edison, Rua do Ouvidor, 107. "Chapas" for gramophones and zonophones with national modinhas sung by the most popular Baiano and the highly appraised Cadete, with guitar accompaniment, and the best polkas, schottisches, maxixes played by the Banda do Corpo de Bombeiros do Rio, under the direction of maestro Anacleto de Medeiros.[19]

Newly established recording companies in Brazil hired professional ensembles of choro musicians to accompany singers. The Banda da Casa Edison and the Grupo do Malaquias were among the first to record.[20]

Many early choro recordings were made by civilian or military bands, which typically provided the wind players found in choro. Because an instrument's volume was crucial for a successful take during the early years of acoustic recording, quiet accompanying instruments such as guitar were often exchanged for louder instruments such as the piano, tuba, or ophicleide. The advent of electric recordings allowed choro musicians to use normal instrumentation and playing styles instead of attempting to accommodate the crude and clumsy technology of earlier times. The development of electric microphones in the 1920s allowed the quiet string instruments of the *regional* to be heard in a variety of performing contexts. After approximately 1915, the pandeiro regularly appears on recordings; the seven-string guitar begins to be heard regularly in the 1920s.

The first radio broadcast in Brazil was September 7, 1922, the centennial of Brazilian independence and the same year as the influential Semana de Arte Moderna. Signifying a new national consciousness, the music in the broadcast included the opera based on Amerindian themes called *O Guarani* by Antônio Carlos Gomes. The program also featured choros by the young choro flautist Pixinguinha and his group, the Oito Batutas. From these early groups came the *conjunto regional*, the professional choro ensemble that became the workhorse of the radio industry in the 1930s and 1940s. These ensembles were based on the choro terno of guitar, cavaquinho, and melody instrument, augmented by pandeiro and the seven-string guitar, and were responsible for accompanying singers and instrumentalists in a wide array of genres and styles. Through radio, the sound of the *regionais* reached even the most remote parts of the nation, where it became known not just as the music of Rio de Janeiro but as the music of the entire nation.

It is likely that these ensembles came to be known as *conjuntos regionais,* or regional ensembles, early in the twentieth century. Before samba predominated as the preferred Carnaval genre, choro ensembles were commonly part of Carnaval festivities; during the 1910s, it became fashionable for these groups to dress in the manner of rural northeasterners and assume northeastern names such as Turunas Pernambucanos (The Fearless Ones from Pernambuco), Turunas da Mauricéia (The Fearless Ones of Mauricéia), and Grupo do Caxangá com Pixinguinha. Since these ensembles evoked the northeast region even though they played in a thoroughly cariocan style, they were known as "regional ensembles." Over time, the northeastern associations were lost and the name conjunto *regional* was assumed by professional radio ensembles with specific instrumentation (guitar, cavaquinho, and pandeiro with a soloist) and repertoire (i.e., pre-1930s popular dance genres and choros). The high demands put on the *regionais* for stylistic versatility and high-quality performances did much to raise the general level of musical skill. New and difficult choros, meant to be played rapidly with a great deal of melodic embellishment, were composed to showcase the soloists of the *regionais.*

The pandeiro and the seven-string guitar, the two instruments added to the terno in the *regional,* deserve some comment, as musicians today consider them both to be part of the "traditional" choro ensemble. In the 1920s, the pandeiro, which is similar to the American tambourine, became the primary percussion instrument of the *regional,* responsible for maintaining the compound sixteenth-note rhythm of choro as well as adding rhythmic accents and effects. Why the instrument was not used earlier is not certain, but it is likely that the strong associations between the pandeiro (and any percussion instrument) and Afro-Brazilian culture discouraged its use. Indeed, upper-class fear of Afro-Brazilian percussion instruments and the religious ceremonies they sometimes accompanied reached such heights that, like the guitar, the pandeiro and its relatives were banned at various times in Rio de Janeiro. Today the pandeiro is used in a number of popular music traditions, including samba, pagode, and choro. The first use of the pandeiro in an established professional ensemble was probably by the Oito Batutas in 1919, although percussion instruments were likely used before that on an occasional basis.

In the 1930s, the seven-string guitar (*violão de sete cordas,* often abbreviated as "v.7") was commonly added to the choro ensemble. In addition to the six strings found on a standard guitar, the violão de sete cordas has an added bass string (usually tuned to C or occasionally B), thereby extending the range of the instrument for playing bass lines. The seven-string guitar player normally assumes the baixaria (bass line), which consists of plucked notes (often in rapid succession) rather than strummed chords. The origins of the instrument are obscure, but it may be derived from the Russian seven-string guitar, a folk instrument popular in the late nineteenth and early twentieth centuries before it was displaced by the introduction of the six-string guitar from Europe. Some believe that Russian immigrants introduced the instrument to Brazil. Another story holds that China, one of Pixinguinha's brothers, first heard the instrument played by gypsies at the famous musical gatherings of Tia Ciata and adopted it himself soon after. It is certain that China played the instrument in the group Os Oito Batutas; a photo of the group in Paris dated 1922 clearly shows China holding a seven-string guitar. Another early player of the violão de sete cordas was Artur de Souza Nascimento, affectionately known as "Tute." It was Tute who inspired guitarist Horondino da Silva to switch from the six-string to the seven-string guitar. Today the name Dino Sete Cordas, as his friends call him, is synonymous with the instrument. His style of playing has greatly influenced other seven-string guitarists, including the late Raphael Rabello, and Dino is credited with popularizing the instrument beginning in the 1950s.

By the 1930s, the recording industry employed large numbers of solo singers and instrumentalists, many of whom were featured on radio broadcasts as well. Radio stations and record companies found it more convenient to maintain their own *regionais,* and some musicians were contracted to play in several of such groups.[21] The *regionais,* some of which consisted of as many as twelve to fifteen players, were usually named after the lead player and were strongly identified with their parent station or company. *Regionais* functioned as in-house orchestras, accompanying singers, playing dance music, and playing "their" music; that is, choro. These groups also provided background music and music to fill in between acts on live radio shows. Radio *regionais* often performed live in front of studio audiences, and some groups even inspired fan clubs, a common sight at radio broadcasts. One of the earliest *regionais* was Gente do Morro (The Guys from the Hill). Formed in 1930, the group featured renowned choro flautist Benedito Lacerda. The most prominent radio stations of the 1930s and 1940s and their *regionais* were:

Rádio Guanabara: Gente do Morro and Jacob e Sua Gente
Rádio Transmissora: O Regional de Claudionor Cruz
Rádio Clube: Waldir Azevedo e Seu Regional
Rádio Tupi: Regional de Benedito Lacerda and Regional Rogério Guimarães
Rádio Mayrink Veiga: Regional do Canhoto
Rádio Nacional: Regional de César Moreno and O Regional de Dante Santoro
Rádio Mauá: Jacob e Seu Regional, Regional de Darly do Pandeiro, and Regional de Pernambuco do Pandeiro.

Regionais were expected to accompany any and all types of songs, including sambas; modinhas or their modern equivalent, canções; and American songs. Usually they provided an improvisatory introduction followed by accompaniment for the singer. For sambas, an introduction was typically played by flute, bandolim, or another melodic instrument; the cavaquinhos, guitars, and pandeiro would follow as the singer began. Because samba and choro arose in similar social milieus and share many style characteristics, even today the guitar, pandeiro, and cavaquinho are viewed as part of the samba tradition, a view that was strongly shaped by the radio *regional*.

Despite the high level of performance expected from musicians in the *regional*, there were still those, particularly guitarists, cavaquinho players, and percussionists, who did not read music. As a result, the earliest *regional* arrangements were characterized by a degree of spontaneity and improvisation in both structure and accompaniment. The usual procedure was a variation of the following: The musicians would gather several hours before a scheduled broadcast or recording session. The pieces to be played that day were selected, many of which were already known to the players, and the key was agreed upon. As in the roda de choro, each instrumentalist would fit his part into the stylistic puzzle: The guitars would pluck or in some cases strum harmonies; the seven-string guitars would improvise a baixaria; the cavaquinhos would provide rhythmic and harmonic color; and a melodic instrument such as a flute, clarinet, or (later) a saxophone would play the melody and embellish on the repeats. If a singer was scheduled for a broadcast, a melodic instrument would improvise an introduction; the other melodic instruments would improvise counterpoint to the melody.

Pixinguinha (1897–1973)

Whereas João Pernambuco participated only marginally in the new opportunities for professional musicians, Alfredo da Rocha Vianna, Jr., better known as Pixinguinha,[22] took full advantage of these and in the process became the best known and most admired chorão in the history of the tradition. Pixinguinha was born on April 23, 1897.[23] His father, Alfredo, Sr., was a flautist, but like typical chorões of the time, he held a day job in the telegraph office. He amassed a great collection of choro scores[24] and held frequent rodas in his home, with the result that his sons grew up immersed in choro; besides Pixinguinha, his brothers Leo, Otávio (known as "China"), and Henrique also became respected chorões.

Pixinguinha demonstrated ability on both flute and cavaquinho and started composing at an early age. By the age of 14, he had composed his first choro, "Lata de leite" ("Can of Milk") and was already an accomplished flute player. That year he began studying composition with Irineu de Almeida, another great chorão and friend of his father's, who used to play with Anacleto de Medeiros and Villa-Lobos at the Cavaquinho de Ouro. In 1913, he made his first choro recordings, including a piece composed by Almeida to show off Pixinguinha's talents on the flute; his teacher accompanied him on ophecleide.[25] By the time he was 15, he was playing professionally,[26] and by the age of 18, he was one of the most popular musicians and choro composers in Rio de Janeiro.

Pixinguinha rose to fame in Brazil during a period when the elite had begun to become intrigued, if only in a voyeuristic manner, with aspects of the "underworld" of Rio de Janeiro. The brief resurgence of the modinha, led by Catulo Paixão de Cearense and João Pernambuco, was a result of this interest, and choro was soon to follow. In 1919, at the behest of Isaac Frankel of the movie theater Cine Palais, Pixinguinha formed the legendary Oito Batutas[27] (The Eight Remarkable Players). The group consisted of flute (and later saxophone), guitars, cavaquinho, bandolim, pandeiro, bandola, and assorted percussion. The Batutas may have been the earliest ensemble to regularly incorporate the pandeiro, which was first heard in a recording the group made from 1921; it was played by Jacó Palmieri, who used it in conjunction with the *rêco-rêco* (gourd rasp) and *ganzá* (shakers). The repertoire of the group was an eclectic blend of popular instrumental and vocal music of the time, including choros, sambas, "tangos," and música nordestina.

The group was enormously successful; it entertained customers in the foyer before film showings and attracted large audiences to the theater. Besides being popular entertainers, Pixinguinha and members of his group were among the first to break the racial barrier that prevented black musicians from performing in upper-class venues. The Batutas even performed at the prestigious Assyrian Cafe, after which they embarked on a tour around Brazil, with stops in São Paulo, Santos, Campinas, Ribeirão Preto, Belo Horizonte, and Curitiba. In 1921, they accompanied Duque and Gaby, the Brazilian dance duo that introduced the maxixe to Paris. Because of Duque's influence, the Batutas were brought to the attention of Arnaldo Guinle, the philanthropist who in 1919 had urged João Pernambuco to join the group. Guinle was a supporter of national culture who encouraged Brazilian artists to visit Paris under his sponsorship.[28] With Guinle's support, the Batutas were to be "musical ambassadors" for Brazil, a mission that created as much enthusiasm in France as it did controversy at home. The importance of presenting the Brazilian face of culture abroad was undisputed; what was at issue was the color of the face that Brazil should show.

The controversy generated by the departure of the Batutas for France in 1921 was not the first time Pixinguinha had been subjected to criticism. A few years earlier, singer and poet Catulo da Paixão Cearense had questioned President Epitácio Pessôa's decision to have Pixinguinha perform for the visiting king and queen of Belgium rather than himself.[29] Although it is not clear if racism was a motivating factor in this instance, race was definitely at the heart of the Batutas controversy. The following editorial was written as a rebuttal to the racist attacks on Pixinguinha:

It was a true scandal when, four years ago, the Oito Batutas appeared. Here were Brazilian musicians performing Brazilian music! All this in the middle of Avenida,[30] in the middle of such dandyism, among all these anemic young men who frequent cabarets, who speak only French and dance only the Argentine tango! Right in the middle of the internationalism of French tailors, Italian booksellers, Spanish ice-cream shops, American automobiles, Polish women, and of cosmopolitan idiotic snobbishness!

Critics of the modest Oito Batutas are not lacking. Critics of the heroic Oito Batutas who set out in a cinema on the Avenida, to sing of the true Brazilian land by means of their music, sincerely, without contrivances and without hamming it up, with the spontaneous sound of their guitars and cavaquinhos.

The war waged against them was ferocious. Even though the musicians were skilled, true "aces (batutas)," magnificent guitarists and singers; even though Pixinguinha's flute-playing was better than any flautist around here with ten diplomas from ten institutions—those spiteful critics began to comment on the color of the Oito Batutas, the majority of whom are black. According to these malcontents, it was a disgrace for Brazil to have a black band on the main avenue of its capital city. What would foreigners think?

I had the honor to defend the Oito Batutas (and the defense I made was the most vigorous of my career in journalism) on that occasion. It was just four years ago. . . . Today however I want to get back to the subject—the "Oito Batutas" departed this week for Paris . . .

—For Paris?

—But this is humiliating!

—How come the Ministry of Foreign Affairs isn't doing anything about it?

—Now Brazil will be completely humiliated!

Silence, you imbeciles. Silence, you patriotic cockroaches. Silence, you pretentious musicians who play music in the entrances of Casa Mozart and Arthur Napoleão.[31]

The Oito Batutas will not humiliate Brazil in Europe. On the contrary. They will carry in their guitars the sung soul of Brazil—the modinha. They will bring all that Brazil is in its feeling and natural beauty. They will bring true Brazilian music, that which has not yet been contaminated by foreign influences and which thrills and suffers and weeps of its own accord, singing of the moonlight in the *sertão* and the eyes of the *caboclos*. They will bring the perfume of our forests, the pride of our jungles, the grandeur of our country, the melancholy of our people, the goodwill and love of our hearts, spoken and sung in simple verse, and the sublime music of the soul of the people. . . . They will bring the true Brazil, unbeknownst by Brazilians themselves, but formidable just the same in the enigma of its forces and aspirations . . .

—But, they are black!

—What does it matter? They are Brazilians![32]

This essay represents a particularly romantic strain of national sentiment. The author condemns the cosmopolitan orientation of the elite and the concern for what foreigners think, yet the music identified as "Brazilian" is the Luso-Brazilian modinha, not choro and not manifestations of Afro-Brazilian culture. The author characterizes "blackness" not in terms of racial heritage but as part of the natural landscape of Brazil that includes the moonlight on the sertão and the green eyes of the Indian-European caboclos. Nevertheless, it illustrates the passions that the Batutas generated as national icons.

Pixinguinha and the Batutas were not only subjected to racial attacks, they were also criticized for being corrupted by the influences of American jazz. When they returned from Paris in 1923, critics interpreted Pixinguinha's incorporation of the saxophone and trumpet and the inclusion of certain North American genres into the repertoire as an indication that they had become *jazzificado* (jazzified). Pixinguinha argued in his defense that the trumpet and saxophone had already appeared in choro groups before the Batutas and that the incorporation of foreign genres was necessary if he was to survive as a professional musician:

> [I]t was that we were playing *commercially,* as professionals, and we'd play every-thing in our ensemble. We used to go to a dance to play what is ours. Every now and then we would include a little fox-trot, for variation. Commercially, we had to play a little bit of everything.[33]

In 1928, and again in 1930, Pixinguinha and Donga were attacked by a record re-viewer who claimed that their recordings of the *choro-canções* (sung choros) "Lamentos" and "Amigo do povo" in 1928 and "Carinhoso" in 1930 were disap-pointing because of the influence of jazz.[34]

In 1921, the Batutas spent six months in Paris. The group opened in the night-club Cabaré Sheherazade and had great success as a dance band. Pixinguinha re-turned to Brazil from Paris with a saxophone, which would become his primary in-strument beginning in 1946. He also brought home a familiarity with French popular music and the American ragtime that was popular in Paris at the time. João Pernambuco was added to the group after the European excursion at the insistence of Guinle, although it retained the name the Oito Batutas. Always sensitive to what the public wanted, Pixinguinha added more instruments to the group and allowed the repertoire to include jazz tunes as well as Brazilian music. At this point, the group became known simply as Os Batutas.

After the European tour, the group went to Buenos Aires, where they were en-gaged to perform at several clubs. They also made several recordings for the Victor label[35] that featured sambas, maxixes, and choros labeled as polkas and tangos, all composed by members of the group (including João Pernambuco, who did not play on the recordings). These recordings, made in 1923, constitute an important histor-ical document of choro; they represent the performance style of the day) and pre-serve several pieces that otherwise would have been lost.

Pixinguinha maintained a busy recording schedule with several different *region-ais,* including Orquestra Típica Pixinguinha, a particularly large *regional.* Despite his as-sertion that he was never very involved in samba, he recorded many sambas. In 1917, he even participated in what many believe to be the first recording of samba, "Pelo

Figure 5.2. Photo of the Oito Batutas. Note that there are actually nine players. The additional musician is João Pernambuco (seated, center). Photo in the collection of the Biblioteca Nacional, Rio de Janeiro.

telefone," which was written by his friend and colleague Donga.[36] As the number of *regionais* continued to multiply with the expansion of the recording and radio industries, Pixinguinha became the arranger and conductor for various bands. His talents were also in demand by many famous singers, including Carmen Miranda and Mário Reis. In this way he gained a familiarity and worked with all of the most popular samba artists.

Pixinguinha was equally at ease as a performer, composer, and arranger. His career as a music arranger began in the late 1920s when the Victor Talking Machine Company hired him as orchestrator and director of the Orquestra Victor Brasileira. From piano scores, Pixinguinha created parts for *regional,* often adding long introductions and variations on the melody, much as the piece would be interpreted in the choro roda. Unfortunately, few of his arrangements were published; those that were usually consisted of instrumental parts without a conductor's score.[37]

By the late 1930s, the size of many *regionais* and the demand for music that incorporated aspects of American music necessitated written-out arrangements. Pixinguinha was one of the few chorões who was a competent arranger as well as a skilled player, composer, and conductor. One of his surviving arrangements is of the popular choro "Ingênuo," published in 1948 by Irmãos Vitale.

The orchestration in Example 5.1 is not that of a typical *regional;* instead, it is scored for three saxophones, two trumpets, flute, trombone, and bass, an ensemble resembling an American jazz band. The arrangement dates from 1947, a time when the influence of American jazz music was strong; pieces such as this were often referred to as *choro de jazz band.* As American jazz music became more and more prominent in Brazil in the 1940s, *regionais* were pressured to adopt the style in order to please audiences. Improvisation decreased as musicians were restricted to playing written arrangements that simulated the sounds and style of jazz. Few choro professionals besides Pixinguinha were willing or able to create such arrangements, and the need was filled by classical composers, including Guerra-Peixe and Radamés Gnattali, who were well versed in popular as well as classical music (see chapter 9).

Despite the instrumentation, the arrangement reflects typical *regional* style. The flute is responsible for the melody, accompanied by saxophones in harmony and in unison rhythm. The trombone part provides timbral punctuation at important places in the structure, in the manner of the six- or seven-string guitar. The bass part is written in quarter notes, but in performance, the baixaria would have been improvised. Although they are not indicated in the score, guitars, cavaquinhos, and percussion would undoubtedly be used in performance. *Regional* musicians would already be adept at improvising from a bass line or by ear; thus, a written part was considered to be superfluous.

In the 1930s, the popular view of choro began to take on nostalgic overtones. There was a feeling among choro musicians and fans that the "golden age" of choro had passed and that the choro of the present was somehow different, perhaps because it was now disseminated by radio and recording. Undoubtedly the increasing presence of American popular music had something to do with this perception; anything emanating from the United States was automatically categorized as contemporary, modern, and sophisticated. In comparison, Brazilian popular music was increasingly viewed as the opposite. The 1930s mark the turning point; after that, Brazilian music would be compared, positively or negatively, to American music. In this decade, Alexandre Gonçalves Pinto wrote his tribute to the old chorões of the past in a distinctly nostalgic manner, and Pixinguinha, at age 35, formed an ensemble with the nostalgic name Grupo da Velha Guarda, the Old Guard Group, in 1932. As if the instrumentation of the choro *regional* were not Brazilian enough, Pixinguinha added a number of Brazilian percussion instruments to those already in use by the Batutas, including *chocalho* (rattle), maracas, *afoxé* (gourds encased in beaded nets), *berimbau* (musical bow), *bombos* (drum), *cuíca* (friction drum), *agogô* (double-headed cowbell), and *prato e faca* (literally, plate and knife). All of these instruments (with the exception of the berimbau) are typical of Carnaval samba groups, and all are strongly associated with Afro-Brazilian culture.

Many of Pixinguinha's compositions are part of the core repertoire of choro. One such standard is the piece "1 × 0 (Um a zero)" ("One to Zero"), written in 1917. The title refers to the score of a soccer match in which Brazil defeated Uruguay for the South American championship, and it exhibits the spirit of *malícia* prized among chorões, including a breakneck tempo, rapid arpeggios, and few pauses for the flautist to take a breath. Perhaps the best known vocal choro, or *choro-canção*, is "Carinhoso" ("Tenderly"), also composed by Pixinguinha in 1917. Because of the negative reaction of critics who charged the piece as being "under the influence of jazz," Pixinguinha did not release it for ten years.[38] In the 1930s and 1940s it was a favorite of popular crooners, including Orlando Silva. It has since become one of the most well-known popular songs in Brazil and is often requested by audiences who want to sing along. Pixinguinha composed in many genres, including the samba, the waltz, the maxixe, and Carnaval sambas.

Throughout the 1930s and 1940s, American music occupied an ever-increasing portion of the music industry. As a result, choro was forced to compete with samba for the shrinking slice of the market dedicated to domestic music. Samba had several advantages over choro: It was vocal, it tended to be direct and used singable melodies and uncomplicated harmonies, and every year it was highlighted during

Carnaval time. By the late 1940s, choro had undergone a severe decline in air time and dissemination, and the *regional* fell out of favor as the all-purpose studio band for recording companies and radio stations. Pixinguinha found it increasingly difficult to make a living, and in a moment of crisis, he sold the rights to his music to his friend and fellow musician Benedito Lacerda. From that time, all of Pixinguinha's music was published under the names of both chorões.

In 1946, Pixinguinha gave up the flute for the saxophone. On recordings made after this time, one hears Pixinguinha creating elaborate counterpoints to the flute melody, almost always played by his partner Benedito Lacerda. Sadly, some of his most famous choros, including "Sofres porque queres" ("You Suffer Because You Want To") and "Um a zero," were recorded with Pixinguinha playing a prominent but still secondary role. In the 1950s and 1960s, choro dropped out of the music industry and from the public view. Pixinguinha spent his time in retirement playing at local parties and special events. Nevertheless, music was still the most important thing in his life. In 1964, Pixinguinha suffered a mild heart attack; while in the hospital he is said to have written some twenty choros with titles such as "No elevador" ("In the Elevator") and "Mais quinze dias" ("Fifteen More Days [in the Hospital]").

Pixinguinha is generally viewed as the most important choro musician, arranger, performer, and composer. He left dozens of choros, many of which remained in the choro repertory during the lean years of the 1950s and 1960s and continue to be favorites today. In addition to the aforementioned works, his best known pieces include "Descendo a serra" ("Going Down the Mountain"), "Rio antigo" ("Old Rio"), "Rosa," "Naquele tempo" ("In That Time"), "Os Oito Batutas," "Cheguei" ("I've Arrived"), "Ele e eu" ("He and I"), and "Segura Ele" ("Hang on to Him"). Before his death in 1973, Pixinguinha witnessed many changes musically and politically: the rise and fall of many different musics including choro, samba, samba-canção, jazz, bossa nova, and rock and roll; the rise of recording, radio, cinema, and television; two world wars; the rise and fall of Gétulio Vargas and the return of dictatorship in 1964; the life and death of Carmen Miranda; and the construction of the new capital city of Brasília from the barren red clay of central Brazil. It is a pity that he did not live long enough to witness the one thing that perhaps would have made him the most happy: the revival of choro and its subsequent reemergence as a valued and permanent Brazilian musical tradition.

Getúlio Vargas, Carmen Miranda, and Popular Music

If the 1920s saw great changes in the realm of popular music and its dissemination, the 1930s were an era of great political change marked by the rise of a government controlled by one man with strong ideas of nationalism. The dictatorial regimes of Getúlio Vargas (1937–1945) were periods of repression, dissent, censorship, reduced personal liberties, and a government that moved progressively to the right. They mimicked some of the traits of European fascist models in a milder version of fascism called corporatism, particularly during the Estado Novo from 1937 to 1945, and focused on nationalism, social welfare, and economic development.[39] During the Estado Novo, a large propaganda machine worked hard to keep Vargas in power. It was a time of intensive educational and artistic reform activities as well, during which the Vargas governments stressed civic pride, patriotism and citizenship, discipline, and physical fitness. Music played an important role; Brazilian popular music was incorporated into official radio programs, and schoolchildren learned Brazilian folk songs as part of their lessons in citizenship and physical fitness.

Like leaders of other totalitarian states, Vargas used the institutions and power of the state to promote his nationalist agenda, placing the state, rather than the intellectual elite, in charge of what nationalism should mean to the ordinary citizen. His regimes formalized the stifling of intellectual creativity through censorship and the repression of dissent while at the same time overhauling the educational system to fit the new aims of the state. Composer Heitor Villa-Lobos was given the important job of creating and putting into place a national system of music education, a job he would hold until Vargas's suicide in 1954. In a decree of April 18, 1931, music education and choral singing were made mandatory in primary and secondary educational institutions throughout the nation, and the office of SEMA, the Superintendência da Educação Musical e Artística, was established with Villa-Lobos as the director. In his new position, he created a method called "orpheonic singing" that used Brazilian folk and popular music as a source and emphasized love of the fatherland, discipline, and physical fitness. To disseminate the programs, he directed a school for music teachers and published various guides related to the topic. Villa-Lobos's ideas of civic musical education were periodically presented to the nation in mass choral spectacles, supported of course by the Vargas government, which embraced the pomp and pageantry of European totalitarianism. These celebrations were usually held on national holidays—Workers' Day, Independence Day, and National Flag Day—in soccer stadiums or other large open-air spaces and included marching, flag-waving, patriotic speeches, folk dancing, and addresses by the president. The largest of these choral spectacles was held in 1943 and involved 44,000 students. Whether or not Villa-Lobos supported the regimes and their goals is irrelevant to our arguments; the fact remains that he held a very important post in the Vargas government for years that gave him a great degree of prominence and exposure, allowing him to continue his work as a composer while advancing his career and Vargas's nationalist agendas.

Ever since the challenge to create modern Brazilian art had been posed in 1922 at the Semana de Arte Moderna, composers had sought ways to express the nation through music. Vargas's rise to power and his nationalist programs provided even more incentive for composers to become more "Brazilian." The acceptance of popular music as an expression of Brazilian national sentiment in the 1920s by elites and intellectuals was the first step in the elevation of Carnaval samba to the status of national symbol in the 1930s,[40] and the heavy reliance of radio stations on the *regional* as the consummate Brazilian performing force grew even stronger in the 1930s and 1940s under Vargas.

THE *HORA DO BRASIL*

From its modest beginnings as a hobby that was cultivated in elite clubs of amateurs, radio became a primary force in shaping Brazilian popular culture of the 1930s and 1940s. As better and more powerful transmitters were installed, radio broadcasts could reach remote areas of Brazil and beyond national borders. The power of radio as a propagandistic tool was quickly recognized and acted upon by the state. Lourival Fontes, future director of the censorial Departamento de Imprensa e Propaganda (DIP, Department of Press and Propaganda) under Vargas, wrote in 1936:

> Of all countries of vast territories, Brazil is the only one without an "official" radio station. All the rest have stations that cover all their territory. These stations act as an agent for national unity. . . . We must not underestimate the impact of radio as a tool of propaganda and culture, most importantly, its effectiveness in reaching the people. It suffices to say that radio reaches those areas where schools and publishers haven't: those points most distant, where it can be understood even by those who are illiterate.[41]

After assuming dictatorial powers, Vargas seized control of the media and turned Rádio Nacional into his government's official mouthpiece and one of the most powerful radio stations in South America. Unlike many other dictators, Vargas did not use propaganda tools to create a personality cult around himself; instead, he channeled his efforts into glorifying the nation and garnering support for his nationalist programs and projects. A powerful tool was the official radio program called *A Hora do Brasil,* which stations were obliged to broadcast. It presented official news and propaganda alternating with musical selections, most notably choro and samba. The execution of the program was put under the jurisdiction of the DIP, the newly created censorial agency that held a tight grip on the output of independent newspapers and broadcasters.[42] In 1936, Vargas made overtures to Nazi Germany, going so far as to broadcast the program to Germany. In order to extend the influence of the Estado Novo abroad, Vargas also ordered the creation of an Argentine *Hora do Brasil* to be broadcast from Buenos Aires; it was produced by Ernani Braga, a composer, colleague of Villa-Lobos, and participant in the Semana de Arte Moderna. The success of the program was a source of controversy back were hired to perform Brazilian music.[43]

A large part of Vargas's success as a leader came from effective propaganda that promoted his image as a populist president who was dedicated to building a unified Brazilian culture. All popular music that passed through the recording or radio industries or was presented in cariocan Carnaval celebrations came under the direct or indirect influence of the Vargas regime. This was new; before this period any concerted action at the national level with regard to popular culture had been impossible because the weak republican government had had no real power over the old order of powerful regional elites.[44]

CARMEN MIRANDA

In 1935, when Vargas made a trip to Uruguay and Argentina, in part to establish versions of his *Hora do Brasil* abroad, he took with him popular singer Carmen Miranda and her backup band O Bando da Lua. Vargas saw in Carmen not only her talent but also a personality capable of capturing the hearts of foreigners as a "musical ambassador" for Brazil. Indeed, no other Brazilian performer achieved the status and fame abroad that Carmen did. She made numerous recordings, starred in a number of movies produced in Hollywood, was featured on talk shows, and lived the life of a celebrity before her tragic death in 1955. In Carmen, Vargas had a powerful ally, for despite the glitz and glamour, she truly believed that her purpose was to be a musical ambassador and to bring the joy of Brazilian music to the world. Carmen is most remembered for the sambas and choros put to words so they could be sung. The most famous of these was "Tico-Tico no fubá" ("Tico-Tico Bird in the Corn Meal"), a choro she spread around the world.

As one of Hollywood's biggest stars in the 1940s, Carmen was famous for her exotic and sensuous image. She was the "Brazilian Bombshell," who in 1946 was the celebrity with the second-highest salary (after Bob Hope) in the United States.[45] It was Carmen Miranda who first introduced most Americans to Brazilian popular music, and the image of Carmen Miranda with a fruit basket on her head was the icon of the vision of Brazil as a sunny, carefree Latin American nation.

One small irony is that Carmen was not even born in Brazil. She was born Maria do Carmo Miranda da Cunha on February 9, 1909, in Marco de Canavezes, Portugal; she is claimed by the Portuguese as one of their own. Her family moved to Rio de Janeiro when she was about 2 years old. As a young woman she worked as a milliner. She was discovered at a talent show, and in 1929 she signed on with the Victor Recording Company, which promoted her heavily to compete with the star of a rival label, singer Francisco Alves. Her career skyrocketed with the spectacular success of the 1930 Carnaval march "Taí (Eu fiz tudo pra você gostar de mim)" ("That's It [I Did Everything I Could To Make You Love Me]"). It was at this time that she met Almirante, a man of many talents including radio pioneer, singer, composer, and folklorist, who was to become one of her strongest supporters and dearest friends (see chapter 6). Carmen and Almirante performed together on stage, in films, and on radio with great success during the 1930s.

Her success as a singer prompted notable songwriters such as Dorival Caymmi to write songs specifically for her. His "O que é que a bahiana tem?" ("What Does a Bahian Girl Have?") of 1939 was one of her most memorable songs. The question "What does a Bahian girl have?" is posed by Bando da Lua, to which Carmen gives a series of replies, including "a silk turban," "golden earrings," and so forth. From this description came her signature costume, which she used both in Brazil and the United States.[46] As was common practice in the United States, the popular singer became an actress and began to appear in movies. She made seven movies in Brazil, starting in the late 1930s, including the film *Banana da Terra,* which featured "O que é que a bahiana tem?"

Carmen's work caught the attention of American producer and manager Lee Shubert, who saw her singing "O que é que a bahiana tem?" in her trademark *baiana* costume in the Casino da Urca in Rio de Janeiro. This event changed the course of Miranda's life and affected the way Americans viewed Brazil in the 1940s and 1950s. When Shubert offered her a lead role in the 1940 Broadway revue *The Streets of Paris,* Getúlio Vargas himself urged the singer to accept the offer, but not without her backup band Bando da Lua. As she told Shubert, "The president didn't think it prudent to come without my group." Shortly thereafter, Miranda starred in her first American film, *Down Argentine Way,* which introduced Betty Grable. It was the first of five big Technicolor spectaculars she would make.

Carmen Miranda was not the first Latin music performer to achieve fame in the United States, although she is likely the most memorable.[47] Latin American music entered mainstream American popular culture with a series of dance fads, beginning with the Argentinean tango and Cuban "rhumba"[48] crazes of the 1910s to the 1930s. By the 1930s, American audiences were being regularly exposed to Latin American music through film and recordings. Despite the presence of Latin bands in New York City (for example, the Cuban group led by Don Azpiazú), few Americans knew or cared about the difference between Cuban rumba and Argentinean tango or understood that Brazilians speak Portuguese and not Spanish. To add to the confusion were performers such as Desi Arnaz and Xavier Cugat, who presented hybridized "pan-Latin" music to American audiences. As a result, Latin American music was most often presented as homogenous, not as music from distinct cultures. To Americans, everything south of the border was the same.

At first, Carmen performed Brazilian sambas and choros with the Bando da Lua. As her film career progressed, however, and she became increasingly ensconced in Hollywood, she was forced to compromise her musical standards to conform with Hollywood's highly inaccurate but extremely marketable interpretation of Latin American culture. The results were often a multicultural nightmare, in which it would not have been a surprise to see the Brazilian singer playing a character named "Murphy" who spoke English badly with an exaggerated accent heavier than her own and dressed in stylized Afro-Brazilian garb while singing "Chattanooga Choo-Choo"—in Portuguese with a samba beat, and accompanied by her Brazilian band dressed as Cubans with Mexican hats—in a Canadian hotel, as happened in the film *Springtime in the Rockies* (1942).

Carmen Miranda brought samba to the United States, but it was not the type favored by poor urban Afro-Brazilians; it was rather music that was favored by white or mulatto radio singers accompanied by *regional,* characterized by subdued rhythms and a smooth vocal style.[49] She also introduced sung choro, which, given its similarity in accompaniment style to samba, was probably indistinguishable as a separate genre to most American ears. Carmen was a talented singer and performer, but the contributions the Bando da Lua made to her performance were of inestimable importance. Had they not accompanied her to the United States, it is likely that her music would have been very different and quite a bit less Brazilian. Among the talented musicians in the group were two notable choro musicians: guitarist-composer Garoto (see chapter 6) and guitarist Aloysio de Oliveira.

Formed in 1931 in Rio de Janeiro, the vocal and instrumental conjunto known as Bando da Lua was the first in Brazil to harmonize voices in the American style. Other groups quickly imitated their style, and the resulting "sophisticated" sound was fashionable for many years in Brazil. Before working with Carmen Miranda, the group made numerous recordings of Carnaval music (thirty-eight releases between 1931 and 1940) and made successful tours of Argentina. The band began to play with Carmen Miranda in the 1930s, and accompanied her on her tour of the United States. As Carmen's band, the group was compelled by studio executives to wear "Latin" costumes, usually a mixture of clothing styles from several cultures, and to perform not only choros and sambas but also Americanized "rhumbas" and merengues. The versatile group remained undaunted, and they in turn absorbed American musical culture. In 1939, the plucked-string virtuoso Garoto joined the group and stayed with it for two years. The band dissolved in 1944 and was reunited four years later by Aloysio de Oliveira as part of the Anjos do Inferno (Hell's Angels). From this point until it permanently disbanded in 1955, the group focused on American songs that they sang in English.

Carmen Miranda was very successful at introducing her own version of Brazilian samba and choro to the American market at the same time that her band members eagerly exchanged tunes and techniques with American musicians. The Bando da Lua was employed by the film industry only while Miranda's films were being made; the remainder of the time the performers were expected to find other jobs. They toured with Miranda and played nightclubs or struck off on their own, playing the music they knew best: choro. In this way a select few Americans were able to hear Brazilian music for what it was without the interpretive filter imposed by federal officials or by Hollywood. Together, Carmen Miranda and the Bando da Lua were responsible for disseminating choro to a new appreciative audience. Some choros even became standards among foreign musicians; the best known example is undoubtedly "Tico-Tico no fubá" by Zequinha de Abreu, which has been recorded by jazz musician Sonny Rollins on tenor saxophone, by a Russian group on traditional Russian instruments, and by a British performer on a Hammond organ, to name only a few.

Although Carmen was constantly pressured to modify her style to conform to what the producers of her films thought would be most profitable, she could at least trust in her band to accompany her in a Brazilian style. One of her biggest hits was the "samba" "Sous' American Way," written by Jimmy McHugh and Al Dubin with English lyrics and featured in the film *Down Argentine Way* (1940). Several days before recording began she was given the song and told to perform it with her band. The band spent the next several days rearranging the tune into something more reminiscent of a Brazilian samba and substituting different lyrics in Portuguese for Carmen to sing. Only the title was left untouched. The song as Carmen recorded it became an instant success, both in the United States and Brazil, and few people, if any, realized that it had American roots.

As a musical ambassador, Vargas could not have asked for a better celebrity than Carmen Miranda. She gave samba and choro an international audience, and she delighted audiences with a happy image of their Sous' American neighbor. That Brazil struggled under the heavy hand of dictatorship was not a message that she was willing to spread. Despite her smiling image, however, Carmen Miranda suffered heavily under her burden. During the years she was away from Brazil, popular opinion was becoming increasingly anti-American. In the period immediately preceding her death, the people of her beloved homeland rejected her as "too American," and she died broken by the stress of living in America.[50]

The American Music Invasion

Americans viewed Brazilian music as performed by Carmen Miranda in the 1940s and 1950s as an exotic novelty, a ripple on the surface of American popular culture. To Brazilians, however, the impact of American music on Brazilian culture was the equivalent of a tidal wave. American music was viewed as sophisticated and cosmopolitan on the one hand, and as a dangerous threat to Brazilian culture on the other. The two attitudes were in fact often held simultaneously, and together they express a basic tension inherent in many Third World nationalisms that simultaneously seeks to embrace and reject the First World way of life.

The sometimes-uneasy love affair between America and Carmen Miranda was the direct result of American policies directed towards Brazil that began during the Second World War. Americans were frightened when Vargas made overtures to the Germans in 1936, and the United States began an intense campaign to convince Brazil to join the Allies. Not only was the United States concerned about which side Brazil would take in the war, it also viewed Brazil and the other Latin America nations as the last remaining market after the closure of Europe by war. Roosevelt's Good Neighbor Policy was a response to the critical situation, developed to foster positive relations with America's southern "neighbors."

During the 1940s, the U.S. State Department sent American filmmakers and other creative artists to Latin America to espouse the American cause and bring back images of Latin American life. The activities of filmmakers such as Orson Welles and Walt Disney came under the strict scrutiny of the Motion Picture Division of the U.S. Office of Inter-American Affairs, which was created in 1940 in order to guide the film industry in Latin American matters and to "develop a better understanding of Latin America." Orson Welles was sent as a creative ambassador in 1942 with the objective of making a film about Brazil. The project was left unfinished after a series of misfortunes.[51]

American musicians also traveled to Brazil as part of the Good Neighbor Policy. In 1940, the arrival in Brazil of the great conductor Leopold Stokowsky, music director of the Philadelphia Orchestra since 1912, caused a great stir, as he had been charged with bringing to the United States recordings of the best popular music of Latin America. Stokowsky consulted with Heitor Villa-Lobos, who suggested the maestro record his friends and colleagues from the worlds of samba and choro. The outcome was a series of recordings featuring Pixinguinha, sambistas Donga and Cartola, and other popular musicians, made in a special studio belonging to the Columbia label aboard the ship *Uruguay*.[52]

American jazz had become familiar to Brazilians long before the cultural exchanges encouraged by Roosevelt's Good Neighbor Policy. As early as the 1920s, recordings of American jazz and dance music were available for purchase in Brazil. Brazilian elites quickly embraced the newest trend from the United States. Imported recordings of American music filled a large niche in the Brazilian market through the 1920s, and by the 1940s American recordings overtook Brazilian recordings in numbers sold and air time on the radio. Over the next few decades, American music came to completely dominate the Brazilian market, even though Vargas had set quotas for radio airplay of Brazilian music. The music of American singers and instrumentalists such as Frank Sinatra, Glenn Miller, Fred Astaire, Duke Ellington and Ella Fitzgerald were not only available on recording and played on the radio, they were also heard in the soundtracks of imported movies and musicals. The presence of American servicemen stationed in Brazil during the war only increased the intensity of exposure. Brazilian musicians started touring the United

States during and after the Second World War, in large part because of the cultural exchanges sponsored by the U.S. Office of Inter-American Affairs. These musicians returned to Brazil bringing with them the latest in American popular music, including bebop and cool jazz, to an eagerly awaiting audience.

Jazz profoundly influenced the style and practice of choro beginning in the 1920s. The *conjunto regional* began to incorporate jazz into its repertory and to increase in size under the influence of American dance bands. Lyrics began to be written and set to choros so that prominent singers could sing them, in the manner of American big band songs of the 1930s and 1940s. Choros with added lyrics were given a new life and choros such as "Tico-Tico no fubá," "Não me toques" ("Don't Touch Me"), and "Carinhoso" ("Tenderly") were popular once again. Besides being sung by famous vocalists such as Carmen Miranda, these choros went through further modifications in instrumentation, which often included the American drum set (*bateria*), which was previously unknown in Brazil. In the 1940s, the large choro *orquestra,* with a wind section, drum set, and electric guitar, became popular. There were even new terms for American-influenced choro: *choro de big band* or *choro de jazz band*. Revitalized by their new presentation, choros that might otherwise have fallen out of the repertory were published as transcriptions for guitar or piano or in lead-sheet form (i.e., melody with chord symbols). It is perhaps ironic that some of the greatest choros were preserved by the foreign influences that precipitated the genre's decline in the 1950s.

In the 1920s and 1930s, choro was swept up in the vast changes affecting Brazil, and its course was altered in ways that flautist Joaquim Calado could never have envisioned. With João Pernambuco the guitar emerged as a solo instrument in choro and was no longer the despised instrument of street musicians. New instruments—the pandeiro and the seven-string guitar—were permanently added to the *conjunto regional* choro ensemble. Recording companies and radio stations created the demand for a new degree of professionalism, which steadily increased over the years as pressures to compete with slick American musical products intensified. Most importantly, however, choro became politicized after its "discovery" by intellectuals and elites in their search for authentic Brazilian culture. No longer was choro what lowlife musicians engaged in to pass the time; now it was the musical embodiment of the most idealistic blending of the races espoused by the doctrine of miscegenation. For musicians such as Pixinguinha, who first and foremost were concerned with their art and with making a living at their art, the controversies that arose about race and foreign influences must have seemed absurd. Nevertheless, Getúlio Vargas understood the power of popular culture, and he specifically used choro (in the forms of the *regionais* that played "national" music on the radio and the performances of Carmen Miranda and the Bando da Lua) to represent his idea of a unified Brazilian culture.

The politicization of choro was also a reaction against the threat of cultural invasion, specifically from the United States. American popular music was envied, imitated, and assimilated by Brazilians, to the chagrin and constant criticism of self-appointed guardians of national purity. Pixinguinha and Carmen Miranda both suffered under the pressures to adopt American stylistic influences in order to remain current while at the same time struggling to preserve their national identity. By the 1950s, choro had succumbed to the wave of new popular musics and new technologies (prerecorded radio shows and the advent of television), and although it had disappeared for the most part from the airwaves and from the general view of the public, it continued to survive in the roda and in the hearts and fingers of a few talented instrumental virtuosi.

The Velha Guarda in the New Brazil
Choro in the 1950s and 1960s

In 1960, the capital of Brazil moved from Rio de Janeiro to the newly constructed city of Brasília, which had arisen from the red clay in a mere three
years. Workers labored around the clock hauling materials, erecting fantastic futuristic buildings, and creating a network of roadways that connected Brasília to
the rest of the nation. The city's location, some 600 miles away from the coast,
was intended to symbolize literally and figuratively the center of the nation, and
the architecture was a bold announcement to Brazil and to the world that the
nation had entered the future. Riding on the wave of optimism in the 1950s,
musicians created a bold new musical style, blending samba and jazz, called the
bossa nova. It was heralded as the first Brazilian musical export with universal
appeal, and it quickly took the world by storm, generating numerous imitations
and derivations. It seemed to many as if the modernist ideals articulated in the
Semana de Arte Moderna in 1922 were finally being realized; Brazil would soon
be able to enter the fraternity of global nations as an equal rather than as a dependent stepchild. Choro and samba, once celebrated as national expressions,
were now viewed as the music of the past. In this brief period of national eu-
phoria, choro was denigrated *because* it was national music; this attitude reveals the inherent contradictions within the Brazilian discourse of nationalism.
Choro advocates and musicians were forced to adopt a defensive position,
which ultimately served to further reinforce the categorization of choro as music
of the past.

During Vargas's regimes, Brazil began a remarkable and radical transformation from a mostly agricultural nation ruled by regional powers to a unified industrialized nation under a central government. In order for Brazil to partake as an equal in the global economy instead of serving as a source of raw materials for wealthy nations, she had to develop an industrial infrastructure. The race to develop Brazil began in the 1940s with the establishment of transportation and shipping networks, power stations, and oil refineries. The period immediately after the war was one of great activity marked by massive public and private building and home construction, great expansion of road and port construction, and the establishment of heavy manufacturing, including steel and automobile industries. Brazil began for the first time to export manufactured goods in addition to agricultural products, and Brazilians began to take pride in their country's strides toward becoming a developed nation.

With the end of the Second World War, Brazilians became restless under Vargas's authoritarian government and the military applied immense pressure on Vargas to relinquish his hold over the country. That Brazil had sided with the Allies in the struggle against fascism only served to highlight the absurdity of the political situation at home. Vargas's promises to hold elections at the end of 1945 were not enough to convince the military, and he was subsequently deposed by the same forces that had enabled him to assume power fifteen years earlier. Although the political climate had changed drastically, the relentless march toward development continued unabated. The huge projects Vargas had undertaken continued without him and new ones were undertaken.

In 1950, the military relinquished its control and allowed presidential elections to take place as promised. Riding on a broad base of support, Gétulio Vargas staged a dramatic return to the office of the president, this time as a democratically elected official. His term would prove to be short, however, because his extravagant spending and heavy reliance on huge foreign loans (mostly American) to fund his huge infrastructure projects led irrevocably to severe economic instability and hyperinflation. The flood of migrants from the impoverished northeast to the industrial southeast in search of work resulted in high levels of unemployment, adding to the social instability. This time, critics were no longer silenced by censorship, and they warned Vargas of dire consequences unless he changed his course. By 1954, Vargas no longer had control over the economy and the military once again prepared to intervene. In the month of August, hours before the military was to remove him from power, Vargas committed suicide. The power vacuum that resulted was filled in the years to come by a succession of weak and ineffectual governments, ending with yet another military coup in 1964.

Despite the economic and political turmoil, Brazilians were for the most part

The Velha Guarda in the New Brazil

optimistic about the future. They had visual evidence of their progress toward industrialization in the form of factories and manufactured goods, and the national pride Vargas had carefully cultivated flourished. Each victory, whether on the soccer field (Brazil won the World Cup championships in 1958, 1962, and 1970) or in the construction of a new industrial plant, was cause for national celebration. President Juscelino Kubitschek (1956–1961) promised the nation "fifty years' progress in five," and during his presidency he strengthened the auto industry, raised industrial production by 12 percent, and created a new futuristic capital city in the middle of the high plains of Brazil's interior. During the 1950s, the economic growth rate of Brazil far surpassed that of its Latin American neighbors and the arts flourished as Brazilian directors, writers, musicians, and scholars were celebrated as national artists.

A significant driving force behind the strong national pride was anti-American sentiment promulgated by intellectuals and radical critics, which reached a peak in the late 1950s and early 1960s. Despite the progress made by Brazil in industrialization and the establishment of infrastructure, the country continued to be plagued by economic difficulties. To explain why Brazil was not yet a First World nation, economists developed the theory of developmental nationalism premised on the assumption that the woes of the nation were a direct result of First World ownership of large sectors of Brazil's economy. As Brazil's largest investor, America was both beloved by government officials seeking financial backing for their projects, and the target of vitriolic attacks from the think-tank ISEB (Superior Institute of Brazilian Studies), the institution that served as the focal point of the developmental nationalist movement. The ISEB and other radical groups blamed the U.S. for "economic colonialism." Similarly, these groups viewed the inroads made by American popular music and culture in the 1940s and 1950s as "cultural imperialism" that threatened to undermine authentic Brazilian culture. Despite the anti-American rhetoric among radical groups, American popular music continued to flow into Brazil during the 1950s and 1960s, blending with existing genres and styles and giving rise to new musics.

The Demise of the *Regional*

Ambivalent, often contradictory attitudes toward American culture are evident in Brazilian discourse and in the consumption and production of music. That the strong government-sponsored nationalism in the 1930s and 1940s allowed for an invasion of American music is indicative of the inherent tension between the mutually exclusive ideas of Brazilian nationalism and cosmopolitanism. American engagement with Brazil occurred on many levels, from the presence of American military airbases in the northeast to assistance from the American government in reestablishing Brazil's rubber industry for the war effort to the quotidian exposure to American music through record sales, airplay, and movies.

The radio system Vargas established remained intact after his removal from power but with two related differences: Government-controlled stations gave way to privately owned stations and the repeal of censorship produced innovative programming that had not been possible during the dictatorship. In the new Brazil, Vargas's nationalist programming quickly faded under the onslaught of newly unleashed market forces. This translated to a significant increase in the volume and influence of American music and the consequent marginalization of Brazilian genres, including choro and samba. In order to survive, the *regional* had to resemble the American jazz band in instrumentation and style. As they adopted more and more prerecorded shows, radio stations no longer needed or cared to support the expense of maintaining their own *regionais,* and choro musicians and composers were forced to seek other areas of employment. Some musicians joined American-style bands; others simply retired as professional musicians.

By 1945, the choro and the *regional* were in decline in terms of radio play and recordings. Under Vargas, the *regional* sound disseminated throughout Brazil by radio had become an index of national culture, both in sound and in repertoire. This association was both a curse and a blessing: It ensured a certain degree of popularity under Vargas, but it meant that it was vulnerable to changes in conceptions of national identity once Vargas was no longer in power. Brazilian popular music genres were no longer typically accompanied by *regional*. Instead, ensembles that had incorporated the "modern" influences of American jazz bands and orchestras became the norm, and their repertoires reflected a blend of American and Brazilian genres and styles.

As Brazilian ensembles expanded to become *orquestras,* the differences in playing style between Brazilian and American became less noticeable. Choros such as "Espinha de bacalhau" ("Codfish Bone"), a technically difficult piece when played fast and often seen as a showpiece for instrumental soloists, were played in arrangements for *orquestras* at a leisurely pace and with no hint of malícia or spontaneity. Hybrid genres began to appear, such as "Boogie-woogie na favela" ("Boogie-Woogie in the Shanty Town") by Cyro Monteiro and "Oh! Suzana" by Monte Alegre, the *cantor cowboy* (the cowboy singer). By the 1960s, most of the famous radio *regionais* had disbanded due to lack of work and competition from new popular musics, including rock-and-roll and bossa nova. The combination of new entertainment media such as television and prerecorded radio programming and the perception that choro was music of the past led to the demise of the *regional*. Nevertheless, new choro musicians continued to arise during the 1950s and 1960s, extending the technical boundaries of their instruments, composing new music, and infusing new life into choro.

The Velha Guarda in the New Brazil

Garoto, the multitalented plucked-string virtuoso who played not only guitar but also banjo, cavaquinho, cavaco (a larger variant of the cavaquinho), viola, violão de sete cordas, bandolim, and tenor guitar (a four-string guitar with metal strings), was a central figure in the history of choro and in Brazilian popular music in general. Although he is often associated with Carmen Miranda's Bando da Lua, he was an important performer and composer in his own right. He was known for his smooth technique, powerful musicianship, and inventive performance and compositional style. His choros are notable for their subtle yet effective blending of the rhythmic and melodic aspects of choro with the harmonic sophistication of jazz. In this respect, he prepared the ground for bossa nova, although he did not live long enough to witness its development.

Garoto began his musical studies in his native São Paulo at age 11, when he received a banjo as a present, an instrument very much in vogue at the time. He was a child prodigy who quickly earned the appellation of *moleque do banjo* (street urchin of the banjo), later changed to simply "Garoto" (the kid). By the turn of the century, choro had spread to São Paulo, and Garoto began his career playing in the Regional Irmãos Armani in the 1920s. By 1927, he had become one of the most popular chorões in São Paulo, in part because of his association with the group Conjunto dos Sócios, in which he sang and played the guitar as well as banjo. He performed both as a solo musician on guitar and as an ensemble player in a variety of venues, including cafés and nightclubs. In 1929, Garoto recorded with one of the other great guitarists of the era, Paraguassú, who at the time was coaching the young guitarist.[1] He also played on the soundtracks for several movies in the emerging film industry, all assisted by Paraguassú, who helped his young protégé to become established in São Paulo and later in Rio de Janeiro.

In 1930, Garoto made his first recordings as a banjo soloist, playing two of his own compositions. Composer Francisco Mignone, who at the time was the artistic director of Parlophon, one of the larger record companies in Brazil, recognized the young instrumentalist's abilities and had him rerecord two selections for commercial release: "Bichinho de queijo," a maxixe-choro, and "Driblando," a maxixe on which he was accompanied by Serelepe, another well-known choro guitarist. Garoto later formed a duo with guitarist Aimoré, and the two were inseparable for many years. Garoto's talents were also utilized for live radio broadcasts for Rádio Record. His fame as a talented instrumentalist spread through records, radio, and live performances. He traveled extensively through the south of Brazil and Argentina, playing the tenor guitar in the *regional* led by guitarist Armando Neves. At about the same time, he picked up two more plucked-string instruments, the cavaquinho and the bandolim. By age 21, he was an accomplished professional

musician on each of his instruments and was in demand for his singing as well as
his instrumental abilities.

In August 1936, he was invited to perform for the prestigious Rádio Mayrink
Veiga in Rio de Janeiro. He stayed in the capital city for several months, but he
worked so much that his health, which had always been frail, suffered. He returned
to São Paulo in December of that year and resumed his work with Aimoré. For the
next several years Garoto found himself making the trip to Rio de Janeiro more and
more frequently, and in 1938 he made the decision to move there permanently. His
association with Rádio Mayrink marked a turning point in his career, for among the
talented musicians employed by the station were Carmen Miranda and guitarist
Laurindo Almeida. With Almeida, he formed the group Cordas Quentes (Hot
Strings), which recorded for Odeon, the biggest record company in Brazil. His big
break, however, came because of his association with Carmen Miranda.

The invitation to accompany Carmen Miranda on her first trip to the United
States was an offer no musician would refuse, and Garoto quickly packed his bags.
On October 18, 1939, he boarded a ship bound for New York City as a member of
the Bando da Lua. His impact on the group was significant, for he not only provided
backup vocals and accompaniments on some half-dozen plucked-string instruments, he also improvised introductions to sambas and choros, assuming the same
role as the flute or clarinet in the *regional.* Several of these incredible performances
can be heard in Miranda's early Hollywood movies, including *Down Argentine Way,
That Night in Rio,* and *Weekend in Havana.* As an accomplished soloist, Garoto
often performed as the opening act for Carmen when she did stage shows, and he
often received separate billing on record jackets and in show promotions.

Garoto, like many musicians of his time, was a devoted admirer of American
jazz. He was particularly fond of Tommy Dorsey and Glenn Miller, and he composed
a choro in honor of Benny Goodman ("Benny Goodman no choro"). Once he
reached the United States, Garoto took every opportunity to learn from, listen to,
and jam with American jazz musicians in what he called *roda de jazz.* He showed
them the inner workings of Brazilian music, and they in turn introduced him to jazz
harmonies, improvisation, and techniques. In New York, he caught the attention of
Art Tatum and Duke Ellington, and soon other jazz musicians were seeking him out.
When Carmen was contracted as a Hollywood film star, she and the Bando made
their way across the country, stopping in Chicago, Detroit, and Pittsburgh. In each
city, Garoto's performances as a soloist or as part of the Bando were enthusiastically received. Once in California, he was contracted to play for a number of Hollywood celebrities, including Judy Garland, Mickey Rooney, and Betty Grable.[2]

Garoto returned to Rio de Janeiro after having spent a year in the United
States. He had high hopes of returning to America, but his contract with Carmen
was not renewed, and he remained behind. In Rio de Janeiro, Garoto resumed his
hectic career as a recording and radio artist. Besides Rádio Mayrink Veiga, he

Figure 6.1. Garoto in 1955. From the collection of Marco de Pinna.

worked for Rádio Nacional, Rádio Tupi, and Rádio Record, and he was contracted to record for several companies including Continental, RCA-Victor, and Odeon, for whom he accompanied various musicians in samba and choro. In 1950, he recorded two solo pieces on electric guitar. In the same year, he made a series of guitar recordings of his own compositions for his friend Ronoel Simões, who kept the acetate tapes in his own personal collection.[3] Although the quality of many of the extant recordings is not the best, Garoto displays a fine technique and a subtle yet highly expressive playing style that foreshadows the bossa nova guitar of the late 1950s and early 1960s.

As a composer, Garoto revolutionized the choro genre. His pieces exhibit a new harmonic sophistication while retaining many of the rhythmic and melodic characteristics of choro. Garoto's musical palette consisted of a wide variety of styles and genres, including choro and samba, jazz, and classical music, and he blended these influences with a masterful ease. In "Debussyana," Garoto pays homage to the French composer in a slow, free-floating piece with melodic fragments reminiscent of "Clair de Lune." The piece "Jorge do fusa" is particularly interesting, as it is a seamless fusion of choro and jazz: The rhythmic structure and bass lines are grounded in choro, while the extended harmonies come from jazz (see Example 6.1).

Example 6.1. "Jorge do fusa," by Garoto.

Garoto's compositions were unlike that of any choro musician before him. He had a strong influence on musicians of his time, and his style was a clear precursor to the harmonic language and subtlety of bossa nova. As innovative as bossa nova composers such as Tom Jobim, Luiz Bonfá, and João Gilberto appeared to be, they were at least in part following a path already laid by Garoto. João Gilberto summed up the contributions of this remarkable musician when he said "Garoto is extraordinary and his guitar is the heart of Brazil."[4]

Bossa Nova and Modernism

In 1958, singer and guitarist João Gilberto released the single "Chega de saudade" ("Enough of Longing"). It featured the highly syncopated guitar accompaniment and sophisticated harmonies that became hallmarks of the new style called bossa nova. Everything about bossa nova seemed new and modern. João Gilberto's syncopated guitar style suggested the rhythmic complexity of an entire samba school percussion ensemble, yet it was played in a subdued manner, never competing with the vocals for attention (see Example 6.2).[5]

Example 6.2. Bossa nova guitar accompaniment composed by Thomas Garcia.

The use of extended harmonies gave bossa nova a sound that distanced it from other Brazilian popular genres, and the understated whispering style characteristic of Gilberto's vocals had nothing in common with the emotional bel canto style used by popular crooners and singers of samba-canção.[6] Lyrics about love, flowers, the sun, and the sea were an expression of the widespread optimism shared by the affluent middle class that had benefited most from economic development and the rising standard of living of the 1950s and early 1960s. Bossa nova was the music of a particular time, place, and people:

> The music emerged in the small clubs and apartments of the beachfront district of Rio's South Zone. The very characteristic of Bossa Nova—intimate, soft, controlled—corresponds to the enclosed physical space in which it grew. Bossa Nova was made by and for middle-class citizens. As one samba musician from Rio's working-class North Zone put it: "It's their samba."[7]

Despite its modest roots, bossa nova quickly became an international style, launched by the 1959 film "Orfeu Negro" ("Black Orpheus"). Adapted from a play by composer, poet, and lyricist Vinícius de Moraes and set to music by Antônio Carlos ("Tom") Jobim and Luiz Bonfá, *Black Orpheus* told the story of the Orpheus myth set in Rio de Janeiro during Carnaval. Soon after the release of the film (it won the prize at the Cannes Festival in 1959), bossa nova became an international craze, and the music of Jobim, Bonfá, and Gilberto set the standard for the latest in popular music. Inspired by its international acclaim, Brazilians proudly claimed bossa nova as a "universal" music originating on their soil. Scholars such as Jomard Muniz de Britto hailed bossa nova as the musical result of the calls for the modernization of Brazilian culture articulated in the Semana de Arte Moderna in 1922. Popular musicians were also inspired by the notion of bossa nova as modern and universal music. Singer/songwriters Gilberto Gil, Caetano Veloso, Gal Costa, Tom Zé, and Maria Bethânia all shared an enthusiasm for bossa nova and a strong respect for modernist ideals. They would make their contribution by founding the iconoclastic modernist musical movement called *tropicália* in the late 1960s. According to Gil, "Bossa nova was for all of us the emblem, [the] signifier of modernity."[8] For Gil and others, modernity implied synthesis and universality:

> João [Gilberto] was the great synthesizer. Maybe the only great synthesizer of Brazilian music, in the modern sense of incorporating in Brazilian music its various interests: an African stream, a European stream, a Latin American stream, and a North American stream. . . . João represented to us this general codification of the musical elements already culturally insinuated in a universal manner.[9]

For the first time in their history, Brazilians celebrated a popular music that was Brazilian *and* modern.[10] Of course, the acceptance of bossa nova by the international community was necessary to legitimate bossa nova in the eyes of Brazilians, and in the end this dependence on the opinion of foreigners reinforced the notion that Brazilian traditional music, including choro, was somehow innately inferior.

The success of bossa nova and the never-ending flow of American popular music into Brazil put choro advocates on the defensive. Even though amateur chorões still gathered in the occasional roda and choro musicians received some publicity every now and then, choro had greatly diminished in popularity in the late 1950s and early 1960s. While the general public embraced American music and its increasing role in Brazilian culture, there were individuals who took it upon themselves to preserve Brazilian music. They viewed American music as a threat to Brazilian national identity, and they focused their activities on educating the public about their musical heritage. Two individuals who were important in shaping the discourse about the preservation of choro were radio broadcaster and singer Almirante and musician Jacó do Bandolim. Both were associated with radio, the most powerful disseminator of popular music from the 1930s to the 1950s.

ALMIRANTE (1908–1980)

Henrique Foréis Domingues, known as O Almirante ("The Admiral"), began his career in popular music as a samba singer in the 1920s and 1930s. He was a close friend to Carmen Miranda, whom he supported in her role as musical ambassador to America. By the 1940s, he had dedicated himself to the radio as a program producer. As an ardent supporter of Brazilian music on the radio, many of his numerous programs were devoted to bringing Brazilian music to the public. One of the most important radio programs produced by Almirante was *O Pessoal da Velha Guarda*, a series of twenty programs dedicated to educating the public and disseminating the compositions written by the Old Guard of Brazilian popular music, such as Chiquinha Gonzaga, Irineu de Almeida, Nelson Alves, and Eduardo das Neves.[11] The pieces, which were played or sung live by guest artists or the house band directed by Pixinguinha, were prefaced by historical commentary about the composers and genres the listeners were about to hear. Almirante was a tireless researcher, and over the years he amassed a large collection of materials pertaining to Brazilian popular music.

Almirante made his position against the adoption of American music clear when he made the following plea to his listeners:

> Men and women singers of popular music, the best thing that you could possibly do is to sing samba as samba, marcha as marcha, waltz as waltz, and don't go around imitating these Bing Crosbys and Frank Sinatras. The effects they introduce in their foxtrots are fine for foxtrots, but not for our music.[12]

For Almirante, Brazilian popular music was a well-defined musical tradition that could easily be corrupted or destroyed by foreign influences. His view of choro

The Velha Guarda in the New Brazil

was not new; rather, it was an outgrowth of the attitudes toward choro Vargas had perpetuated in the 1930s. Once choro had become a "national" music, it was lifted from its original context as a dynamic musical tradition and became a static entity to be defended and preserved. Within this context, Almirante used the terms "*auténtico*" (authentic) and "Brazilian" interchangeably to describe Pixinguinha and the music in his shows. For Almirante, authenticity was strongly linked to national sentiment and the *regional* sound that had been disseminated under Vargas. As one scholar noted,[13] the logic behind Almirante's assertion was circular—choro was authentic because it was Brazilian, and it was Brazilian because it was authentic. Despite the flaws in reasoning, this perception of choro strongly affected musicians and fans, and the idea that choro was in danger of being eradicated went unchallenged.

In 1954, Almirante produced a gala event, the three-day Festival da Velha Guarda, in São Paulo to honor the birthday of Pixinguinha and to celebrate samba and choro composers of the past. The project was carried out in collaboration with Rádio Record and the planning committee for the fourth centennial celebration of the city of São Paulo. The festival began on April 23rd, Pixinguinha's birthday, with a dramatized performance of the life of Pixinguinha that was broadcast live on the radio. The second night featured live performances by great choro musicians, many of whom came from Rio de Janeiro for the occasion, including Pixinguinha, Benedito Lacerda, Waldir de Azevedo, and Jacó do Bandolim.[14] The festival continued on the following day with a "tribute to old São Paulo" that featured *paulista* composers and seresteiros.[15]

The following year Almirante succeeded in organizing a second Festival da Velha Guarda, during which "rare recordings" of choro, according to *O Estado de São Paulo*, were offered for sale.[16] One of Almirante's goals in promoting these festivals was to demand that Brazilian recordings be given equal airplay with foreign ones. (The desire was realized in the 1970s, but without enforcement many radio stations continued to play mostly foreign music.) Like the first festival, the second was not restricted to narrow definitions of samba and choro. Instead, it resembled a musical revue, with the Velha Guarda of São Paulo playing first (including the guitarist Paraguassú), followed by the Velha Guarda of Rio (including Pixinguinha, Donga, João da Bahiana, Jacob Palmeiri, Salvador, and Bororó). Nelson Souto played "Desperta da montanha" on piano, and Dircinha and Linda Batista sang songs composed by their father, Batista Junior. Other musical guests included composer and pianist Radamés Gnattali, guitarist Dilermando Reis, and pianist Carolina Cardoso Menezes.

Almirante's efforts to preserve and promote Brazilian popular music were monumental. Because of his work, choro musicians who had not played in public for years were at least temporarily reconnected with appreciative audiences, and his radio shows, which have been preserved by the Museu da Imagem e do Som

CHORO

JACÓ DO BANDOLIM (1918–1969)

Another tireless supporter of choro was bandolim virtuoso, composer, and radio producer Jacob Pick Bittencourt, better known as Jacó do Bandolim. He was a chorão who was highly respected by his peers for his playing style, his composi-tions, and the rodas de choro held at his home in Jacarepaguá (in the western zone of Rio de Janeiro). For a time, Jacó supported himself with a variety of jobs, includ-ing working in a pharmacy. He dedicated the rest of his time, however, to perfecting his skills as a musician, recording, teaching, and performing on radio, television, and the stage. Jacó produced radio programs featuring Brazilian music, including choro, at a time when American influence reigned supreme over the airwaves. He shared Almirante's views of Brazilian and American music and worked to educate his radio listeners in a manner that resembled Almirante's.

In 1955, Jacó worked as a radio announcer for Rádio Record and TV Record, for whom he produced and participated in a number of programs. Like Almirante, he was inspired to produce a grand event to promote Brazilian popular music. To that end, TV Record in São Paulo invited him to produce a television special called "Noite dos choristas" ("Evening of Choro Players"), which aired on December 5, 1955. Although the show featured live performances by Pixinguinha and Jacó ac-companied by the TV Record *regional,* Jacó wanted to highlight new musical talent among ordinary people in the manner of the old radio talent shows common in the 1930s and 1940s. He held open auditions; one simply needed to fill out a form and go through the audition process. From the applicant pool he selected several indi-viduals to perform solo numbers. The soloists either provided their own accompani-ment or used the studio group. The remainder of the applicants played in an end-of-program *regional* that numbered more than seventy participants. In 1956, Jacó produced a second "Noite dos Choristas" that ended with an orchestra of over 130 participants.

Due to the meticulous statistics Jacó kept and preserved in his archive at the MIS in Rio de Janeiro, the professions of each of the participants of the festivals are known. Other than Alexandre Gonçalves Pinto's book in 1936, documents provid-ing a glimpse into the demographics of ordinary choro players are exceedingly rare. Of the 245 combined participants from the festivals of 1955 and 1956 that listed a profession on their application forms, 46 percent were employed by service or light industries, 32 percent worked in heavy industry, and 15 percent were in sales. It is interesting that only 4 percent listed their occupation as "student," even though the age range for the finalists of the 1956 festival matched the young general age of participants: ages 14 to 32. The most popular instruments among the partici-pants were guitar, cavaquinho, bandolim, and pandeiro.

Jacó also developed a live radio show for Rádio Guanabara called *Jacó e seu Bandolim* (Jacob and his bandolim).[18] Each show opened with a refrain from the choro "Despertar da montanha" by Eduardo Souto, then Jacó played five or six numbers with explanatory remarks about the composer and style of each piece. The publicity material for the show refers to the enormous collection of sheet music Jacó had collected and to his own immense performing repertoire: "[T]his artist could perform in 400 programs, during eight years, without repeating a number." Indications are that listeners could call the station and make requests, although the scripts included in the program materials indicate that the more commonly requested numbers may have been ignored for the sake of variety.

Besides the musical content of the show, certain remarks in the radio scripts are interesting because they help us understand the popular perception of choro in the mid-1950s, the era just before the birth of bossa nova when Frank Sinatra and Sinatra-style crooners were the rage:

> There are those who believe that music from the past only pleases old people, nostalgic people, those that lived in the era in which these melodies were inspired. It falls to us, then, to reply that this is not the case with our program. Old people, young people, men, and women, from Copacabana or from São João de Merití, request that we play [choros] "Farrula," "Flor do abacate," "Soluçando," "Brejeiro" of [Ernesto] Nazaré, or "Tres Estrelinhas" by Anacleto [de Medeiros].

There is even a plea for old guard chorões to get together, pick up their forgotten instruments, and form a roda de choro as in the past:

> Chorão of the old guard. . . . Why don't you get together with your old friends for a choro session next Sunday instead of sleeping in? Put some new strings on your guitar, start warming up tonight and play in front of the group tomorrow. . . . We bet that every one of you has already had this idea. . . . All that was lacking was a little motivation. . . . So here it is. . . . Get going, chorões, whether you choose C major or A minor. . . . Picks, reeds and fingers ready to serve good Brazilian music.

Jacó do Bandolim was an important link between the old *regional* groups and the new generation of instrumentalists, many of whom he encouraged in the rodas held at his home. He even predicted the demise of the old radio *regional* style, which he blamed on a lack of creativity on the part of musicians. Jacó was unparalleled in his dedication to the choro genre and style as an important part of Brazil's cultural heritage. So highly regarded are Jacó's efforts to preserve choro and Brazilian popular music in general that in 2003 the Instituto Jacó do Bandolim was founded with the stated purpose of working for the "defense of Brazilian popular music." As a composer and performer, he was greatly admired by the choro community; his compositions are adored by bandolinists and many are considered classics of the tradition. Jacó's death in 1969 seemed to many to mark the end of an new groups such as Os Carioquinhas, Galo Preto, Camerata Carioca, and Nó em Pingo D'Água that continued the tradition inherited from the *regional*.

Choro Musicians of the 1950s and 1960s

JACÓ DO BANDOLIM

Although Jacó did much to preserve choro through his radio and television broadcasts, it must not be forgotten that he was also one of the most accomplished virtuosi of his generation. The bandolim has been a popular instrument in choro only since the 1950s, most likely due to his recordings and performances. The bandolim shares the four double courses of strings of the mandolin[19] but differs in shape and playing technique. It is characterized by an oval shape and a flat back with a somewhat deeper body than a mandolin and is played with a pick made of tortoiseshell or plastic. Although the technique of tremolo, or passing the pick rapidly up and down to give the impression of a single sustained note, is used at times, the plucking of individual notes is more common.

Of all the instruments in the choro ensemble, the bandolim has the strongest associations with the style since it is rarely used in other traditions. According to the musicological literature and the numerous recordings available, the bandolim historically played an important role as a solo instrument in choro, yet Pinto was acquainted with only six bandolim players out of the 365 chorões he listed. It is likely that the instrument became popular only later in the history of choro and was not present in great numbers before 1935. The bandolim seems to have been a twentieth-century addition to the choro ensemble, replacing the larger bandola used in nineteenth-century groups. Before this time, the flute seems to have been the most common solo instrument. One of the earliest proponents of the instrument was Luperce Miranda, who played in several early professional radio and recording groups.

Jacob Pick Bittencourt was born in Rio de Janeiro on February 14, 1918. His mother gave him a violin when he was 12, which he attempted to play by plucking the strings. Shortly thereafter he was given a bandolim, which he taught himself to play. In 1933, he appeared on Rádio Guanabara in a group he formed with some friends. Resolving to dedicate himself to the bandolim, he appeared again a year later on a radio talent show. The jury, which consisted of famous singers Orestes Barbosa and Francisco Alves and choro flautist and *regional* leader Benedito Lacerda, was impressed with his talent and gave him first prize. From this point on, Jacó continued to perform on various radio shows, winning many prizes. He formed a *regional* called Jacob e Sua Gente in 1937, within which he perfected his talent as a performer. In 1947, he made his first recording as a soloist, playing one of his own pieces ("Treme-Treme") and one by Bonfiglio de Oliveira (the waltz "Glória").

In his professional career, Jacó passed through many of the most famous *regionais,* performing live on nearly every radio and television station in Brazil. He quickly became known for his high standards and his studious approach to performance. He also became known among chorões for the rodas he held at his home in Jacarepaguá. These gatherings were by invitation only and attracted the best of local talent and international guests, all of whom were subject to Jacó's strict rule of silence during performances. Throughout his life, Jacó was close friends with Donga, who had helped him during periods of financial difficulty, and Pixinguinha, whom Jacó aided in a similar manner.

Jacó wrote 103 compositions that he modestly described as "little pieces that fit well on the bandolim"; many of these pieces make up the standard repertoire for the instrument.[20] Jacó's pieces and playing style were influenced by many choro musicians of the past, including Pixinguinha, whom he especially admired for his unparalleled playful spirit (malícia). He was acquainted with the new harmonic vocabulary of American jazz and Brazilian experimental musicians, such as Garoto. As a nationalist, Jacó publicly proclaimed his distaste for "foreign" modern harmonies, but his conservative incorporation of certain extended harmonies gives his works a sound that distinguishes them from choros of the previous decades, representing a considerable enrichment of the choro repertoire.

An example of his harmonic style can be found in one of the his most famous pieces, the choro "Noites cariocas" ("Cariocan Nights"), composed in 1957 and considered since then to be a part of the core repertoire (see Example 6.3).[21] His use of diminished triads and seventh chords in the piece set a new standard for choro compositions, a style that many continue to embrace.

Besides his recordings, his compositions, and his rodas, Jacó's contribution to the choro tradition also includes the last group that he formed before his death. Época de Ouro (Golden Age) was formed in 1961, consisting of musicians hand picked from the regulars at his rodas, including Horondino da Silva ("Dino Sete Cordas" on seven-string guitar), César Faria and Carlos Leite (six-string guitars), Jonas Pereira (cavaquinho), and Gilberto D'Ávila (pandeiro).[22] At first he called the group Jacob e seu Regional, as was the custom, but given his distaste for *regionais,* it is not surprising that in 1966 he changed the name permanently to Época de Ouro.

Jacó was a perfectionist, and he insisted that the groups in which he participated rehearse regularly. Because singers whom *regionais* accompanied demanded rehearsal schedules that accommodated them alone, Jacó became frustrated at the lack of time musicians had to rehearse instrumental numbers. The status of the *regional* as a studio ensemble that was used for accompaniment and to fill in dead time on the air angered Jacó, who believed that the music and the musicians deserved greater respect.

Example 6.3. "Noites cariocas," by Jacó do Bandolim.

Under Jacó's guidance, Época developed a professional style that balanced precision with spontaneity and malícia. The group disbanded in 1969 with the unexpected death of Jacó. Few members at the time would have predicted the comeback of Época in the 1970s and the role the ensemble would play as purveyor of the choro tradition for countless numbers of aspiring young choro musicians.

WALDIR DE AZEVEDO (1923–1980) AND THE CAVAQUINHO

As new virtuosi on the guitar, bandolim, and flute arose in the 1930s and 1940s, the cavaquinho was developed as a solo instrument by Waldir de Azevedo. Like the bandolim, the cavaquinho has Portuguese roots. Since the earliest days of the colony, Portuguese instrumental preferences were adopted in Brazil with local modifications; in this way the Portuguese *cavaco* became the *cavaquinho* (and, incidentally, the *ukulele* in Hawaii, an island group much visited by the Portuguese). In early choro, the cavaquinho provided most of the rhythmic support, allowing the guitar player to improvise freely within the texture. Later the cavaquinho came to be used upon occasion as a solo instrument, but exactly when this new role came into fashion is unclear. On a recording made by the Oito Batutas in 1923, the cavaquinho improvises countermelodies to the solo flute part and takes an occasional solo,[23] and recordings of other professionals of the period exhibit the cavaquinho played in similar fashion.

The most famous player and composer for the cavaquinho as a solo instrument in choro is Waldir de Azevedo. He began his studies on flute and bandolim but later settled on cavaquinho, on which he perfected his talent to an unprecedented level. He began his professional career in 1940, and in 1945 he joined the *regional* led by guitarist Dilermando Reis on a program of the Radio Club of Brazil. Two years later, he assumed leadership of this ensemble. Waldir de Azevedo was a tireless recording artist: In the 1950s and 1960s he recorded twenty LPs (one of them with Jacó do Bandolim) and more than fifty singles. In 1971, he moved to Brasília and helped the new city build a strong choro tradition of its own.

De Azevedo was responsible for creating a repertoire of choros that featured the cavaquinho as a soloist. Among the best known is "Delicado," which became an international hit in 1950 and 1951; it was even recorded by Percy Faith, who had the first number-one hit in Brazil by an American artist. Another showpiece for the cavaquinho is "Brasileirinho," rhythmically a *baião* rather than a choro (see Example 6.4).[24] The piece is harmonically simple, allowing the listener to focus on the arpeggios and melodic runs. The alternation between an A6 chord and an A minor 6 chord

Example 6.4. "Brasileirinho," by Waldir de Azevedo.

is reminiscent of riffing or comping techniques used in jazz, and undoubtedly this aspect aided its popular appeal. Although it was written for cavaquinho, all choro soloists are eventually asked to play this standard at some point in their career.

DILERMANDO REIS (1916–1977), ALTAMIRO CARRILHO (B. 1924), AND OTHER CHORÕES

Although choro was no longer in the forefront of popular music in the 1950s and 1960s, it continued to evolve during these years under the hands of the new generation of virtuosi who pushed the boundaries of their instruments and the choro genre. One of the most important guitarists after Garoto was Dilermando Reis, who was a celebrated instrumentalist and composer in his day. He began his career in the 1930s, when he moved from the interior of São Paulo to Rio de Janeiro. There he gave guitar lessons at the Bandolim de Ouro and A Guitarra de Prata music stores and made the acquaintance of fellow educator João Pernambuco. He worked sporadically at Radio Guanabara and in 1945 formed the *regional* for the Radio Club of Brazil that included Waldir de Azevedo on cavaquinho. In 1956, he signed a contract with Rádio Nacional, where he remained until 1969. He recorded many successful LPs of his own compositions and arrangements, including "Penumbra" (bolero), "Alma Nortista" (waltz), and "Calanguinho" (choro). In 1970, Radames Gnattali dedicated his *Concerto #1* to Reis, who recorded it that same year. In 1972, he recorded the LP *Dilermando Reis Interprets Pixinguinha* and in 1975 released *The Brazilian Guitar,* two of the most successful choro recordings before the revival. He was known by the great chorões of the day, including Horondino da Silva, who accompanied him on one of his LPs, and he gave concerts abroad, including a performance in New York City on CBS television. His legacy includes many professional and amateur students, the most famous of whom was the president of Brazil, Juscelino Kubitschek (1955–1961).

Reis composed many solo pieces for guitar, including choros and waltzes. Although they are not adventurous in terms of harmony or form, they are appreciated by guitarists as pieces that are particularly suited for the instrument and a pleasure to play.

The flute has been the preferred solo instrument in choro since its rise in the 1870s. Joaquim Calado was the forerunner of the flute tradition, followed by Pixinguinha, Benedito Lacerda, Dante Santoro, Carlos Poyares, and Altamiro Carrilho. Carrilho has been called a living legend; as this book goes to press, he is still an active performer. He demonstrated a talent for flute as a youngster, and like Jacó do Bandolim, he began his career after winning an amateur talent competition when he was a youth. He worked in a pharmacy during the day and studied his instrument in the evenings. After forming his own ensemble, he had a television show on TV Tupi in 1952. Altamiro's talent extended to classical music as well as popular, and beginning in the 1960s he was invited to give various concerts throughout the world. He has made an extensive number of recordings and has written approximately 200 pieces for flute.

Altamiro Carrilho, Garoto, Jacó do Bandolim, Waldir de Azevedo, and Diler-mando Reis are proof that choro did not disappear in the 1950s and 1960s. What had changed, however, was public opinion concerning choro. Although there was no question in people's minds that choro was "authentic" and "Brazilian" music, it seemed to belong to a different time and place. What choro there was in the 1960s was eclipsed by increasing social unrest, political radicalization, and the mobiliza-tion of sectors of the population into trade unions, student organizations, and peas-ant leagues. Choro had little to do with the powerful sensibilities and the youthful audiences for the new modern musics flooding the soundscape, such as bossa nova, rock and roll, protest music, and a new popular-song genre called *música popular brasileira* (MPB).[25] In the context of social upheaval and political crisis, it is no wonder that choro advocates feared that their music, and their way of life, would be completely forgotten.

The Radical Sixties and the Rediscovery of the Traditional

Following the mysterious resignation of President Janios Quadros after only seven months in office, Vice President Goulart stepped into the presidency in 1961. Goulart was not looked upon kindly by the military, who took exception to his friendly gestures toward Fidel Castro. Like Quadros, Goulart believed that Brazil was best served by playing the United States against communist countries, including China and Cuba. Continuing the heavy spending of his predecessors, Goulart ignored the galloping inflation that threatened to plunge the country into economic chaos. As Goulart pushed radical proposals that leaned farther and farther to the left, the moderate middle class began to fear popular uprisings and urged the military to intervene. In 1964, with inflation spiraling out of control and increasing social unrest and protest of President Goulart's policies, the military sided with the conservatives and seized control of the government. The military dictatorship lasted for twenty-one years, during which time Brazil experienced repression, censorship, torture, and social turmoil.

Despite the censors and the repressive actions of the government, popular music in Brazil flourished as never before. Huge festivals of MPB, jazz, and rock were held in Rio de Janeiro and São Paulo, and the music industry underwent unprecedented growth to handle the demands of a new young consumer class. Popular music with a political and social message began to arise, and bossa nova was injected with a new strain of social awareness by singers such as Geraldo Vandré and Chico Buarque. Students, artists, critics, and musicians eagerly took on the task of reforming middle-class society and values through music, theater, and film, creating a loose social movement based on the notion of "cultural resistance."

The most important musical manifestation of the cultural resistance movement was a new interest in working-class samba, or *samba de morro* (samba from the hills). As music of an economically disadvantaged class of people,[26] it satisfied the political requirements of the resistance movement. *Sambistas* (samba singers and musicians) who had previously been ignored by the music industry, such as Clementina de Jesus, Zé Keti, Cartola, and Nelson Sargento, were sought out to make recordings and give shows. To scholars and intellectuals, the "discovery" of these purveyors of authentic, "pure" Brazilian culture was revelatory; Vasconcelos calls it the equivalent of the missing link for anthropologists. His view of samba de morro in this case is strikingly similar to the reaction Gilberto Freyre had to choro in the 1920s and illustrates the persistence of the notion that authentic national culture is to be found only among the poor uneducated folk.

In 1963, the sambista Cartola and his wife Zica opened a restaurant that shortly became renowned as a meeting place for old and young sambistas, artists, and intellectuals. The Zicartola Restaurant was the site for intense discussions and debates about the renovation of Brazilian culture between the young sambista Paulinho da Viola (the son of Época de Ouro's guitarist César Faria), critic Sérgio Cabral, and cultural producers Hermínio Belo de Carvalho and Albino Pinheiro. It was Hermínio's idea to launch a musical show that featured Old Guard samba singers accompanied by veteran choro and samba musicians. The result was the stage show *Rosa de Ouro* (*Golden Rose*), which featured sambistas Elton Medeiros,

Nelson Sargento, Jair do Cavaquinho, and Paulinho da Viola. Several of the accompanists were respected choro musicians, such as guitarists Horondino da Silva (seven-string guitar) and Meira (six-string guitar). The show provoked an outpouring of praise from critics, won several awards, and toured Brazil for two years.

Despite marginalization by the music industry, samba de morro was cultivated and disseminated for its political potential within the cultural resistance movement. In this context, it was introduced to the middle class that had once favored samba-canção crooners over the rough-voiced sambistas from the favelas. This new audience meant that singers from the morro were recorded, many of them for the first time in their lives, to the accompaniment of traditional instruments (e.g., cavaquinho, pandeiro). The discovery of samba de morro by the middle class set a precedent for choro, which would follow a similar path a decade later.

The cultural resistance movement relied on a blend of popular and traditional styles and instruments in order to show support for the disaffected Brazilian masses, or *o povo*. The musical stage show *Opinião* (*Stubborn Opinion*), which opened in Rio de Janeiro in late 1964, exemplifies the musical hybridity of the movement.[27] It consisted of samba de morro (samba from the hillside favelas sung by ordinary people and accompanied by only a few traditional instruments such as cavaquinho, guitar, and/or pandeiro), música nordestina, politicized bossa novas, American protest songs, and film music from the avant-garde cinema novo movement.[28] Choro is conspicuously absent from the cultural resistance movement even though it had been strongly associated with Brazilian nationalism since the 1920s. There are several possible reasons for its omission. The most obvious is the fact that as an instrumental genre, choro could not serve as a vehicle for protest lyrics. The increasing demand for professional musicians and the unspoken prejudice against blacks meant that the majority of players in any given *regional* tended to be white or light-skinned. Therefore, unlike samba de morro, choro was not associated with an oppressed class of people. Finally, the Americanized style and instrumentation of choro ensembles in the late 1940s and 1950s had come to be viewed as mainstream music without political value. It is an irony that the disappearance of choro from the Brazilian soundscape in the 1960s seemed to aid its reappearance and repoliticization in the form of the choro revival a decade later.

The 1950s and 1960s were a period of great change in choro. New trends in Brazilian music were infused with American influences, including the harmonic sophistication from jazz movements from the 1940s and 1950s, brought home by returning Brazilian musicians such as Garoto and American musical imports. New technologies, including the rise of television and the advent of prerecorded radio shows, changed the face of popular entertainment and caused the decline of the professional *regional*. The trend toward increasing professionalism in choro continued, however, and new virtuosi, such as Garoto, Jacó do Bandolim, Waldir de

Azevedo, Dilermando Reis, and Altamiro Carrilho, significantly enriched the repertoire for their instruments with new compositions and the highest standards of performance on recordings and live appearances.

Despite the anti-American sentiments that arose as a by-product of developmental nationalism, the influx of American popular music continued unabated. By
the mid-1950s, choro was no longer part of everyday Brazilian culture despite the
attempts of Almirante and Jacó do Bandolim to recapture its earlier glory, and by
1960, choro had completely disappeared from the airwaves, where it was supplanted by songs of Presley and Sinatra. The arrival of rock and roll and the rise of
bossa nova in the late 1950s had a revolutionary effect on Brazilian popular music;
both were considered to be modern manifestations of culture which further served
to marginalize choro. As Brazil focused on industrial development as the path to
the future, the attitude toward choro underwent a fundamental shift. No one denied that choro was a "national" music, but it was now a music associated with a
past that had nothing to do with modern Brazil.

7

The Choro
Revival

On May 26, 1977, a grand choro concert with an audience of almost 4,000 people was held in São Paulo. It was the realization of an idea by critic and cultural producer J. E. Homem de Mello, who was inspired to produce a choro spectacle after hearing a performance at a meeting of researchers of popular Brazilian music the previous year. Mello was fortunate enough to have heard a group of highly skilled choro musicians that included guitarist Canhoto de Paraíba.[1] Canhoto's *regional* had disbanded in the 1960s, like so many other *regionais*, because of the lack of performing opportunities. When Mello first suggested that he reunite his group for a public concert, Canhoto replied skeptically, "Look, a lot of people have already tried that. I'm retired, we don't play anymore in public." Nevertheless, plans for the concert went forward, and when the moment arrived, Canhoto and his group were reunited once again: "One by one, Canhoto's group [appeared]. They entered the stage the way they had been all day: smiling, bursting with happiness. They played for us with all the experience and emotion of being together again after 20 years."[2]

Canhoto and his group were not the only choro musicians to return to the concert stage after having seen choro fall into obscurity. Veteran choro trombonist Raul de Barros opened Mello's show with his choro "Melodia celestial" ("Celestial Melody"). São Paulo's oldest and most respected choro group, Conjunto Atlântico, shared the stage with Paulo Moura, the versatile clarinetist who is as well versed in classical music and jazz as he is in choro. Although older choro musicians who had been active in the 1950s dominated the show, the concert organizers wanted to show the continuity of the choro tradition with the younger generation. To do this, they engaged A Fina Flor do Samba, a group of young choro musicians, and presented them to the audience in a way that left no doubt about the importance of their role; as Conjunto Atlântico played Jacó do Bandolim's beloved "Noites cariocas" ("Rio Nights"), the members of Fina Flor entered the stage one by one and switched places with the older musicians, all without interrupting the music.

Throughout São Paulo and Rio de Janeiro older choro musicians dusted off their instruments and reunited the members of their groups to play public concerts. Even young people showed an interest in choro, forming new groups and attending choro concerts, rodas, and events. Many spoke of the *renascimento,* the rebirth of choro in the Brazilian musical consciousness, and indeed Brazil was in the midst of a choro revival. Older choro musicians were guarded at first but thrilled at the sudden attention and prestige their art brought them. Critics who warned about the dangers of cultural imperialism in popular music were ecstatic that choro had "returned": In this vein, critic José Ramos Tinhorão urged the public to "take advantage of the choro boom to finally hear good music."[3]

The movement began in the mid-1970s and was spearheaded by a cultural elite of academics, journalists, and critics. The revival arose in the city of choro's origin, Rio de Janeiro, and quickly spread to the cities of São Paulo, Brasília, and beyond. The founders of the revival all shared a concern about the apparent decay of authentic Brazilian music in the face of imported popular musics. Some of the revivalists were themselves choro players, and all hailed from the middle sector of Brazilian society from which choro had emerged 100 years earlier. By the late 1970s, their efforts were applauded by the middle class and financially supported by the government, which resulted in a full-scale revival. The outward signs of the revival were unmistakable: Old Guard musicians, forgotten since the 1950s, were sought after once again as performers and conveyors of the tradition; new groups of aspiring young instrumentalists were formed by the dozens; choro clubs sprang up in practically every major city in Brazil; huge festivals and competitions that attracted dozens of groups and thousands of spectators filled theaters and auditoriums in Rio de Janeiro and São Paulo; and record producers, recognizing a new market, scrambled to release new choro recordings. On the surface, one would not have guessed that the revival took place under the shadowy wing of military dictatorship in which censorship, random arrests, and torture had become a part of daily life. Yet this context is fundamental to the particular historical formation and the trajectory of the choro revival.

Music Revivals

Music revivals are social movements that strive to restore a musical system believed to be disappearing or completely relegated to the past.[4] Regardless of when or where they occur or what type of music they involve, music revivals have a great deal in common in terms of motivation, sources, and activities. Music revivals are initiated and maintained by a dedicated individual or small group of core revivalists who base their knowledge of the tradition on a combination of resources that includes interaction with representative artists and/or studying recorded examples of the music. Core revivalists and participants tend to frame their goals and activities in terms of preserving the tradition and maintaining its authenticity. For a revival to be a social movement, it must have a group of followers, which typically consists of fans and musicians. Participants may engage in a variety of revivalist activities, such as organizations dedicated to the tradition, festivals, and competitions. Finally, many revivals generate nonprofit and/or commercial enterprises catering to the revivalist market. Some of the products these enterprises may create are recordings, magazines, sheet music, instructional materials, and instruments for purchase.

Core revivalists are those who are interested in preserving or resuscitating a musical tradition. To do so, they seek out living musicians who are representative of the tradition and collect source materials, such as recordings, photographs, musical scores, song lyrics, and historical instruments. A revivalist community coalesces around the core revivalists, and together they take on the task of educating each other and the public about their musical tradition. Even though they emphasize historical or cultural authenticity, revivalists inevitably create a new tradition, one that is different from the tradition that they seek to revive. Revivalists place a heavy emphasis on the history of their tradition and the importance of preserving their music. Unlike other musicians who perform for a variety of reasons, including pleasure and money, revivalists perform music in order to preserve the tradition. Their concern with clearly defining the tradition and separating it from other musics means that they tend to use a strict set of stylistic parameters based on recordings, scores, or the performing styles of certain musicians believed to be authoritative bearers of the tradition. In this way, revivalists hope to safeguard the purity of their tradition while ensuring its cultural continuity. Revivalists usually have in mind more than the restoration or preservation of particular styles, genres, or instruments. To them, a musical tradition represents a way of life, a cultural alternative to present-day society and mainstream culture. Restoring a musical tradition instills a different perspective and a different set of values in people. For this reason, revivalists position themselves in opposition to mainstream culture, which represents to them a number of negative traits that include mediocrity, commercialism, falseness, and decadence.

The choro revival exhibited all the hallmark traits of a musical revival movement situated in a specific time and place: Brazilian society and culture in the 1970s and 1980s. Choro revivalists generally believed that choro, along with other forms of "genuine" Brazilian popular music (including samba and MPB), were threatened by new commercial genres modeled on the American and British pop music that was flooding the airwaves. They blamed the scarcity of choro recordings and the fact that youths growing up in the 1960 and 1970s were unacquainted with choro on the unwillingness of recording companies and concert promoters to produce and disseminate a genre that was not lucrative. Revivalists also felt that choro was caught in a double bind: Without adequate dissemination, the public was unaware of choro, yet without public demand, choro remained unmarketable. They were convinced that a large potential audience for choro already existed; it was simply a matter of educating the public and creating a space in the media for it. They believed that without their efforts, traditional music as a cultural link to the past was in real danger of being entirely and irrevocably forgotten. The links choro revivalists made between the past and the present are evident in the following remarks by critic Ruy Fabiano:

> For those who are not familiar with the subject, it is worth remembering that choro is one of our richest and most creative musical manifestations. Perhaps [it is] the only genre of progressive national music, at certain times crossing boundaries between the popular and the erudite. For all that it offered in the past, including the shaping of our best instrumentalists, and for all that it will certainly bring to MPB, it is worth recalling its history and reflecting upon its return and its contact with musicians of the new generation.[5]

Returning choro to the realm of popular culture by securing a space for it in the music industry was seen as a step toward the goal of restoring Brazilian culture and reestablishing musical and social links between the past and the present.

The Return of Choro

In 1973, a musical show produced by Sérgio Cabral was performed in the South Zone of Rio de Janeiro. The concert, called *Sarau*,[6] consisted of samba de morro songs alternating with instrumental choros and featured Paulinho da Viola backed by his father's choro group, Época de Ouro. Época had disbanded after the death of its founder Jacó do Bandolim in 1969, but the members reformed the group for *Sarau* with Jacó's student, the young bandolinist Déo Rian, as soloist. A similar show also written by Sérgio Cabral had been produced in the mid-1960s, but the reaction to *Sarau* was unanticipated. Although the samba numbers were warmly applauded, it was the "accompanists" that received the most enthusiastic response. The reaction to their instrumental numbers was so great that Época de Ouro was obliged to give several encores. For revivalists, this event marked the beginning of the choro revival.

It is no surprise that the show involved many of the same people who had been involved ten years earlier in introducing samba de morro to the cariocan

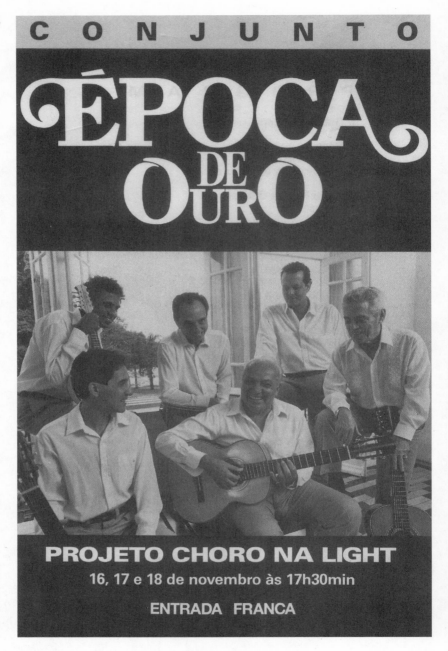

Figure 7.1. Época de Ouro. Publicity photo, 1994.

middle class. The most significant was Paulinho da Viola, who grew up hearing samba and choro at family gatherings with chorões Jacó do Bandolim and Pixinguinha. His father, César Faria, is a choro guitarist who remains an active member of Época de Ouro. Despite his fame as a sambista and the demands of being a recording artist, Paulinho is a tireless advocate for choro, and he served as a spokesman and a performer in the revival.

Sérgio Cabral, the writer and producer of *Sarau,* was an educated and outspoken critic of Brazilian music and culture. He was a respected journalist and columnist for the *Jornal do Brasil, Tribuna da Imprensa, Diário Carioca,* and *Correio da Manhã,* and his ties to the media proved invaluable in promoting the revival. In addition to music criticism, Cabral also wrote and directed several musical productions in the 1960s and 1970s that featured samba and choro, reflecting his concern with preserving and promoting traditional Brazilian popular music. He is the author of several books on popular music and is often cited as an authority on the subject. Cabral also produced recordings of Brazilian traditional music for the Marcus Pereira label and RCA, and was one of the founding members of the Choro Club of Rio de Janeiro in 1975.[7] During and after the choro revival, Cabral was especially concerned with promoting choro as a musical and cultural alternative to rock and roll for Brazilian youths. In one of his many writings about choro, Cabral described it as "a type of music that requires talent and competence from instrumentalists" and warned that "electric guitarists accustomed to the poverty of rock and similar music shouldn't try to play it lest they risk cramps in their fingers." He continues, "[A]nother suggestion is for instrumentalists that are looking to develop themselves using resources offered by American music: play choro, for it is richer than you can imagine."[8] Many young instrumentalists appeared to take Cabral's advice as they flocked to concerts and scrambled to find bandolims, cavaquinhos, and guitars.

Building the Revival Tradition

YOUTH INVOLVEMENT IN CHORO

By 1976, there were no less than seven choro groups in Rio de Janeiro consisting entirely of players between the ages of 15 and 20.[9] Many of the young choro musicians we encountered during our research in the 1990s recall having first become interested in choro in the 1970s. Although some, such as guitarist Raphael Rabello, became inspired to play choro upon hearing it played at home by older relatives, others were first introduced to choro by attending concerts during the early years of the revival. The influence of these public choro concerts on youth was significant: Many aspiring musicians resolved at that point to dedicate themselves to the instruments they heard performed and to form their own choro groups. At a concert of choro, one young spectator was overheard saying, "Man, this is cooler than Woodstock." Bandolinist Marco de Pinna admits that his father forced him to attend a concert given by the cavaquinho virtuoso Waldir de Azevedo in 1977. To his surprise,

> I was moved to see Waldir play so well. What's funny is that I didn't want to go to that concert. It was when rock was big and at 13 years of age, I thought it was old-fashioned to go to a choro concert. The day after the show, I asked to have a bandolim, and a week later I was playing pieces by Jacó do Bandolim by ear.[10]

Raphael Rabello, who was 14 years old at the beginning of the revival, describes the general reaction to choro:

> What I know is that people really get into it when they hear choro. People my age think it's weird to play this music, but they all just go crazy over it. It's just that they've never heard this music before on radio or on television, and they don't have any prejudice against the music.[11]

To older chorões and revivalists, these young players were an important symbol that represented the historical continuity of choro and assured its survival in the future. They also helped dispel the commonly held notion that choro was "old people's music" or "music of the past." To those who grew up in the 1960s hearing the Beatles, the music of the Jovem Guarda,[12] rock, and other transnational popular styles, choro was something new, an alternative path for those looking to develop their skills on a particular instrument. For many, the sudden interest of youths in choro was highly surprising:

> The seclusion of choro for almost three decades in the backyards of suburban cariocas is as mysterious as its sudden revival, identified with a [young] generation produced by a controversial and tumultuous period in history. In fact it was unthinkable until just recently that a generation born under the mantle of rock and roll . . . would derive their creative inspiration from the distant and bucolic music of choro, a genre which was thought to be dying out, condemned to disappear with the last of its cultivators.[13]

Young revivalists were for the most part from middle-class homes. Many attended college and received degrees. Some abandoned their original career path for music, while others kept their careers but continued to play choro in their spare time. Most of the young revivalists were male; the few women who participated in the revival gravitated toward instruments commonly believed to be suitable for women, such as flute or piano. The lack of Old Guard female choro musicians (with the exception of Chiquinha Gonzaga) as role models and a general feeling among male chorões that women are incapable of being good choro musicians is likely to have affected the gender imbalance of the revival. Even so, there were some notable exceptions to this bias, and the revival produced some excellent female choro

musicians, including Luciana Rabello (cavaquinho), Dolores Tomé (flute), and Bete
Dias (flute).

RODAS DE CHORO

The roda de choro was in many ways the most important facet of the revival. From a revivalist perspective, the roda served as a pedagogical tool, obviating the need for formal instruction or method books. In the roda, young players learned by listening and imitating older musicians. In addition, they learned the social etiquette and values of the roda, which served to perpetuate choro within a context similar to that of the past. In the 1970s and 1980s, established rodas attracted new players as well as spectators, and new rodas formed by the dozens in bars and homes. In São Paulo, the established rodas at the Casa del Vecchio music store and at the home of Antônio D'Auria, leader of Conjunto Atlântico, were suddenly inundated with new players and spectators.

The best-known roda de choro during the revival took place on Sunday afternoons in a small bar called O Sovaco de Cobra (The Snake's Armpit) in Penha, in the North Zone of Rio de Janeiro. The neighborhood was, and continues to be, made up of lower-income families and has a higher percentage of Afro-Brazilians than in the wealthy South Zone. In his survey of the history of choro, Ary Vasconcelos describes the Sovaco de Cobra as "the great cariocan temple of the [choro] genre" that had become "the meeting place for all chorões" during the revival.[14] Musician Jorge Simas recalls that in the years before the revival, the bar was simply a place where music-lovers would get together on Sundays to play. Around 1976, however, the Sovaco suddenly became a fashionable destination; even those from the upper middle classes of the South Zone would make the trip to Penha to hear the great names of choro, including clarinetists Paulo Moura and Abel Ferreira, flautist Altamiro Carrilho, guitarist Horondino da Silva, and other members of Época de Ouro. Young musicians flocked to the Sovaco in order to learn from the best players and debut their talents. Members of the youth group Os Carioquinhas, which included Raphael Rabello and his sister Luciana, first "cut their teeth" as participants in the roda at the Sovaco de Cobra. Young bandolim player Marco de Pinna was another such disciple; besides refining his talent, he met Jorge Simas at the bar and formed the group Nó em Pingo D'Água. Cavaquinho player Henrique Cazes and his brother Beto were also inspired and influenced by these rodas.

By 1977, the Sovaco de Cobra had become such a popular and lucrative venue for choro musicians and audiences that imitations had begun to spring up throughout the city. A particularly blatant example was the opening of a new bar and restaurant that assumed the name Sovaco de Cobra and hired choro musicians to play there to make it appear as if a spontaneous roda was in session. The outcry it provoked among those who patronized the real Sovaco was evident in a review of the restaurant in the prestigious newspaper *O Jornal do Brasil,* which blasted the

Figure 7.2. Roda de choro at the Sovaco da Cobra. From the collection of Marco de Pinna.

new bar as a "lamentable and gross imitation" and a "false" gathering for choro musicians.[15] This event and the rise of new bars featuring choro musicians were symptomatic of the choro boom: No one was sure it would last, so businesses had to act quickly to turn a profit from it. In Jorge Simas's opinion, the plethora of new choro bars had a deleterious effect on the roda at the Sovaco, thinning the crowds and complicating the schedules of renowned chorões.[16] Whether or not this was the case, choro fans and musicians had very clear ideas of what constituted authentic choro; the fact that the imitation Sovaco was an attempt to profit from the choro revival was considered just as distasteful as the fact that musicians were paid to perform there to give the appearance of a roda. This type of venture was all too common in hyperinflationary Brazil, where businesses exploited a trend or fad for immediate profit with little regard for future stability.

CHORO CLUBS

Choro clubs were founded with the mission of preserving and disseminating choro as a valuable part of Brazilian cultural history and defending it against mass-mediated foreign-dominated popular musics. Choro clubs were typically involved in organizing and sponsoring concerts and festivals, and a few even provided a physical location where choro musicians could congregate and play on a regular basis.

The earliest choro club, the Clube de Choro do Rio de Janeiro, was formed in 1975.[17] Among the founders were Paulinho da Viola, Sérgio Cabral, musicologist and government official Mozart de Araújo,[18] and music producers Albino Pinheiro and Juarez Barroso. All of these individuals were involved in various other choro activities, such as adjudicating competitions in and around Rio de Janeiro. As the choro revival quickly spread throughout Brazil, similar clubs sprang up in Brasília and Recife (established in 1976), and in São Paulo and Salvador (established in 1977).

The Choro Club of Rio de Janeiro sponsored numerous concerts and events commemorating past and present choro musicians. Its first production in 1975 was the Week of Jacó do Bandolim, which commemorated the donation of the choro musician's extensive popular music archive to MIS. The club was fortunate to be sponsored by the MIS, which in turn was funded by the secretary of culture and the state of Rio de Janeiro.[19] Few other clubs were able to rely on such sponsorship, but this did not deter them from forming throughout Brazil.

An exceptional club is the Clube do Choro de Brasília, which is unique in several ways. The club has its own building, and many of its members are government officials in various capacities. The tendency for cultural manifestations in the nation's capital to become enmeshed with the state is noted by a reporter who says: "In Brasília, choro has a legal personality: that is, the Choro Club is legally constituted and ready to continue the battle."[20] The club went though a period of financial hardship in the mid-1990s but is today one of the most active choro clubs in Brazil, led by Reco do Bandolim (Henrique Lima S. Filho), president of the club since 1993.

It seems strange at first that a city literally created out of nothing on the vast uninhabited high plains of Goias between 1956 and 1960 should have an active choro scene. Brasília houses many federal agencies and their officials, many of whom were forced to relocate when the capital moved from Rio de Janeiro. As a planned city designed by the futurist architect Oscar Niemayer, Brasília is architecturally impressive, but it is thought by many to be sterile and cold. Instead of the neighborhoods with markets, bars, and houses within walking distance that are so typical in Brazil, in Brasília, large housing developments are located far away from businesses. These physical features make it difficult for spontaneous music-making to occur in public places. To enliven the city, various concessions were made to bring choro and samba musicians to Brasília. Some were expressly invited by President Juscelino Kubitschek (1956–1961), including Canhoto de Paraíba, who became one of the president's guitar teachers;[21] others came in search of work, such as virtuoso Waldir de Azevedo. João Figueiredo, the last president of the period of military rule (1979–1985), also invited musicians to live in Brasília. In one instance, he created a government position for an out-of-work saxophonist and sambista he admired.[22] In some respects, Figueiredo was simply continuing a tradition that allowed choro musicians to draw modest salaries for little or no work. Pixinguinha was given a modest government pension, and Quincas Laranjeiras, a popular chorão in the 1920s, was paid a salary and a pension for a civil service position with no duties.

By 1977, interest and support for choro was sufficient not only to organize a club but also to have a meeting place dedicated to choro built; the city paid Sergio Bernardes to design and construct the new building. In keeping with the futuristic architecture Brasília is known for, the Clube de Choro building is distinct: the main quarters are sunk underground while above is a cement "roof" that projects up and out like the inverted stem of a wine glass. The building is equipped with a bar and cooking facilities to recreate the favored environment of choro musicians. Despite many years of disrepair and neglect due to lack of funds shortly after opening, the club building is once again animated by the sounds of choro.

CHORO RECORDINGS

Recordings of choro were released by several different types of organizations, including the state-run agencies MIS and the Fundação Nacional de Arte (National Foundation of Art, hereafter FUNARTE), national labels (Marcus Pereira, Eldorado, CID, Copacabana, Continental), and transnational labels (RCA, CBS, Warner, EMI, and Polygram). A few recordings were also produced by private businesses for promotional purposes; these were frequently given away for free. When the choro revival produced a sudden demand for recordings, companies scrambled to produce as much as they could quickly and cheaply. Although some new recordings were produced, many were simply re-releases of old archived choro recordings of *regionais* from the 1940s and 1950s. By 1977, critics had begun to complain about the number of re-releases, arguing that national and transnational companies should invest in studio recordings and take an active role in supporting current choro musicians instead of taking advantage of prerecorded material. Of the recordings released in 1977, approximately one-fourth consisted of reissues. These archived recordings were mostly of the great *regionais* of the past, including groups led by Altamiro Carrilho, Abel Ferreira, Waldir Azevedo, Jacó do Bandolim, Canhoto, and Pixinguinha. Because these recordings of the 1940s and 1950s were an important source young musicians used to develop their style, they largely defined the "traditional" revival sound of the 1970s.

Although it was not significant in terms of sales, the prolific work of independent producer Marcus Pereira was indispensable to the revival because of its focus on local artists and traditional music. Pereira was motivated to open a performing venue and a record label dedicated to Brazilian music in order to disseminate it and preserve it for future generations. About his bar O Jogral in São Paulo that featured traditional music, he said:

> It was the first real attempt to combat the domination of foreign music, and to showcase first-rate Brazilian music. Not only urban music of the kind called MPB, but also regional music, music of the interior of Brazil, outside of the Rio-São Paulo axis.[23]

In 1968, he started an independent record company in order to preserve and disseminate "authentic" Brazilian popular and folk music that other companies were ignoring. Like John and Alan Lomax in the United States in the 1930s and 1940s, Pereira traveled throughout Brazil with portable recording equipment capturing the sounds of unknown musicians and rural traditions. He was also the first to record urban samba legend Cartola, thereby stimulating interest in samba de morro in the 1960s. His LP *Brasil: Flauta, cavaquinho, e violão*[24] was the first in a series of recordings dedicated to choro. Pereira related how the idea of recording local choro artists came about:

> In 1968 . . . we returned to the idea of recording a disc. The choro ensemble that played [at the Jogral] was an obvious choice for the recording.[25] The festivals had made amends to a certain type of Brazilian music, but Carlos [Paraná] was not satisfied; he frequently lamented that the beautiful genres of instrumental music—like choro—or the rich and representative genres—like *música sertaneja*—continued to be forgotten, disparaged and maligned. After looking in vain for a sponsor, I decided . . . to record a disk of *chorinho* and to distribute it as an end of the year gift from my defunct promotions business.[26]

In 1973, two years before FUNARTE was created and given the task of officially preserving Brazil's cultural legacy, Pereira had the idea of "mapping" the musical heritage of Brazil and preserving it on discs.[27] Between 1973 and 1976, he released sixteen discs on the Discos Marcus Pereira label of rural regional music traditions sung by unknown musicians and contemporary MPB singers. Despite the immensity of this project, he did not neglect choro and released five choro albums between 1973 and 1976. In 1977, he released no less than eleven new albums that featured a variety of instruments from piano to guitar to the standard *conjunto regional*. Between 1978 and 1982, he produced only two more choro albums, no doubt a result of increasing debt, difficulties with distributors, the lack of sponsors, and a lack of support from the Ministry of Education and Culture.[28] In over ten years of production, Marcus Pereira produced 144 recordings.

Choro on Stage: Competitions and the Discourse of Authenticity

The roda was important for the transmission of the choro style and ethos to young musicians, but choro concerts, competitions, and festivals were the most important means of disseminating the music to the general public. The style of choro music played in concerts, festivals, and competitions tends to differ from that of the roda; in a concert, the musicians are concerned with entertaining an audience rather than each other. This affects their choice of repertoire, instrumentation (which shows a concern for balance), and playing style. In preparation for a concert, musicians tend to plan ahead what they will play and how they will play it. Because the emphasis is on sound as a product, there is generally an emphasis on precision of playing. Yet another layer is added to the process in a competition, when a panel of experts judges pieces and performances. Revivalist choro competitions offer a fascinating window on the politics of musical style, as implicit assumptions of authenticity are made public and challenged. It was in the public realm of choro competitions that the debate between preservation and innovation within the choro tradition was carried out most fiercely. (This is a point of tension within all music revivals, and the debate almost always heralds the eventual dissolution of a revival as a musical movement based on tenets of authenticity and preservation. The choro revival was no exception.)

In 1977, two huge choro festivals were held in São Paulo. Such festivals had their roots in the events promoted by Almirante and Jacó do Bandolim in the 1950s. The difference was that in the 1970s the nation was in the grip of a revival and the response to the festivals was overwhelming. The festival held in May, which featured the Regional de Canhoto and São Paulo's own Conjunto Atlântico, attracted thousands of people. Only a month later, another festival, called the first Encontro Nacional do Choro (National Choro Meeting), was organized by independent record producer Marcus Pereira and sponsored by the prominent media network Rede Bandeirantes. Participants included choro greats Waldir de Azevedo and Pernambuco do Pandeiro, and, in a symbolic gesture of approval, Paulinho da Viola and MPB artist Chico Buarque made guest appearances. Like Paulinho, Chico Buarque was an outspoken advocate of Brazilian popular music who had written songs in the choro style.

The year 1977 also marked the rise of choro competitions. Although these events were reminiscent of Jacó do Bandolim's television special "Noite dos Choristas" in that they gave novice musicians an opportunity to play for a large public, they differed in the rigor of the judging and the debate they engendered. Two series of choro competitions were launched in this year: The first was sponsored by the Ministério da Educacão e da Cultura do Rio de Janeiro (Ministry of Education and Culture of Rio de Janeiro, hereafter MEC), the second by the Bandeirantes Television Network in São Paulo. Each offered cash prizes for the best unpublished choro and the best performance by an ensemble. According to its government sponsor MEC, the competitions in Rio de Janeiro were intended to promote the formation of new choro groups by offering incentives to compete. Juries were comprised of a panel of musicologists, critics, and musicians, such as choro musicians Horondino da Silva, bandolinist Déo Rian, and clarinetist Sebastião Barros ("K-Ximbinho"). The Rio competition proved to be so popular that it was held for three more consecutive years and was hailed as a successful way to promote choro among young people.

Choro competitions were also held in São Paulo in 1977 and 1978. Contrasting with the modest facilities and low level of media coverage of the festivals in Rio de Janeiro, sponsorship by one of the largest media networks in Brazil, Rede Bandeirantes, made for high-profile, heavily publicized events. The First National Festival of Choro was a competition for the best unpublished choro. In all, approximately 1,200 unpublished choros were entered; thirty-six entries were selected for the final round and were performed live. These choros and the ensemble that debuted them were broadcast simultaneously on TV Bandeirantes in the cities of São Paulo, Rio de Janeiro, Belo Horizonte (Minas Gerais), Recife (Pernambuco), and Porto Alegre (Rio Grande do Sul). A live recording was also released of the twelve finalist choros on the Bandeirantes label; it sold 7,000 copies in two months.[29] The Second National Festival of Choro rivaled the first in terms of number of participants and media coverage. Producer Roberto Oliveira opened up the entire floor of the huge Teatro Bandeirantes in order to recreate an atmosphere suggestive of a roda de choro. The contestants were seated at bar tables at which they could drink beer while waiting for their turn to play.[30] The competitions provided a goal for younger musicians and disseminated the work of older established musicians. The celebrated youth group Os Carioquinhas and Nó em Pingo d'Agua received accolades and groups from outside the Rio de Janeiro–São Paulo nexus rose to the forefront of the competitions, such as Rossini Ferreira and Os Ingênuos.[31]

Ensembles that chose to compete in the performance category of the competitions typically chose a well-known choro so the jury would focus on the performance, not the piece. Typical selections in this category were "Tico-Tico no fubá" (by Zequinha de Abreu), "Apanhei-te cavaquinho" (by Ernesto Nazaré), "Dôce de côco" (by Jacó do Bandolim), and "Vou vivendo" (by Pixinguinha). The Department of Culture provided a survey of data on the sixteen ensembles that participated between 1977 and 1978; it illustrates the extent to which *regional* instrumentation permeated the revival.[32] Fifteen out of sixteen ensembles included cavaquinho and pandeiro, and all included at least one guitar. Eleven complemented the six-string guitar with a seven-string guitar. The most popular solo instrument was flute (eleven groups chose this instrumentation), followed closely by bandolim (nine groups chose this instrumentation). The other groups featured clarinet, trombone, or trumpet as soloist. The reliance of revivalist choro groups for style and instrumentation on the *regionais* of the past instead of, for example, the *orquestras* was a conscious decision that illustrated concerns about authenticity. By the 1970s, the flute, guitar, bandolim, cavaquinho, and pandeiro were seen as metaphors for authentic Brazilian culture; they were often contrasted with the electric guitar, which represented the "cultural imperialism" of the United States. As professional ensembles once endorsed by Vargas and praised by Almirante, whose sound was disseminated throughout Brazil on radio and recordings, *regionais* defined the sound of choro.

In these competitions, groups were rated in a number of categories, including execution of the piece and intonation. Competing choros were also judged on a numerical scale regarding arrangement, melody, and development of the theme. The large number of groups that formed with the primary intention of competing and the enormous quantities of pieces submitted for consideration demonstrated that competitions were an important, if not a central, aspect of the revival.

Most of the compositions chosen as finalist pieces displayed characteristics of choro of the previous decades. A few pieces experimented with introducing aspects of *música erudita,* or classical music, in instrumentation and arrangements that emphasized contrapuntal motion; others experimented with dense harmonies and chromaticism. A primary point of tension within revivalist competitions was the degree to which one could innovate yet remain within the choro genre. One group in particular challenged the judges not only with their highly chromatic piece but also with their instrumentation. The Bahian group A Cor do Som (The Color of Sound), founded by bandolinist Armandinho, shocked judges and audiences with its instrumentation, which consisted of amplified bandolim, keyboards, electric guitar, and drum set, and the original composition they performed. The group was influenced by the northeastern amplified style of Carnaval music called *trio elétrico;* the father of the bandolinist was a pioneer of the style in the 1950s.[33] Their choro, called "Espírito infantil" ("Childish Spirit") is more reminiscent of northeastern *frevo* than choro: its melody is comprised of chromatic riffs full of stops and starts played at breakneck speed.[34] Certainly it would have been difficult for the judges to separate the piece from the performance in this case, since a traditional *regional* would have had great difficulty in playing the piece. Although A Cor do Som was not the only competing group that used a drum set and electric instruments, the group's performance was a focal point for the debate between conservatives, who refused to accept electric instrumentation and a drum set in choro, and progressives, who argued that *regional*-style choro was already outdated and needed to be modernized to reflect contemporary popular music trends. Some charged the group with succumbing to the influence of foreign rock and roll, while others praised the group as a sign of "healthy modernization." The competition organizers encouraged the judges to select "modern" pieces as well as "traditional" choros in order to sustain the interest of youths in choro. A judge who supported this action warned of the dangers of enforcing traditional-style limitations on choro:

> People who say that choro is monotonous are right. The interpretations repeat themselves and choro remains as a thing of the past, it wasn't being renovated like samba. During the Festival, we commented to the other members of the jury that for the next year, there should be an emphasis on innovation. We don't have the right to limit choro [to traditional style].[35]

Other judges refused to select a piece simply because it was nontraditional, and they insisted on voting for pieces using their own standards. Paulinho da Viola challenged the assumption of some critics that modernization simply required the use of "modern" (i.e., electric) instruments:

Choro is not obligated to be modernized. The form and design [*desenho*] of choro should be maintained. As for the introduction of new instruments, I think that it is of little importance, because if you give an electric guitar to Dino [Horondino da Silva of Época de Ouro], for example, he's not going to play rock.[36] And if you give a bandolim to a rocker, that won't be the reason he'll play choro. . . . Above all, it is necessary to love and understand choro. . . . You need to love choro first, then learn to understand it, then try to modify it.[37]

Nationalist critic and popular music scholar José Ramos Tinhorão offered a different view of the modernization debate. He argued that the festivals offered a window on the types of choro currently being played throughout Brazil. He correctly points out that the majority of the choro heard during the festivals and competitions was traditional choro, the style played by the great *regionais* of the 1930s and 1940s. The few competition organizers, judges, and music critics who criticized the lack of "progress" in choro were dwarfed in number by those interested in hearing and playing traditional choro. Tinhorão characterizes the calls for modernization as a preoccupation of the bourgeoisie that had little relevance to the reality of the lower classes. He states:

[T]he choro that musicians from the Brazilian masses are playing at this moment is exactly that which we are hearing over the Bandeirantes television network. Whoever wants something different can invent a Festival of Choro of the Vanguard for talented members of the upper middle class. Or, they can just dispose of the *povo* [masses] that inconvenience them with their poverty, their daily grind, their lack of culture, their adhesion to oral traditions, their old-fashioned instruments, and their talent for being authentic. As long as the reality of the totality of the Brazilian people is the reality of underdevelopment, it will continue to be this way.

He summarizes his argument by stating:

What is behind all of this is firstly a preoccupation with the new for the sake of novelty by musicians, journalists and intellectuals who are alienated from the middle class. And secondly it is their solidarity with the multinational entertainment industry.[38]

The modernization-versus-preservation debate also applied to choro recordings. As new releases proliferated during 1977 and 1978, critics began to complain of a certain monotony in sound. Certainly the complaint is justified for those recordings that limited themselves to choro standards such as "Carinhoso," "Noites cariocas," and "Tico-Tico no fubá." Yet plenty of recordings featured lesser-known works by the masters and new works by contemporary musicians. It seems that it was the sound of the *regional* to which some critics (and musicians) objected.

We have seen that choro is not restricted to any particular instrumentation so long as certain musical roles are fulfilled. Nevertheless, the reification of the *regional* as the typical choro ensemble began with the rise of radio bands in the 1940s and 1950s. During the revival, choro became inseparable from the *regional*, the ensemble that appeared most often in contests, festivals, concerts, and recordings. The distinctive instruments associated with the *regional* (acoustic plucked strings, flute, and pandeiro) came under attack for preventing the development of the genre. Critic Echevarria believed that choro should develop along the lines of jazz. Others believed that the "erudite" side of choro should be emphasized.[39]

Traditional choro in the 1970s and 1980s was criticized partly because of the sudden emergence of a consumer market for this music. Although the majority of those participating in choro groups were happy simply to learn the core repertoire and develop their skills playing together, the choro consumer quickly grew tired of hearing the same old pieces over and over on stage and on recordings: They wanted something new and different, something modern. Brazilian intellectuals concerned about the direction and development of national cultural forms were proponents of this attitude. They found the apparent lack of development in choro during the revival deeply distressing. On the one hand, they were pleased that young people were rejecting American and British cultural imperialism in the form of rock and roll in favor of an authentic Brazilian form of music. On the other, they worried that if the music didn't modernize fast enough, young people would lose interest. But even this does not explain why it was so important to some that choro modernize.

What was really at stake in these debates was the issue of national identity. With the revival, choro had reentered the realm of popular culture and became a site of conflict between nationalists, the state, and the middle class. The question for all involved was how to develop an authentic Brazilian national culture that was modern, and hence on par with that of North America and Europe, yet still distinctly Brazilian. The emphasis on the modern in the mainstream clashed with the revivalist focus on preservation of the traditional, a term which since at least the 1950s, if not before, had connoted mostly negative ideas, such as "static," "unchanging," "outdated," "nostalgic," and distinctly "antimodern."

The Revival and the State

The choro revival owed a great deal to the interest and involvement of the state. Government organizations such as MIS, MEC, and FUNARTE were important sponsors of recordings, concerts, and competitions. The Secretaria Municipal de Educação e Cultura de Rio de Janeiro spearheaded an ambitious program called Projeto Concerto do Choro, whose goal was to preserve the cultural heritage of choro through education. A secondary goal of the project was to redirect the interest of youth who, according to an official pamphlet, were "completely wrapped up in the process of massification from foreign pop music, to the detriment of the legitimate art of the country." To this end, the youth groups Os Carioquinhos and A Fina Flor do Samba were both heavily supported by the state so that they could serve as examples for the nation's young people. Concert programs were designed to present new as well as established choro groups at different locations throughout the city such as public squares, schools, theaters, and samba school rehearsal areas. The project sponsored twelve concerts between 1975 and 1976. Other state-funded concert series were important to the choro revival. Among them was the Projeto Pixinguinha, which offered concerts of choro and MPB at affordable prices throughout the nation. The municipal government of Rio de Janeiro even attempted to establish a regular roda de choro. In 1978, one night each week was reserved for choro jam sessions at the city's planetarium.[40]

The choro revival was part of a complex web of relationships between individuals and audiences, national and multinational organizations and enterprises, and the state. Each sector had differing yet intersecting goals that sometimes complemented each other's activities and aims and at other times contradicted them. Underpinning these networks of relationships was the notion of revivalism. The benefits to Brazilian society and especially to young Brazilians inundated by imported and domestic pop music were clearly stated by a government anxious to win support from the middle class; these same goals were affirmed by revivalists threatened by the new popular musics and unsettled by political and social turmoil.

One might ask why the state chose to support choro at this particular juncture in the mid-1970s. We are not aware of previous attempts by the Brazilian government to revive a particular musical style, so the choro revival seems to be a unique event in Brazilian history. There is little doubt that the actions of the state were closely linked to the economic and political climate created by the administration of General Ernesto Geisel (1974–1979). Geisel's policies, in turn, were heavily influenced by the economic and social crisis brought on by heavy borrowing begun by President Juscelino Kubitschek and continued by the military presidents to fund economic expansion and the protests against government violations of human rights that grew in number and degree between 1968 and 1974.

In the early years of the military regime, repression was directed toward manifestations of lower-class rebellion; protests were severely crushed and the leaders were imprisoned and/or tortured. By 1968, however, the mobilization of middle-class leftists and students posed a new threat to the regime; as a result, crackdowns and censorship were directed toward a new sector of society, the middle class. The Fifth Institutional Act, which gave dictatorial powers to the president, was promulgated in 1968, placing all communications media, including radio, television, music, theater, literature, and the press, under heavy censorship. Police brutality was directed toward members of the middle class, and individuals were encouraged to denounce friends, family members, and acquaintances. Repression was accompanied by an inundation of nationalist propaganda, including "a proliferation of Brazilian flags, of propaganda leaflets, and the setting up of courses in gym-

148   nastics and civic values for university students."[41] In order to strengthen its grip on the nation, the state became increasingly active in establishing programs of "cultural development" which were intended to integrate the nation both culturally and economically.

Upon accepting the appointment of president in 1975, General Ernesto Geisel was forced to confront the growing popular demand for the return of civilian rule, an inflation rate that grew higher on a daily basis, and the crumbling support of the middle class. Geisel's administration had four basic objectives: to maintain support for the administration within the military, to control subversives, to maintain rapid economic growth, and to prepare for the return to democracy. Geisel believed, as did the first leader of the military regime, Humberto Castelo Branco, that the "emergency government" instated by the military coup of 1964 was a temporary measure until conditions became adequate to return power to civilians.[42] In order to appease protestors, he promised to initiate a policy of *distensão* (decompression) in which the military government would begin preparations for the return to civilian rule. In another move to consolidate middle-class support and, perhaps more importantly, to boost the economy by looking at cultural commodities as a valuable economic asset, Geisel created several new powerful cultural organizations. He appointed Ney Braga as head of the Ministry of Education and Culture, the umbrella agency for cultural activities. The appointment of Braga was a calculated political maneuver on Geisel's part. Braga, an ex-general who had made a successful career in regional politics, was a member of a powerful group of leading businessmen. He also had connections with prominent leftist intellectuals and artists to whom he had granted special favors during his political career. These connections helped Geisel create the image that he supported culture and maintained the appearance that his government provided stability to the Brazilian people. FUNARTE, which was established in 1975, was the most important of the cultural organizations created during the Geisel administration. With this and a series of related programs, Geisel continued the expansion of state involvement in culture that had begun in earnest in the 1960s.

Huge choro festivals and concerts fit in well with the regime's plans. As an instrumental genre, choro escaped the wrath of the censors. Moreover, it seems to have been seen as completely apolitical by both the state and (at least overtly) by revivalists. Critic Roberto Moura went as far as to call choro "anti-protest music": "[It] certainly is not a coincidence that exactly at the time when all the Brazilian arts are in a climate of tension, MPB has taken upon itself the resurrection of a genre that is typically instrumental—in which it is not necessary to say anything."[43] Another aspect that made choro palatable to state officials was its racial composition; by the 1960s, it was predominantly played by "white" (light-skinned) males and thus would be associated with the middle and upper classes rather than the possibly dangerous lower and disenfranchised classes of society (e.g., Afro-

Brazilians, Brazilians of Indian heritage, or immigrants from the northeast). For
these reasons, we suggest that the state intended to use the choro revival as an
overt attempt to win over the conservative middle class that was beginning to side
with the radicals in their demands for democracy.

The Decline of the Choro Revival: 1980s

In 1985, the long-awaited transfer of the government from military to civilian rule
finally took place. The "New Republic" was honored in Carnaval celebrations, and
Brazilians looked forward to the new era with hope. Besides political changes, 1985
also heralded a renewal of the rise of rock and roll as the preferred music of youth.
The ten-day Rock in Rio concert attracted over a million people and demonstrated
the parity of Brazilian rock with British and American groups. No longer supported
by the government and overshadowed by new popular musics such as rock, soul,
funk, and disco, choro activity declined significantly. Nevertheless, the revival appears to have stimulated new choro-based styles, and instrumentalists continue to
be attracted to the genre for its musical possibilities.

Economic instability and the worsening of social ills characterized the 1980s
and early 1990s. Inflation reached a staggering 2,000 percent annual rate. A new
economic plan was introduced when Fernando Collor de Mello was elected in 1990
and the currency was changed to the *cruzeiro*. As part of his economic austerity
program that also included privatization and deregulation of industries, Collor de
Mello froze all personal savings and corporate assets for a period of eighteen
months. Working-class Brazilians were outraged and labor unrest was rampant.
Two years later, Collor de Mello stepped down under accusations of corruption and
embezzlement of federal funds; corruption scandals continued to plague the Brazilian government. In 1994, the new currency, called the *real*, was implemented, moving the country to the dollar standard and resulting in relative economic stability.[44]

With the changes of administration and the accompanying financial and social
turmoil, arts organizations suffered. The Ministerio da Cultura, which was created
in 1953, was reduced to a secretariat in 1990. Fiscal incentives for private-sector in-
vestment in the arts were abolished. Both FUNARTE and the agency that supported
Brazilian cinema, EMBRAFILME, were disbanded; this was a reversal in the previous relationship between the Brazilian state and culture.[45] Despite the decrease in
number and strength of state arts organizations, a few survived and continue to
patronize the arts. The Projeto Pixinguinha, which was originally developed to promote MPB musicians, still exists, and the Arts Foundation of the State of Rio de
Janeiro (FUNARJ) has managed to fill some of the void left by FUNARTE in promoting local arts.[46]

The withdrawal of state support in the early 1980s had an immediate and negative impact on choro. No more festivals were organized until the 1990s, and groups that had formed for the purpose of competing disbanded. Choro clubs dissolved or became inactive, with the exception of the Clube do Choro de Brasília. Interviews with choro musicians indicate that rodas de choro in private dwellings were still common in the 1980s, but with the escalation of urban violence in the 1990s, there was a distinct drop in the number of rodas. Without the high public profile of choro provided by subsidized concerts and festivals, the music industry reduced the number of choro recordings they released. The withdrawal of state support was not the only factor in the demise of the choro revival. Social stratification became more pronounced due to economic disparity, frustration and class conflict erupted in violence, and new groups of popular music consumers arose that challenged the notions of racial integration and national identity that were tacitly endorsed by choro. Mass-mediated musics such as national rock, *axé* music,[47] pagode, sertaneja, and funk became the expressions of these newly defined groups, for which choro was of little interest.

The choro revival in Brazil is an example of a music revival as a response to intense feelings of dissatisfaction among a number of social groups because of shifting social, political, and economic circumstances. Revivalist practices are meaningful because they offer revivalists the opportunity to actively create music that represents historical continuity and authenticity. In making music, revivalists present not only a vision of how they view themselves and their role in creating a better society but also how they want to be perceived by society at large. Music revivalism is a cultural movement that strives to restore a particular musical genre, instrument, and/or style that is perceived or imagined to be rapidly disappearing and to promote its reception and practice as an alternative lifeway among the general public. Such movements are characterized by an ideology of authenticity and the belief that restoration of historically valuable cultural practices can benefit society. The choro revival occurred at this social and political juncture because it offered middle-class Brazilians a powerful vision of an alternative reality at a time when contradictions between national sentiment and political repression threatened to undermine their identity as Brazilians. The revival's nostalgic evocations of a happy past filled a void in the expressive culture of sectors of the middle class and created a musical community that helped restore a sense of optimism and national pride. As a musical movement, it reinvigorated choro by attracting and educating new dedicated players who continue to explore its musical potential and establish new style trends, including "traditional" and "progressive."

Contemporary Choro

Brazilians heralded the transition from military rule to democracy in 1985 as a watershed moment in their history. As if to signal the beginning of a new era, Brazilian rock, which had been forced underground by the series of military dictators that succeeded President Goulart as a dangerous foreign influence, emerged as the dominant popular music of the nation's youth. Groups such as Os Paralamas do Sucesso (The Mudflaps of Success), Legião Urbana (Urban League), and Titãs (Titans) rose to the top with a successful blend of British and North American rock conventions and local styles and meanings. Radio play and record sales of national rock rivaled and in some cases surpassed imported rock. As the economic situation continued to worsen, however, and violence and corruption plagued the nation, the jubilation over democracy quickly turned to bitterness and sarcasm. Choro revivalists experienced a sense of betrayal and abandonment as the government support they enjoyed during the 1970s withered away, leaving them to fend for themselves in a harsh, money-driven economic climate. Choro retreated once again to the margins, surviving as before in rodas in homes and bars, and professional choro musicians either abandoned choro in favor of other more lucrative styles or left the country to seek their fortune. We began our fieldwork in Rio de Janeiro in the mid-1990s, a period when choro was nowhere to be seen. When asked about choro, most cariocans replied with a puzzled look, surprised that a gringo (foreigner) knew about such things. Choro was absent from the newspapers, the magazines, the record stores, and the airwaves. Information about the few concerts and rodas that did occur were spread by word of mouth. Nevertheless, the tight social network of choro musicians and fans that has historically characterized the choro community was as strong as ever, providing an excellent, if well-hidden, resource.

Since the turn of the millennium, there has been a renewed enthusiasm for rodas de choro that was absent in the late 1980s and the 1990s. Many professional musicians who were too busy or disinterested to attend rodas five or six years ago are rediscovering the joy of playing without the concerns and restrictions of live performances and recording sessions. Rodas held in public places are faithfully attended by young and older musicians and fans, and even young women are beginning to make inroads into this historically male tradition. For casual musicians, the roda serves as the primary opportunity for musical interaction, whereas for professionals, it is a welcome, relaxing change of musical context. Although they never completely ceased even during periods when choro disappeared from the daily soundscape, the strength and number of rodas today in the major cities of Brazil illustrate the renewed strength and vitality of the choro tradition.

By the late 1990s, choro had rebounded with a force that still shows no signs of weakening. The young musicians who got their start during the revival have matured into professional musicians engaged in a wide variety of choro-related activities. Choro concerts are once again frequent and affordable, festivals and competitions have returned, and a new choro industry has emerged, aided by the advent of relatively inexpensive recording and communication technologies. The nineties saw the rise of independent record labels mostly or completely dedicated to choro and the publication of choro books, music, and method books. Beginning in the year 2000, choro schools and institutes were established with the aim of educating young players. The availability and affordability of new recording technologies enabled musicians to create and produce their own recordings. With the advent of affordable computers, the Internet became the medium of choice for musicians and fans to advertise and discuss concerts, events, and recordings. As a result, choro has quickly spread beyond the borders of Brazil, and communities of choro devotees and musicians have arisen in Japan, the United States and elsewhere. The rise of "world music" as a lucrative popular music category outside Brazil in the late 1980s and the activities of prominent popular musicians such as Paul Simon and David Byrne have stimulated an interest in Brazilian music, resulting in increased exposure for Brazilian artists. As choro recordings became available outside of Brazil, instrumentalists such as mandolinists and guitarists eagerly incorporated choro into their own repertoires. Abroad and at home, choro enjoyed an unprecedented level of interest and dissemination in a variety of forms that have revitalized and strengthened this Brazilian genre and style. The conversation between instruments now crosses linguistic, ethnic, and national borders.

In this chapter, we consider the varied facets of contemporary choro, including live and recorded choro, stylistic trends, choro publications, choro pedagogy, choro on the Web, and choro abroad.

In cities throughout Brazil, choro performance in some form is a daily event. Nowhere is this truer than Rio de Janeiro, the original home of choro that remains the center of the style and genre. Many restaurants have evenings of choro on a regular basis, such as Sindicato do Chopp in two neighborhoods (Humaitá and Barra da Tijuca), where choro is heard every Sunday, and Empório Arabe in Leblon, which has live choro every Thursday. Resort towns such as Buzios, Paratí, and Visconde de Mauá have choro in several restaurants and bars on a regular basis. There are regular rodas in São Paulo at bars such as Bom Motivo and Café Society. In Pernambuco, choro is best represented by the Conjunto Pernambucano de Choro. Brasília enjoys a crop of homegrown musicians, and residents are able to hear the best chorões from throughout Brazil at the Clube de Choro de Brasília. This is not to say that being a professional choro musician is a comfortable profession. Chorões must play at several venues in order to make a living, and most find that they must also play genres such as samba, samba-canção, and pagode to make ends meet. For the most part, the repertoire heard in public venues features old standards by Pixinguinha, Jacó do Bandolim, Ernesto Nazaré, and the like. Occasionally the performer will add a few of his (or her) own compositions, since most choro musicians compose as well as perform, but these are usually balanced with more familiar pieces.

Before his death in 1969, Jacó do Bandolim remarked that a primary difference between the Old Guard players of the traditional *regional* and young players is that "the kids [today] study music, they take courses in music, they're orchestrating and composing pieces."[1] Bandolinist Pedro Amorim agrees:

> Choro musicians are more informed about other types of music, about music [itself], they know how to read music. There was a time when the musicians played only by ear; these days everyone knows how to read and write music, at least the younger musicians can. At the time of Camerata Carioca [1979] and on, from Os Carioquinhas [1977] and later, the musicians were interested in studying and getting to know the tradition at the same time that they were learning the technique, [they] were studying musical theory, and this brought about an enrichment . . . of the genre. This has affected not only the general level of sophistication of newly composed choros, but also the style of arrangements, the quality of recordings, and the quality of live performances.[2]

Musical literacy has had a noticeable effect on the choro tradition of the past thirty years; it has facilitated the exchange of stylistic influences between choro, jazz, and classical music and extended the boundaries of the choro genre and the style.

CONCERTS

Since the mid-1990s, choro in Rio de Janeiro has most often been heard by the public in concert performances. The types of ensembles and variety of styles repre-

Contemporary Choro

sented in staged shows are impressive. One can find *regionais* performing traditional choro in universities, concert halls, and even shopping malls; choro performed in a jazz format at upscale jazz venues; choro musicians accompanying MPB and samba singers; "progressive" or "modern" choro played by ensembles with mixed electric and acoustic instrumentation; "erudite" choro performed on the piano or on choro instruments accompanied by string orchestra; choro performed as part of a musical revue; or choro played by an orchestra of Brazilian folk instruments. Each of these choices represents different stylistic directions that choro musicians pursued during or after the revival and represent a combination of individual stylistic preferences, current economic conditions, and the availability of resources.

"Erudite" choro is a category used by choro musicians to describe choro played in a classical music venue such as a concert hall or performed by instruments normally associated with European art music, such as solo piano, wind quintet, string orchestra, or chamber ensembles. The term can also be applied to the playing style and arrangements of ensembles with *regional* instrumentation, characterized by sparse textures and an emphasis on precision over virtuosity. Erudite choro is performed while seated, sometimes with the musicians reading from musical scores; concerts may feature arrangements of classical compositions or choros that are more intricate and complex in harmony and melody than the choro standards. During the revival, erudite choro was eclipsed by traditional choro based on the *conjunto regional*. Nevertheless, a small number of musicians and groups continue to work within this stylistic framework, and it forms an important part of the choro tradition. The influence of composer Radamés Gnattali and his group Camerata Carioca on erudite choro cannot be overestimated.

Camerata Carioca was formed when bandolinist Joel Nascimento persuaded Gnattali to arrange his suite *Retratos* (*Portraits*), which was composed in 1965 for Jacó do Bandolim and scored for bandolim and string orchestra, for a small group based on the *conjunto regional*. The suite consists of four dance movements based on popular forms associated with particular choro composers of the past. The first movement is a choro entitled "Pixinguinha"; it is followed by a waltz ("Ernesto Nazareth") and a schottische ("Anacleto Medeiros"). The suite ends with a corta-jaca dance ("Chiquinha Gonzaga"). When the arrangement was ready, Joel gathered together some friends that had accompanied him previously and surprised maestro Gnattali on his 73rd birthday with the first performance for *conjunto regional*.[3] The group that formed for this occasion was christened Camerata Carioca, which Maurício Carrilho described as "a new style of performance, an instrumental group which combined the spontaneity of traditional choro with the technical quality and balance of chamber music."[4]

The group O Trio is a direct outgrowth of the example set by Camerata Carioca. The ensemble consists of bandolim, six-string guitar, and clarinet played by

Pedro Amorim, Maurício Carrilho, and Paulo Sérgio Santos, respectively. Pedro began playing bandolim in 1978 as a university student in physical education. Inspired by shows and rodas with bandolim players Déo Rian and Rossini Ferreira and groups such as Época de Ouro, Pedro decided to pursue a career as a professional musician.[5] Guitarist Maurício Carrilho began playing with the youth group Os Carioquinhas during the revival. Like Pedro Amorim, he was strongly influenced by the traditional style of Época de Ouro. Perhaps the greatest influence on his style was his work under Radamés Gnattali with the chamber ensemble Camerata Carioca. Maurício believes that Gnattali's emphasis on tight arrangements performed with the technical precision characteristic of chamber ensembles should be the path for the modernization of choro. This belief and style have had enormous consequences on subsequent artists. According to Luciana Rabello:

> [Camerata Carioca] influenced everyone. Musicians who came after it were concerned with arrangements, with a theoretical knowledge of music. I don't want to say that they evolved, because I think evolution in music isn't completely dependent on theoretical knowledge. But I see that younger players have sought to sophisticate their interpretations.[6]

The classical training of Paulo Sérgio Santos enhances the chamber possibilities of O Trio. "With this formation, we play some pieces organized as if for a chamber ensemble, others we play in a traditional style, like a *regional*, and others we improvise and have no idea ahead of time where we are going."[7] The recording *O Trio* was made in a Paris studio in 1993 and released by SACI (Sociedade de Artistas e Compositores Independentes). It features an eclectic repertoire including ragtime by Scott Joplin, a tango by Astor Piazzola, a work influenced by música nordestina by Newton Rangel and João Lyra, and choros by Gnattali, Pixinguinha, and Jacó do Bandolim. According to Maurício, O Trio recorded Piazzola and Scott Joplin because

> of their deep relationship to us. They are musical cousins [and] we wanted to demonstrate their affinity. Instrumental [genres] of music from Argentina, from the USA, from Columbia, Venezuela, the Caribbean, all arose in the same epoch as ours, from similar origins, and because of this, they have a lot to do with us.[8]

The recording won two of the coveted Sharp prizes for best instrumental ensemble and best instrumental recording and is notable for its imaginative and refined arrangements and polished performances.[9] The style of O Trio is directly influenced by the musical ideal of the Camerata Carioca: the spontaneity of traditional choro combined with the technical quality and balance of chamber music.

Many choro musicians have noted the similarities in style between choro and European art music from the Baroque period, specifically the use of small chamber ensembles, contrapuntal textures, and the prominence of an active bass line with contrapuntal sections. The ensemble Vibrações, which is directed by multi-

156 instrumentalist Marco de Pinna, produced a show entitled *De Barroco ao barracão* (*From the Baroque to the Straw Hut*) in the mid-1990s, which progresses from European art music to choro. Selections from Vivaldi, Bach, and Handel are followed by a chronological survey of choro beginning with Calado and ending with recent works by the founding members of the group, Marco and his father Sérgio. In one performance of the show, the concert opened with a darkened stage with only the cellist present. Within a small circle of light, he played a short work by Handel. He was subsequently joined by two more players, guitar and bandolim, for another selection from the art-music repertoire. With the addition of the cavaquinho and pandeiro player, the repertoire switched to traditional choro. Although it was not meant to show a historical connection between the two traditions, the gradual transition from Baroque music to choro was an effective demonstration of the chamber-music possibilities of choro first explored by Camerata Carioca.

Progressive choro is a wide category that includes jazz and rock influences in harmony, melody, improvisation, and instrumentation. It often makes use of electric instrumentation (such as electric bass and/or electric bandolim), extended improvisatory solos based on jazz-type harmonic progressions, and arrangements that feature alternate sections of the ensemble rather than everyone participating equally throughout the piece, as in traditional choro. Members of ensembles often

CHORO

Figure 8.1. Marco de Pinna with some of his instruments. Photo by Andrew Connell.

perform standing up and virtuosity is emphasized. In the mid-1990s, the progressive trend was represented by a number of groups, including the shows produced by bandolinist Armandinho and Raphael Rabello. Before his untimely death at the age of 33, Rabello was one of the most promising young guitarists in Brazil. He made numerous recordings and was versatile in a number of styles. Nevertheless, he always claimed to be most comfortable in the idiom he grew up with, choro. His shows with Armandinho, soloist of the revival group A Cor do Som, were a lively blend of the harmonic and rhythmic sensibilities rooted in choro and Armandinho's pyrotechnics on the bandolim, which were heavily influenced by the popular genres *frevo* and *trio elétrico* (which were predominant in the city of Salvador, Bahia).[10] In 1995, the duo appeared at Jazz-mania, a jazz club with an expensive cover fee. The elegantly dressed audience was upper middle class, and although a few were obviously interested in the music, most seemed more absorbed in quiet conversation. The same show was presented later with dramatically different results at an outdoor theater at the Arpoador, a spit of rocky beach separating Copacabana from Ipanema that is favored by serious surfers. No admission was charged and the audience was notably younger. Despite problems with the sound equipment, the show was charged with energy; both audience and musicians were clearly enthused, which resulted in more-extensive improvisations from Raphael and Armandinho and several lengthy encores.

A number of progressive choro groups have emerged since A Cor do Som and the revival of the 1970s. The group of young artists known as Nó em Pingo D'Água was founded in 1977 by bandolinist Marco de Pinna and guitarist Jorge Simas. The original members of the group included Marco on bandolim, Jorge on seven-string guitar, Mário Sève on flute, Artur Roman on six-string guitar, Jorge José on cavaquinho, and Celso Silva on pandeiro. When Marco left the group, Pedro Amorim joined as bandolinist. In 1983, they produced a recording of the works of João Pernambuco with pianist Antonio Adolfo and guitarist Maurício Carrilho; the pieces were arranged for different ensembles of instruments ranging from solo piano to *conjunto regional* and were performed with the precision and clarity of erudite choro. Current members of the group include Rodrigo Lessa on bandolim, Rogério Silva on guitar, Mário Seve on saxophone and flute, Leonardo Lucini on electric bass, Celso Silva on pandeiro and percussion, and Leo Leobans on percussion.

The album entitled *Receita de samba* (*Recipe for a Samba*), released on the Visom label in 1990, marked a departure from the group's earlier erudite style toward a new style that combined the sound modification and manipulation using technology found in most recording studies with acoustic and electric instruments and upbeat dance rhythms. The tight, jazzy arrangements of the works of Jacó do Bandolim were provided by band members Rodrigo Lessa and Rogério Silva. The instrumentation was based on the *regional* with addition of electric guitar and bass. A variety of percussion instruments, such as ganzá, rêco-rêco, agogôs, surdo drums, congas, bongos, batã drums, and bells, added color to the arrangements. An impressive list of musical guests, including Horondino da Silva from Época de Ouro and Rildo Hora on harmonica, helped to provide an ever-changing array of timbres and styles.

Livingston-Isenhour first heard bandolim player Rodrigo Lessa at a roda in the Santa Teresa neighborhood of Rio de Janeiro, and asked him about his jazz-influenced improvisations. Rodrigo explained that his style was a conscious attempt to modernize choro and make it relevant to his generation. As part of Nó em Pingo D'Água, he went even further in his pursuit of a modern sound, creating a recording that didn't sound anything like their live choro. For this group, modernization also meant choosing a recording style that depended on multitrack recording so that aspects of the sound product could be modified to produce the desired result.

By 2001, the attitude of many choro musicians had changed significantly. The viability of choro was no longer in question and its future no longer seemed threatened by competition or lack of interest. As the economic climate stabilized and musicians found it somewhat less difficult to make a living than in the 1980s and early 1990s, the fierce competition relaxed enough to allow a variety of styles of choro to emerge and prosper. Musicians gained better control over their image and their music by producing their own recordings and advertising on their own websites, thereby circumventing many of the major obstacles to production and dissemination choro musicians in the 1980s and earlier had encountered. Choro musicians born after the revival are not particularly concerned with issues of modernization, authenticity, or national identity, and their music reflects a new degree of confidence and optimism that their endeavors will be heard and appreciated.[11]

Tira Poeira is a new young group that has defined a progressive style with a hard edge that distinguishes its style from jazz-influenced groups such as Nó em Pingo D'Água. The ensemble is comprised of five young, aggressive musicians: Caio Márcio on guitar, Sérgio Krakowski on pandeiro, Samuel de Oliveira on saxophone, Fábio Nin on seven-string guitar, and Henry Lentino on bandolim. All of the musicians were in their twenties at the time of this writing, and all exhibit extraordinary skill on their instruments. Several members were grounded in choro by family members or by training: Caio Márcio's father is the choro clarinetist Paulo Sérgio Santos; Sérgio Krakowski studied with Jorginho do Pandeiro of Época de Ouro and has worked with chorões such as Pedro Amorim and Dirceu Leite; and others have performed with choro musicians from an early age. Their music is a fusion of traditional choro with funk, jazz, heavy metal, rock and roll, and Brazilian popular genres delivered with virtuoso technique and a "bad boy" attitude.

Garcia saw Tira Poeira perform in May 2003 at the Clube do Choro de Brasília to a full house of appreciative choro fans. The show included some of Jacó do Bandolim's standard choros performed at breakneck speed with aggressive articulation, powerful bass lines, and highly amplified pandeiro, providing a power and timbre not associated with traditional choro. The result is a fresh and vibrant sound that may well herald the future of choro presented on stage. The group maintains a well-organized website[12] and has enjoyed excellent reviews. Their first CD, which was self-titled, has already won several awards in Brazil.

One of the most energetic young musicians of the progressive wing of choro is Hamilton de Holanda, the son of choro guitarist José Américo de Oliveira. Hamilton began his studies on the bandolim at 6 years of age and formed a group with his brother Fernando called Dois de Ouro. In 1995, he was selected as best musician in the Second Festival of Choro of the State of Rio de Janeiro. His aggressive playing style and phenomenal technique astonished the audience and marked the beginning of his career as a choro prodigy. His group Dois de Ouro has released two recordings: *Destroçando a macaxeira* (1997) and *A nova cara do velho choro* (1998). In the year 2000, Hamilton played at the Free Jazz Festival of Rio de Janeiro. His repertoire included an eclectic mix of choro, contemporary Brazilian instrumental music, and popular genres such as baião. In December of 2001 he won, by unanimous vote, the Prêmio Icatu Hartford de Artes (the Icatu Hartford Arts Prize) as the Best Brazilian Instrumentalist, the award for which was a one-year residence in Paris at the Cité Internationale des Arts.

FESTIVALS

Although they are no longer a focal point for choro musicians, festivals and competitions are still a part of the contemporary choro scene in Rio de Janeiro and São Paulo. In format and intent, they are similar to revivalist festivals, although on a much smaller scale. Competitions continue to serve as a way for younger players to gain recognition and disseminate their work to a broad listening audience. In São Paulo, a noncompetitive four-day event called Chorando Alto was held in 1996 and 1997. The first festival took place in May and June, in commemoration of the centennial of Pixinguinha's birthday; the second festival was held the following year in August. While it was organized to celebrate choro, the second festival also featured performances by sambistas Paulinho da Viola and Martinho da Vila and MPB musicians Wagner Tiso and Edu Lobo. The pairing of choro with other Brazilian popular genres is common and illustrates the desire of choro musicians to appeal to a broad audience.

In 1994 and 1995, the Museum of Image and Sound Foundation and the Arts Foundation of the State of Rio de Janeiro produced a series of two Festivals of Choro of the State of Rio de Janeiro. Each festival was dedicated to a choro musician of the past. As in the festivals of the 1970s, cash prizes were given for the best unpublished pieces and for best arrangement and group. Historical continuity was once again demonstrated by the pairing of an ensemble of the new generation of chorões with a veteran ensemble for the concert portion of the festival. In 1995, the

Figure 8.2. Hamilton de Holanda in the Clube do Choro de Brasília.
Photo courtesy of Hamilton de Holanda.

group chosen was Água de Moringa, which was paired with the legendary Época de Ouro, an ensemble that, to many, still serves as a living example of the *regional* style of the past. Many of the members Jacó do Bandolim originally chose in the 1960s continue to play in the group.

These competitions were an attempt to revive the format of the 1970s with one difference: lack of funding. Only a few months before the festival was to begin, the Museum of Image and Sound Foundation notified the organizers that their budget had been cut in half. As a result, the guest ensembles received only half of what they had been promised. There was no money to pay the jurors, so each night the makeup of the jury changed.[13] Despite these hardships, the organizers from the MIS produced a competition that was similar in quality and format to those of the revival.

As in the revivalist festivals, winners of awards for best interpreter and best compositions sometimes were the same individual. Young virtuoso bandolinist Hamilton de Holanda from Brasília won the prize in 1995 for best interpreter; his choro "Destroçando a macaxeira" ("Devouring the Mandioc Root") was awarded second place. Hamilton's distinctive manner of performance drew as many remarks as his technical prowess; dressed in neon colors, he strutted around the stage while playing in a manner not unlike the electric bandolinist Armandinho of A Cor do Som, who had shocked audiences and judges twenty years earlier.

Most of the groups in contemporary competitions continue to rely heavily on *regional* instrumentation, but the style of their compositions and arrangements are more diverse than during the revival. Groups tend to fall into three broad categories: traditional, erudite, and progressive. The boundary between these style categories is often unclear; they may overlap, and sometimes they are defined as much by the attitude of the performers as by arrangements, instrumentation, and manner of interpretation. Participants in the competitions were mostly within the traditional and erudite style categories, suggesting that the competition format no longer attracts a cross-section of choro musicians.

Choro Recordings

The stable economy ushered in by the anti-inflationary *real* plan Cardoso introduced in 1994 allowed Brazil's record industry to jump to the sixth largest in the world by 1997.[14] Compact discs have become the predominant medium for recordings, followed by cassettes (many of which are pirated and sold on the streets). The upswing in the economy gave blue-collar Brazilians greater purchasing power, and they contributed to skyrocketing sales of popular genres. CID, EMI, RCA/Victor, and BMG released a few recordings of choro, many of which were remastered back issues of archived recordings of past choro musicians. Independent labels proliferated during the boom years of the nineties; many took advantage of profitable economic conditions by cutting distribution deals with the multinationals, which helped solve a problem that had been endemic in the Brazilian music industry since the 1960s.[15]

The late 1980s and early 1990s saw the rise of several independent labels that have produced choro recordings, including Kuarup, Cajú (Milestone in the United States), Visom, and SACI (the Society of Independent Artists and Composers Ltd.). Nimbus released a few recordings of Os Ingênuos and the Orquestra de Cordas Dedilhadas de Pernambuco in the United States, Europe, and Japan, yet these were not made available in Brazil. The Revivendo label, which was founded in 1987, is dedicated to the preservation of all genres of Brazilian popular music by remastering original recordings from its vast archive of some 120,000 recordings. They have revived many otherwise-lost recordings by major artists, including chorões, from the early days of recording technology.

Despite the expansion of the recording industry, practices of exclusion and privilege carried over from the 1980s into the early 1990s. Choro and instrumental music in general shared a small fraction of the market, often making it necessary for artists to record with an established industry artist if they wanted break into the promotion circuit. On a recent CD, singer Marisa Monte contracted Época de Ouro to accompany her on a choro track.[16] According to Horondino da Silva, it was only because of Monte's influence with the recording industry that the song was played at least twice a day on the radio. Choro recordings of the 1990s differ from their revivalist predecessors in a number of ways. Although live recordings and catalog issues still present cheap alternatives to studio costs, the number of studio recordings, many of which are produced by or in collaboration with established artists, has increased significantly. Two factors account for this: Brazil's recording industry and economy is robust and the new generation of choro musicians and consumers has grown more sophisticated. The poor sound quality of many live recordings is becoming less acceptable to an audience used to the high quality of CD imports. A third factor is the development of new styles of choro that are intrinsically dependent on mixing, overdubbing, synthesized sounds, and rhythm tracks. The result is a distinct move away from sounds produced in the roda and in live recordings to something that can be manipulated and refined as an autonomous aesthetic object.

The styles of choro produced in studio recordings range from the traditional *conjunto regional* sound to highly processed combinations of choro and other popular idioms. A recent recording that ventures far from choro's roots is *Beatles no choro*, which was arranged and directed by Henrique Cazes and released on the Deck Disc label in 2002. The recording features songs by the Beatles arranged for a choro ensemble of some of the best choro recording artists today, including Hamilton de Holanda and Paulo Sergio Santos. Its popularity prompted a second recording of Beatles songs arranged for choro ensemble, which was released in 2003.

Although the diversity of contemporary recordings makes it difficult to define a "studio style" of choro, most of them share two characteristics: an emphasis on a clean sound and a reliance upon constant variation of sounds, textures, and styles. These concerns arise because of the necessity of producing something that will maintain interest for a passive listening audience. It is also part of broader trends that characterize contemporary Brazilian instrumental music. Professional musicians tend to be educated in music, and they often incorporate a broad variety of national and transnational styles.

In Brazil, as in the United States and elsewhere, major record companies give contracts to only a small number of musicians and singers. Most artists turn to smaller independent labels or start their own recording companies in order to disseminate their music. In Brazil, even well-established groups such as Nó em Pingo D'Água and soloists such as Gilson Peranzzetta, who have recorded on major labels, must self-publish to disseminate the majority of their work. As sophisticated recording technology becomes more affordable, new choros and choro groups are finding it easier to reach a large audience. The two most significant independent labels for choro are Kuarup Records, which is owned and operated by Mario de Aratanha, and Acari Records, which is run by Luciana Rabello and Maurício Carrilho.

KUARUP RECORDS

Kuarup Records was established in 1977 and is known for its extensive catalog of choro and other Brazilian popular musics. It boasts the largest Villa-Lobos collection of any label in Brazil, and choro is one of the most important genres in their catalog. The founder is Mario de Aratanha, a regular contributor to *Roda de Choro* magazine and a staunch advocate of the preservation and dissemination of all forms of Brazilian popular music. When asked about the name of his company, de Aratanha replied,

> The *kuarup* is a ceremony of the Xingú Indians that celebrates death. Those that live incorporate all the virtues and teachings of those that went before them. . . . The death of an elderly Indian is necessary, but it is also important to relive the best that person had to offer. Kuarup [Records] works from this premise: to bring our best musical values to the new generations. New music is nice, but we will not forget what existed before.[17]

The label offers both old and new popular musics and a selection of classical music. Mario de Aratanha is also interested in furthering erudite choro, and his catalog includes a recording of the music of Villa-Lobos performed by choro musicians.[18] During a period when many recording companies wanted nothing to do with choro, Kuarup released a recording of live concert performances of the "choro all-stars" performing at the Teatro Municipal, Rio de Janeiro's most important and prestigious concert hall, released in Brazil under the title *Noites cariocas* (Kuarup

KCD040, 1990).[19] The recording was made of sold-out concerts in 1987 and 1988 that featured choro greats such as trombonist Zé da Velha and flautist Altamiro Carrilho and some of the new generation of musicians who had participated in the choro revival movement, including Paulo Moura, Maurício Carrilho and Joel Nascimento. Recently, Kuarup released a related recording, *Noites Cariocas—15 Anos Depois* (*Rio Nights—15 Years Later*) (Kuarup KCD182), recorded live in Rio de Janeiro on January 2, 2001. The performance was part of a project dedicated to choro directed by Valéria Colela and Mario de Aratanha, and it featured choro musicians Alexandre Maionese on flute, Cesar Faria on guitar, Déo Rian on bandolim, and others.

Kuarup has earned wide admiration for the quality and breadth of its recordings. The prestigious newspaper *Jornal do Brasil* credited the label with engaging in the most important cultural recording work in the country, and Reco do Bandolim, president of the Clube de Choro de Brasília, has said "whomever closes his eyes and extends his hand to a shelf of Kuarup recordings can be certain that he is taking home a first-class product."[20]

ACARI RECORDS

Another new independent record label is Acari Records, founded in 1999; it has the distinction of being the only large recording company dedicated exclusively to choro. The owners and founders, Maurício Carrilho and Luciana Rabello, are among the most respected chorões in Brazil. Both have family connections to choro: Luciana's brother is the late Raphael Rabello, one of the greatest choro guitarists of all time; and Maurício is the nephew of flautist Altamiro Carrilho, himself a master of choro who has been performing for more than fifty years. According to its promotional material, the objective of Acari Records is to document through recordings the principal composers and interpreters of choro throughout the country, spanning the entire history of the tradition. They have produced recordings of both progressive and traditional choros and have done much to disseminate and promote the genre.

The musical sensibilities of Luciana and Maurício were shaped and refined during the choro revival. Maurício studied six- and seven-string guitar with Horondino da Silva and renowned guitar instructor Jaime Florence Meira. Luciana and her brother Raphael began their studies of choro guitar with their maternal grandfather. Both siblings took quickly to the instrument and avidly devoured recordings of past choro masters. They began to participate in rodas, where they met Maurício and found a supportive group of musicians who advised and encouraged them. In the mid-1970s, the siblings found that their friends were unacquainted with choro, believing it to be "old people's music." Nevertheless, they forged ahead and formed a group called Os Carioquinhas. Raphael convinced Luciana to take up cavaquinho, since the group was without one. Maurício Carrilho strong almost thirty years later.

Maurício and Luciana have taken a unique approach with Acari; their goal is to gather and disseminate as many lesser-known works as possible in order to span the breadth and depth of the choro tradition. Their greatest achievement to date is the series *Princípios do choro,* a fifteen-disk collection of choros composed between 1870 and the 1930s that includes ample and informative liner notes about each of the pieces. They are currently engaged in recording the next series of choros, which will cover the 1930s to the present. They also intend to release sheet music of all of the pieces recorded, thereby preserving music that might otherwise be lost, expanding the existing choro repertoire, and providing younger musicians access to choros of the past. Acari has also released a recording of choros by women, illuminating another little-known aspect of the choro tradition. Their website, which includes sections devoted to choro history and iconography, serves the dual purpose of promoting their products and educating the growing number of choro fans.

Choro Instruction and Pedagogy

One of the most significant trends in choro of the past decade has been the establishment and growth of formalized choro instruction in the form of schools. For most of its history, choro was primarily an oral tradition that transmitted repertoire and playing style through the roda. Although choro wind players might have received formal education in a music conservatory, the pandeiro, guitar, bandolim, and cavaquinho were considered to be unworthy of serious attention until recently, and programs of study on these instruments were not available in the nation's institutes of music education. Without the benefit of music instruction, most choro composers were incapable of writing their compositions down; as a result, those choros not passed on in the roda context or recorded had a slim chance of survival beyond the lifespan of their composer. This has changed considerably, and today many younger choro musicians have at least a grasp of fundamentals of theory and composition.

The increasing popularity of choro in the last decade has produced a steep rise in the number of musicians who want to participate in choro in its most participatory form: the amateur roda. The subsequent demand for teachers has led to the establishment of choro schools such as the Escola de Choro Raphael Rabello, which was established in Brasília in 1997. The school was the idea of Reco do Bandolim, who was forced to teach himself bandolim (including inventing his own tuning systems) when he was unable to find an instructor. The school was named in honor of guitarist Raphael Rabello, who fully supported the project but whose demanding work schedule as a recording and performing artist precluded involvement in it.

After years of hard work, Reco finally succeeded in gaining support from the Ministry of Culture, and in 1997 the school became an official division of the Clube de Choro de Brasília. The school is based on the conservatory model of instruction and offers formal training in choro technique and performance. Students study a chosen instrument and familiarize themselves with theory, performance technique, and the great choro masters of the past. Potential students need only to register and await the beginning of classes (which depends on the availability of instruments and teachers). The monthly fee is R$50, or roughly US$14. In 2003, thirty groups of students from the school performed onstage at the Clube do Choro de Brasília.

The Oficina de Choro (Choro Workshop) in Rio de Janeiro uses a different model of choro instruction. Founded in 2000 by Luciana Rabello and Maurício Carrilho (the owners of Acari Records), it is associated with the Escola Nacional de Música (National School of Music) of the Universidade Federal do Rio de Janeiro and uses that institution's annex facilities in downtown Rio de Janeiro on Saturdays. The program includes mornings of group lessons followed by rehearsals of large and small groups. One of the most interesting facts about the Oficina is the range of age of the students: When Garcia visited the Oficina in 2003, the youngest student was 8 years old and the oldest was in his 70s. The level of ability is equally diverse: Some retirees are rank beginners and some very accomplished players are

Figure 8.3. Oficina do Choro, housed in the annex of the Federal University of Rio de Janeiro School of Music (2003). Photo by Thomas Garcia.

teenagers. The instruction and program are informal, deliberately so. According to Rabello, informal learning is an important part of the choro tradition. The Oficina has become so popular that a second branch opened in the outlying suburb of Ramos in 2003. Each location has approximately 100 students, and enrollment continues to swell.

Another organization that participates in choro education is the Instituto Jacó do Bandolim, founded in February of 2002. The objectives of this virtual institute are the education, preservation, distribution, and production of Brazilian instrumental music, especially choro, the genre to which Jacó dedicated his life. The institute seeks to preserve and disseminate to the general public the large collection of sheet music and recordings Jacó do Bandolim left behind. Founders of the institute include Maurício Carrilho, Déo Rian, Hermínio Bello de Carvalho, Sergio Cabral Santos, Pedro de Moura Aragão, and Joel Nascimento. Egeu Laus is the director of events and designed most of the graphics used in its website. In 2004, the institute began sponsorship of the Escola Portatil de Choro (Portable Choro School), a free school located in the Glória neighborhood of Rio de Janeiro. The school was originally founded in 2002 as the Oficina de Choro. It operated in a small space owned by the School of Music of the University of Rio de Janeiro in Lapa. Since its move to the new larger space, enrollment has increased to approximately 500 students, all of whom receive free instruction and music.

Method books in choro have begun to appear with some regularity. Included among recent titles are *Método do bandolim brasileira,* by Afonso Machado (Rio de Janeiro: Escola Brasileira de Música, 1986); *A percussão dos ritmos brasileiros: pandeiro,* by Luiz Almeida da Anunciação (Rio de Janeiro: Escola Brasileira de Música, n.d.); *Escola moderna do cavaquinho,* by Henrique Cazes (Rio de Janeiro: Lumiar, 1998); and *Vocabulário do choro,* by Mário Sève (Rio de Janeiro: Luminar, 1999). There are also some methods in English that concern choro, including *Inside the Brazilian Rhythm Section,* by Nelson Faria and Cliff Korman (Petaluma, Calif.: Sher Music, 2001) and *The Brazilian Guitar Book,* by Nelson Faria (Petaluma, Calif.: Sher Music, 1995). The choro school phenomenon reflects a larger trend: the formation of schools for the study of Brazilian popular music in general. Several such institutes have been created throughout Brazil, including the Conservatório de Música Popular in Curitiba, the Escola de Chôro Jorge Cardoso in Brasília, the Conservatório de Música Alberto Nepomuceno in Fortaleza, the Universidade Livre de Música Tom Jobim in São Paulo, and many other private conservatories throughout Brazil.

Choro education and teaching has a global component as well. Many choro musicians are living outside Brazil and have taken choro with them. Choro performances throughout the United States and Europe are a result of this musical interchange, which has stimulated an interest in learning and performing choros. The growing number of Latin American studies programs in American universities has brought attention to Brazilian culture, and there are increasing numbers of Brazil-

Figure 8.4. Instituto Jacob do Bandolim logo. Courtesy of Instituto Jacob do Bandolim. Used with permission.

INSTITUTO JACOB DO BANDOLIM

ian music events in college towns. One of the most prominent programs is at City University of New York's Bildner Center, which is dedicated to Latin American studies. In October 2003 it sponsored a choro workshop featuring Nó em Pingo D'Água. The group explained their understanding of choro history, performed traditional and modern choros, and led a long and enthusiastic question-and-answer session. In conjunction with the workshop, the group played the following night at the club Jazz Standard to two sold-out shows. Music camps and schools are taking an interest in Brazilian popular music, and choro will undoubtedly be part of future curricula.

RODA DE CHORO MAGAZINE

Roda de Choro magazine was the only serial publication devoted to choro. In its two years of existence, it sold approximately 800 copies by subscription and newsstand sales and even gained a readership in France and Germany. Egeu Laus and Rodrigo Ferrari founded the magazine in 1995 as a means of informing and educating the readership about the history and development of choro. It featured articles about choro history and performance by a variety of authors from different viewpoints, including Luciana Rabello and Maurício Carrilho of Acari Records; Mario de Aratanha of Kuarup Records; chorões such as Henrique Cazes and Pedro Amorim; scholars such as Luiz Antonio Simas, Ary Vasconcelos, and Ilmar Carvalho; and the publishers of the magazine.[21] Each issue featured an article on a choro instrument by a well-known practitioner, notices and reviews of choro publications and recordings, notices of concerts all over Brazil, and important dates in choro history. Music was also included, with pieces in lead-sheet format arranged by Maurício Carrilho. The last page of each issue was devoted to brief biographies of choro masters such as Garoto, Raphael Rabello, and Pixinguinha. In 1997, production expenses outweighed income from subscriptions and sponsors, and the magazine was forced to cease publication. The editors hope to resume publication in the near future.

Egeu Laus (b. 1951) is an important figure in contemporary choro. Laus is active in a number of endeavors relating to choro and might best be described as a social chorão. He is a graphic artist by profession and specializes in design related to marketing popular music. He has created the artwork for more than 200 recordings for artists as diverse as Paul McCartney, bossa nova artist João Gilberto, and the Brazilian rock group Legião Urbana. He has produced dozens of choro CD covers and artwork and graphic design for books on Brazilian popular music. Laus has amassed a large collection of historical record-cover art, which serves as a resource for his numerous articles, and he has mounted exhibits of the collection in Rio de Janeiro and São Paulo. Laus has engaged in a number of activities relating to the preservation and dissemination of choro, including producing choro events, founding *Roda de Choro* magazine, and assuming the position of director of events for the new Instituto Jacob do Bandolim. As an avid fan of choro, Laus is a familiar face at choro concerts and rodas.

CHORO CLUBS

Since the revival, the Clube do Choro de Brasília has been the strongest and longest-lasting choro club in Brazil, the first to obtain a building for its activities. By the mid-1990s, the club building had been closed for years due to lack of funds for repairs and maintenance. When Reco do Bandolim was elected president in 1993, he made reopening the building a top priority. It was renovated in 1997, and in 2003 it was refurnished and retrofitted with much-needed air conditioning. Today the building is used frequently for choro events sponsored by the club. In 2000, President Fernando Henrique Cardoso attended a ceremony at the Clube do Choro to dedicate April 23 (Pixinguinha's birthday) as National Choro Day.

Figure 8.5. Cover of *Roda de Choro* 5 (1997). Courtesy of *Roda de Choro* magazine.
Used with permission.

There are choro clubs in virtually every large city throughout Brazil, including
Fortaleza in the northeast, São Paulo, and Curitiba. This phenomenon is not, how-
ever, limited to Brazil. As choro spreads beyond Brazil's borders, clubs often form.
Current examples are the Choro Club of Japan (not to be confused with the Japa-
nese choro performing group called Choro Club) and the Club de Choro de Paris.
There are several choro clubs in United States, including at least three in the Miami
area (Clube do Choro de Miami, North Bay Village Clube do Choro de Miami no
Bayview Café, and the Miami Beach Clube do Choro).

Figure 8.6. Interior of the Clube do Choro de Brasília. Photo by Thomas Garcia.

SHEET MUSIC

The proliferation of published sheet music is another aspect that distinguishes contemporary choro culture from that of the revival. Although one can find published sheet music of single pieces (usually scored for piano), the vast majority of choro sheet music is published in collections dedicated either to a particular composer or period. Most are scored in lead-sheet style or for piano.

This is not to say that sheet music was not available historically. A great deal of guitar sheet music was published over the years, and to some extent the choro tradition was preserved in these publications. Publishers such as Ricordi Brasileira, Arthur Napoleão, and Irmãos Vitale have published guitar choros since the 1930s. Few remain in print, but there are significant numbers of these arrangements in circulation. Most of the works by Nazaré and Pernambuco have been published, and a good percentage of the works by Pixinguinha is readily available. Several lead-sheet–style collections were published in the 1950s, most notably of works by Jacó do Bandolim. Recent interest in composers from Garoto's generation has led to published transcriptions based on recordings made in the 1940s and 1950s.

The greatest increase in choro sheet music has occurred since the 1990s. Before this time, musicians who needed sheet music circulated photocopies of the most common choro pieces, such as "Tico-Tico no fubá," "Doce de côco," "Um a zero," "Carinhoso," "Noites cariocas," and "Brasileirinho." The source of the pho-

tocopies was often unknown, and the process of making photocopies of photocopies tended to degrade the image. As the number of musically literate choro musicians increased, the demand for high-quality sheet music rose. Today, collections of choro sheet music are published regularly. The forerunner of contemporary published collections was *84 choros: O Melhor do choro,* featuring choros by Pixinguinha, Zequinha de Abreu, and many others. For many years, this was "the choro bible" for musicians. The collection, however, appears to have been hastily assembled, as it is replete with mistakes. Subsequent publications have a more polished look and are generally more accurate. The series *O Melhor* with titles such as *O Melhor de Pixinguinha* (*The Best of Pixinguinha*) includes choro and samba standards in lead-sheet form with melody and chord changes. Publications for piano include the *Centenário do choro* (*100th Anniversary of Choro*) series, which includes some choro standards in sophisticated arrangements. In an attempt to revive interest in historical choros, Acari Records is publishing sheet music that accompanies their *Princípios do choro* CD collection, enabling the public to own both a high-quality professional recording and sheet music of historically important pieces, and it is publishing a series of collections called *Caderna do choro.*

CHORO AND THE WORLD WIDE WEB

The growing number of websites dedicated to choro performers, composers, and recordings is indicative of its current vitality and marks the greatest difference between choro of the past decade and choro of previous years. Choro websites are created for a variety of reasons, from promoting artists and groups to educating the public about choro history and activities. Of the many hundreds of websites that are currently active, the most significant is the Agenda do Samba & Choro (http://www.samba-choro.com.br), which, among other things, publishes a list of choro performances in Rio de Janeiro, São Paulo, and other cities. The online calendar is updated regularly and contains links directing the reader to a variety of choro and samba sites and events. Also included on this site are pages for news and notices, biographies of artists, musical scores of traditional and new choros, sound files, articles, reviews, a billboard, discussion lists, photos, a list of choro CDs available for purchase, and other choro-related items. Most material is submitted by readers and there is minimal editorial control of the site, which results in both timely information and a variety of perspectives (and the occasional lapse in accuracy).

Choro musicians eager to promote themselves and their work have particularly appreciated the advent of the World Wide Web. By the late 1990s, computers had become affordable enough to be used as a viable means of communication. Many groups and soloists have established websites that range in quality and content but give musicians a forum from which to demonstrate the state of choro and their own particular strengths. Groups such as Tira Poeira (http://www.tirapoeira.hpg.ig.com.br) and Nó em

Pingo D'Água (http://noempingodagua.com.br) have established sophisticated, informative sites. Soloists such as Marco de Pinna (http://www.marco.pinna.mus.br) and
Hamilton de Holanda (http://www.doisdeouro.com) have established sites that include
biographical and musical material and information about choro history and tradition.
Many websites include audio and even video clips of choro performances and contemporary and historical photographs.

Besides Brazilian websites, a number of choro sites are hosted in the United
States, Europe, and Japan. Some are dedicated to a specific composer or portion of
the repertory; others are general music sites that include choro. An increasing number of choro CDs are marketed on the Web, and many of these sites include information about choro or links to other informative sites.

Choro Outside of Brazil

In 1987, British record producers coined the term "world music" in order to create
a category in music stores for recordings emanating from Africa, Latin America, and
other non-Western countries. A year earlier, singer/songwriter Paul Simon had produced his groundbreaking album *Graceland,* which featured collaborative pieces
and performances by Simon with several other North American and South African
musicians. The subsequent exposure that record sales and tours brought to the
South African musicians was significant and heralded a new trend in which well-
known British and American pop stars functioned as cultural mediators, collaborat-
ing with and introducing local groups to a new international market. Although the
"world music" label was applied most often to new hybrid genres such as Afro-
pop, it also helped Brazilian music and musicians achieve a foothold in markets
outside of jazz, the genre with which it has most often been paired since the international success of bossa nova.[22]

A number of global pop stars such as Paul Simon and David Byrne helped disseminate Brazilian popular music and artists to international audiences in the
1980s and 1990s. Byrne, best known as the co-founder of the rock group Talking
Heads, released a series of compilations called *Brazil Classics* on the Luaka Bop
label (founded in 1988) that featured MPB, samba, and *forró* (popular music from
the northeast). Byrne's interest in Brazil even led him to direct a documentary
called *Candomblé* in 1989 about the Afro-Brazilian religion. Paul Simon recorded
the track "The Obvious Child" on *Rhythm of the Saints* in 1990 with the samba-
reggae group Olodum from Salvador. That same year the Verve label released a series of compilations of samba, bossa nova, and música nordestina. In the early
1990s, a few choro recordings were available in the United States to those who
were lucky enough to find them in music stores. As an instrumental acoustic genre,
choro seemed to defy the classification schemes of the music industry; as a result,

it could be found filed under a variety of labels, including "world music," "new age music," and "jazz."

American instrumentalists were the first to become more than superficially interested in choro. An argument can be made that the spread of choro in the United States has been driven by two forces: guitarists and mandolinists interested in the solo and the ensemble possibilities choro presents. American classical guitarists have been influenced both by the guitar works of Heitor Villa-Lobos (see chapter 9) and by recordings that introduced Brazilian guitar music of other composers. Guitarist Sharon Isben includes a number of Brazilian works on her recordings *Dreams of a World* and *Journey to the Amazon*,[23] the latter featuring choros by Pixinguinha. Her recording *Brazil, With Love*[24] with Brazilian guitarist Carlos Barbosa-Lima includes four choros by Pixinguinha and five by Ernesto Nazaré. Paulo Bellinati, a guitarist originally from São Paulo, has made several recordings of Brazilian guitar music, including a recording devoted to the works of Garoto (1991) on the Guitar Solo label. The Los Angeles Guitar Quartet, always in search of new music from around the world, has performed and recorded choros and music by Bellinati, composer and multi-instrumentalist Egberto Gismonti, and virtuoso Brazilian guitarist Sergio Assad. Sheet music by composers such as Pernambuco and Zequinha de Abreu have worked their way into the American market, and recent publications by Paulo Bellinati of Garoto's solo guitar choros and Laurindo Almeida's original choros and arrangements have helped increase choro activity outside Brazil. Choros in guitar tablature have even been published in the United States.

Bluegrass legend David Grisman was so taken upon hearing the music of Jacó do Bandolim that he produced a series of two CDs of forty-three re-releases of Jacó's original recordings. These recordings, released on Grisman's Acoustic Disc label in the early 1990s, introduced other mandolinists to choro. Some mandolinists, including Mike Marshall, began to incorporate choro into their recording and performance repertoires. Marshall, a former member of the original David Grisman Quintet and founder of the Modern Mandolin Quartet, is known for pushing the limits of the bluegrass style. He is also a passionate admirer and advocate of choro music. His trip to Brazil in 1995 in search of the source of choro resulted in the CD *Brasil (Duets),* featuring Marshall in a variety of instrumental combinations that explored the timbral possibilities of new and traditional choro. The recording features a number of highly talented American and Brazilian musicians, including pianist Andy Narell, virtuoso banjo musician Bela Fleck, bassists Edgar Meyer and Michael Manning, and keyboardist and flautist Jovino Santos Neto. Marshall's appreciation of Brazilian music inspired him to create a new label called Adventure Music, which allowed Brazilian and Latin American acoustic musicians to reach new audiences in the United States and beyond. "From samba and jazz to folk and world beat, a singular sound is emerging that connects the music of string band musicians from around the Americas. 'Adventure Music' is harnessing the beauty of that sound and giving it to the world," states Marshall.[25]

Other instrumentalists besides mandolinists and guitarists have also been captivated by the sounds of choro. Flautist Paula Robison includes a number of Brazilian works and genres in her repertoire, including choros. Her recording *Rio Days, Rio Nights* borrows its title from the famous choro by Jacó do Bandolim, "Noites cariocas" ("Rio Nights") and includes several choros. One of the most significant artists to look for new sources of inspiration from both classical and popular traditions around the world is Yo-Yo Ma, arguably the most famous contemporary cellist in the world. Having mastered the standard orchestral, chamber, and solo literature for the instrument, he has ventured outside the confines of European art music in search of new challenges. In recent years, he has released several CDs that reflect his interest in eclectic genres and styles, many of which involve folk and urban popular music: *Silk Road Journeys—When Strangers Meet,* explores Asian musical traditions; *Appalachian Journey* ventures into American folk and traditional music; and *Soul of the Tango* presents the music of Argentine composer Astor Piazzola. In 2003, Ma released the recording *Obrigado Brazil,*[26] featuring collaborative work with many of Brazil's most respected musicians, including Egberto Gismonti and the guitar duo Sérgio and Odair Assad. The recording explores various classical and popular Brazilian genres and includes four famous choros discussed in previous chapters: "Brasileirinho" by Waldir de Azevedo, "Um a zero" and "Carinhoso" by Pixinguinha, and "Doçe de côco" by Jacó do Bandolim. It also includes "Alma brasileira" and "A lenda do caboclo" by Villa-Lobos and "Dansa negra" and "Dansa brasileira" by Guarnieri. Ma and friends followed up this CD with a live recording made in Zankel Hall in New York's Carnegie Hall called *Obrigado Brazil Live in Concert.*

As Brazilian musicians come to the United States to study, they inevitably inspire American musicians to study and incorporate Brazilian music into their own work. In certain cases, the fusion of American and Brazilian styles and musical sensibilities has led to new explorations of choro. Cliff Korman is an example of a New York–based pianist and composer who has embraced both jazz and Brazilian instrumental music. Many of his compositions blend choro with jazz, resulting in a fusion that transcends national boundaries. Recordings such as *Mood ingênuo* (with Paulo Moura), *Bossa Jazz,* and *The Brazilian Tinge* are examples of Korman's synthesis of Brazilian and American instrumental styles and genres. Korman has collaborated with a number of Brazilian instrumentalists in Brazil and the United States and has given seminars and workshops in jazz at a number of Brazilian universities.[27]

There are a number of amateur choro groups in the United States. Some members immerse themselves in Brazilian culture, studying the language and traveling to Brazil, and others have only a superficial knowledge of Brazilian music but are inspired to play choro. Several of these groups can be found in the San Francisco Bay area, one of several locations in the United States with a large Brazilian population. Crying High is one such group whose founding members were introduced to choro by a Brazilian friend. ChôroTime is another American group "dedicated to the recreation, preservation and promotion of this wonderfully rich vein of music, because it's fun to play and we love it."[28] Founder Ron Galen was trained as a classical guitarist in California and Spain. He discovered choro when he was introduced to Brazilian guitarist Paulinho Nogueira's music in the early 1970s. As a result of his obsession with the music, Galen formed ChôroTime, which gained a following for their regular performances in a Berkeley nightclub. Although the group officially disbanded in 2004, Galen and other members of the group continue to play choro in a casual atmosphere resembling a roda. A passionate lover of Brazilian music and choro, Galen hopes to see more Brazilian choro groups introduced to the United States, perhaps as part of bluegrass festivals.

This chapter focused on contemporary choro, its development over the past several years, and various aspects of choro performance, dissemination, pedagogy, and reception. Today choro is enjoying a popularity that it has not seen since the 1920s. Although a great deal of energy was focused on choro during the revival of the 1970s, it seemed for a time that the revival had failed and that choro would remain marginalized. As the economic situation in Brazil stabilized in the late 1990s, choro again increased in visibility and popularity, as indicated by a growing number of choro events, and groups and soloists again performed throughout Brazil. New choro recordings were released with some regularity and the history of choro was the subject of a national television broadcast.

Despite the increased visibility and activity, public perception of choro did not change much in the early 1990s. To a large extent, choro was still viewed as "traditional music" with all the negative associations of the term. By the turn of the millennium, however, the perception of choro had changed dramatically, due in large part to the new generation of chorões. Musicians born after the revival do not have the same concerns about modernity and relevance as their forerunners. With the shackles of tradition broken, choro seems to know no limits.

Choro has come far from its roots in the bars and simple homes of Rio de Janeiro. New media and technologies and the exchange of musicians and music between national borders has led to revolutionary changes in many aspects of Brazilian culture, including choro. The genre and style are once again fluid and dynamic, ready to absorb new influences. The spread of choro across the globe has yielded interesting fusions, ensuring the future of this vital music.

Choro and the Brazilian Classical Tradition

For any and all Brazilian instrumental music,
if it is really Brazilian in origin, we must
consider choro as its basis.[1]

Defining the boundary between music composed within the Western art-music idiom (here referred to as classical music) and popular music can be difficult in many instances. Stylistic differences are often a factor, and social issues such as class associations, intent, and meaning often play a defining role. In Brazil the lines are often indistinct, a result of musicians freely borrowing musical resources across genre and class lines for more than two centuries. Beginning in the nineteenth century, genres such as the lundu and modinha existed as salon traditions (for voice with piano accompaniment) and as popular genres (sung to the sounds of guitars, flutes, and cavaquinhos). Some pieces were by known composers, others were anonymous, some were published as sheet music, and others existed in oral tradition. The distinction between *música erudita* and *música popular* in many cases lies in the instrumentation and contexts as much as in differences in styles and genres.

As one of the first urban popular musics to emerge from the nascent middle classes of society, choro represents the confluence of classical and popular traditions. Choro performance practice is the result of collaboration between musicians educated in the conservatory and those educated on the streets, and its repertoire exhibits the improvisation, the spirit of malícia, and the synthesis of European harmonies and melodies with Afro-Brazilian rhythms. Perhaps because of its natural affinity with classical music, no other popular music since the 1870s has been utilized as extensively by Brazilian composers as a musical resource.

For many composers, choro is an attractive source of quintessentially Brazilian music. National sentiment has been a driving force in Brazilian classical music since the nineteenth century. In the 1860s and 1870s, when Germany and Italy were constructing unified nations from small, disparate states and the beginnings of national identity were awakening in Eastern Europe, similar sentiments were growing in the Americas; in 1822, Brazil was one of the first Latin countries to declare independence from its European colonial master. Just as Brazilians were confronted with the task of building a nation from the remnants of colonialism, so Brazilian composers imposed upon themselves the task of breaking away from European models and creating a musical voice that was distinct to Brazil. Popular and folk musics—with and without African influences—served as sources of inspiration and a means of developing new musical traditions.

Throughout Europe and Eastern Europe, composers such as Liszt, Brahms, and Glinka sought out local musics as a means of defining and distinguishing their national voice from others. Whereas these composers looked to rural folk music as the source for their authentic national voice, Brazilian composers relied heavily on urban popular musics, specifically the lundu, the modinha, the samba, the maxixe, and the choro. References to indigenous music are largely absent in Brazilian classical music, a feature that distinguishes it from the classical music of many Latin American nations such as Mexico and Peru. The overwhelming number of Africans and mulattos in Brazil compared to the small number of indigenous peoples and people of mixed indigenous blood (caboclos) is at least partly responsible for this fact. Indigenous cultures were, however, a source of inspiration to early Brazilian literary movements and are still invoked from time to time as a powerful national symbol, even if their cultures have had minimal influence on the dominant culture.

Nationalist sentiment can be expressed in music in a number of ways. A composer may add verbal cues to a piece of music, such as an evocative title or subtitle, or performance markings, such as "*no tempo de samba.*" Within a composition, the composer may use stylistic references to characteristic aspects of folk or popular melodies, harmonies, or rhythms. Musical quotations of existing folk and popular melodies may be incorporated, and a score might include folk or popular instruments in addition to standard Western symphonic instrumentation. Brazilian composers before Heitor Villa-Lobos tended to be conservative in their approaches to creating Brazilian classical music. Most composers used verbal cues and rhythmic patterns associated with popular music instead of incorporating actual quotations of folk and popular musics. Although the reliance on European standards had been criticized since the early nineteenth century, there was little agreement about what should replace them. In addition, shedding European influence meant disa move that few artists were willing to wholeheartedly embrace.

The hold of French culture on the urban upper classes of Brazil during much of the country's history cannot be overstated. Many European countries also played a role in the musical culture and intellectual development of Brazil, but French influences dominated Brazilian high culture during and after the imperial period (1822–1889). According to E. Bradford Burns:

> Always susceptible to the influence of European thought, the Brazilian elite, particularly in the cities, was brought into closer contact with it by the more frequent and rapid steamship service and by the submarine cable. The expanding middle groups also succumbed to European influence. France continued to shape Brazil's intellectual and cultural life. Three French cultural missions—the first in 1816 and the last in 1840—succeeded in strengthening a preference for Parisian values. French became the second language of the educated classes, who read French literature avidly and knew it better than their own. Polite society as well as the intellectuals animatedly discussed the novels of Gustave Flaubert, Honoré de Balzac, and Emile Zola. Their words dominated the bookshops. In the stores of the major cities, every Parisian luxury could be found. Shops on one of the principal streets in the capital, Ouvidor Street, almost exclusively displayed French wares. Ladies vied with one another in copying the latest Parisian styles. . . . Hypersensitivity to foreign criticism further prompted the elite and [the] middle class to adopt unquestioningly in the tropics all of the trappings of a temperate-climate civilization. Beset with a feeling of inferiority, they sought to be more European than the Europeans.[2]

Brazilian music schools were based on the French conservatory system, and musicians were often sent to France to complete their music training, a practice that continues to this day. In the nineteenth century, French opera was almost as popular as Italian opera, and French opera troupes had their choice of five opera theaters in Rio de Janeiro at the turn of the century, including the prestigious Theatre Lyrique Francais.[3] In the aristocratic salon, the elite enjoyed the piano music in vogue in France, and Chopin (who was of French and Polish heritage) remained the most popular European composer until the 1960s. French composers such as Saint-Saens, Frank, d'Indy, Debussy, and Ravel dominated the repertories of orchestras and chamber music ensembles.

Brazilian classical composers were faced with a dilemma. To be respected in upper-class social circles, one needed to assume European styles of composition, including composing operas in French or Italian. Yet many composers felt the need to create a music that was relevant to their own land and people. The problem was how to simultaneously break away from European models yet create something that would still be accepted at home and abroad as equal to, but separate from, the European classical tradition. Heitor Villa-Lobos and other composers of nationalist music began to receive some recognition in the 1920s, but only during the Vargas era were inroads made against the prejudices of the elite against the lower strata of Brazilian society.

Nationalist Composers Before 1922

Brazilian national sentiment is premised on the idea of the melting pot, in which the three main influences are African, European, and Brazilian Indian. In the nineteenth century, nationalist authors and composers first turned toward the Indian in their search for a national voice. In literature, the quest for national identity was carried out within the boundaries of local culture. The local was frequently expressed as the tropical environment, and the conflict between European culture and the Brazilian landscape was the subject of many nineteenth-century novels. Early nationalist authors often used aspects of indigenous culture to represent the untamed exotic Brazilian land. Romantic writer José de Alencar (1829–1877) wrote three novels prominently featuring the Brazilian Indian, *O Guaraní*, *Ubirajata*, and *Iracema*,[4] in which the Indian protagonist is torn between the exoticism of nature and the civilizing influences of Europe.

Indigenous themes were also found in musical settings, the most famous example of which is the opera *Il Guarany*, based on Alencar's *O Guaraní* and composed by Antônio Carlos Gomes (1836–1896), the most prominent Brazilian composer of the imperial period. Despite the plot, the music and the libretto of the opera are fully within the Italian opera tradition; they were composed in Italy while Gomes was studying with Italian composers. Nevertheless, Gomes was one of the first to show an interest in incorporating Brazilian subject matter in his works, if only superficially. Like Gomes, Alberto Nepomuceno and Francisco Braga also used indigenous themes in their settings of dramatic music. None, however, alluded to indigenous culture in their music.

Most Brazilians believe that indigenous peoples contributed heavily to Brazilian music and culture. Amerindians are upheld for their cultural importance, which is often celebrated at Carnaval as a source of pride and national identity. In practice, however, the government and industry have treated Brazilian Indians as a hindrance to *ordem e progresso,* the "order and progress" displayed on the national flag. Indigenous culture was for the most part ignored or rejected by scholars during the colonial period and throughout most of the imperial period, and colonization, conversion, and assimilation did much to obliterate many Indian cultures in Brazil. Because little research has been devoted to it in Brazilian musicology, indigenous influence on Brazilian music is difficult to ascertain. Most of the extant studies on folk music tend to ignore indigenous culture, other than to acknowledge the incorporation of Amerindian folk tunes and instruments (such as the chocalho, maracas, and rêco-rêco) into Brazilian popular music and dance.[5] Only in recent

decades have significant ethnomusicological studies been undertaken to understand and preserve Amerindian music in Brazil.[6]

Gomes and his contemporaries were fascinated with Brazilian popular music with
African influences. Composers were much more likely to incorporate popular genres,
such as the waltz, polka, and schottische, that had been "Brazilianized" and modified
by chorões than they were to incorporate Amerindian melodies that had little to do
with their European sensibilities. To highlight the exotic aspect of these familiar genres,
composers often added titles referring to black music. An example is an early piece
Gomes wrote for piano that dates from his student days, titled "Cayumba" (1857) (see
Example 9.1). The piece is subtitled "*a dança dos negros*"[7] and strongly resembles a
lundu. Gomes also composed a suite, consisting of a quadrille, a mazurka, a galop, a
polka and a schottische, which he gave the exotic name of *Quilombo*, a term referring
to a community of runaway slaves.[8] Many of Gomes's other piano pieces have whim-
sical or exotic titles, including "Picola polka" (1867), "Mormorio" (1871), "Niny"
(n.d.), and "Salalalyu: polka carateristica" (1867).

Example 9.1. "Cayumba," by Antônio Carlos Gomes.

Brasílio Itibere da Cunha (1846–1913) was a composer, diplomat, and accomplished pianist who was popular in the salons of the empire. He is best remembered
for his 1869 piece for piano employing choro rhythms called "A sertaneja," based
on the popular tune "Balaio, meu bem, balaio." Like Gomes, da Cunha also used

colorful exotic titles: *sertaneja* refers to someone from the rural backlands of Brazil, and *balaio* was a dance from the Azores Islands, popular in the south of Brazil. "A sertaneja" quickly become a favorite piece in the elite salons, leading some musicologists to call da Cunha the first nationalist composer in Brazil.[9] As a diplomat, da Cunha traveled abroad regularly and moved in elite European social circles. He shared his music freely, with the result that "A sertaneja" became known in Europe and was played by the great pianist and composer Franz Liszt.

Alexandre Levy (1864–1892) was one of the most important European-trained Brazilian composers. His father owned a music store in São Paulo, a popular gathering place for musicians who played a variety of styles and repertoires. The young composer first heard da Cunha's "Sertaneja" at one of these sessions. Levy's childhood was immersed in French culture, which was typical for upper-class children. His parents were French and French-Swiss, and he spoke French at home. He studied with Emile Durand (who later taught Claude Debussy) in Paris in 1887. The nationalism he encountered in France affected Levy, who began to consciously seek a more Brazilian style of composition. He believed that each country had its own characteristic music and that Brazil had yet to find her voice.

In 1889, the year the new Republic of Brazil was declared, Levy had composed several nationalist compositions, including the "Tango brasileiro" for piano (see Example 9.2). Cited by Béhague as the "first known characteristic nationalist work written by a professional musician,"[10] it reveals many of the characteristics that are associated with choro, including the use of contrasting sections, and uses melodic and rhythmic patterns that are idiomatic to the genre and style.

That same year Levy composed the *Suite Brésilienne* for orchestra. Although the title given by the composer is in French, the final movement of the suite is titled "Samba" and is based on the same popular tune, "Balaio, meu bem, balaio," used earlier by da Cunha, and "Se eu te amei," another urban popular song. Since the urban popular genre known as samba would not develop until the early twentieth century, it is most likely that Levy used this word to evoke rural black dance rather reference a specific genre. Other pieces with nationalist references include the *Symphony in E minor* and the *Variations on a Brazilian Theme*, both of which quote from the popular melody "Vem cá, Bitú" ("Come Here, Bitú"). Despite exotic references and the incorporation of a few popular rhythms, most of Levy's works do not stray far from European harmony and orchestration norms. It seems likely that Levy was exposed to the new stylistic trend championed by Calado and other chorões, but the time when composers would make extensive use of choro in their own compositions would not come until after the turn of the twentieth century.

Henrique Alves de Mesquita (1830–1906) was another French-trained composer who used popular genres and stylistic components in some of his music. As a young man studying at the Paris Conservatoire, Mesquita acknowledged his Brazilian roots in his graduation piece, "Soirée Bresilienne." In 1871, Mesquita com-

Example 9.2. "Tango brasileiro," by Alexandre Levy.

posed a piece for piano called "Olhos matadores" that he designated a tango. Despite the designation, the piece clearly uses the Afro-Brazilian rhythm in Example 2.3, distinguishing him as the first Brazilian composer to apply this term to refer to an Afro-Brazilian style. Among Mesquita's other works that reference Brazilian popular music are "Beijos de frade" (lundu), "Batuque" (tango), "La brésilienne" (polka), "La coquette" (quadrille), and "Quebra, quebra minha gente" (polka).

One of the most important early Brazilian composers to embrace and incorporate elements of popular music was Alberto Nepomuceno (1864–1920), who was born in the northeastern city of Fortaleza and moved to Rio de Janeiro with his family in 1872. As was customary for aspiring Brazilian composers, he left in 1886 to study composition in Italy and in Germany, where he worked under a friend of Johannes Brahms, Heinrich von Herzogenberg. As early as 1887 he composed "Dança de negros," which he later used as the basis for the fourth movement of his *Serie brasileira*, "Batuque," yet another reference to African dance. He married Walborg

Bang, a student of Edvard Grieg, and in 1893 traveled to Norway, where he stayed in Grieg's house. In 1894, he was invited by the Berlin Philharmonic Orchestra to conduct his own works, a major achievement for a Latin American composer. His music of the period had a strong European flavor, and only on his return to Brazil in 1895 did he begin to seriously incorporate Brazilian popular music influences in his works. That year he composed "Galhofeira" for piano, a piece that exhibits clear references to Brazilian popular music, including choro melodic and accompaniment style and rhythms (see Example 9.3).

Example 9.3. "Galhofeira," by Alberto Nepomuceno.

In 1897, Nepomuceno composed his four-movement *Serie brasileira* for orchestra, which exhibits the influences of several popular genres. The distinct rhythmic patterns of the maxixe are evident in the third movement, subtitled "A sesta na rede" ("A Nap in a Hammock"). The last movement, subtitled "Batuque," is based on his earlier piano work, "Dança de negros." Nepomuceno went farther than any of his contemporaries to "Brazilianize" his works, even going so far as to include a rêco-rêco, a Brazilian percussion instrument of Amerindian origins, in the score. The scandal it created among his elite audiences foreshadowed the reaction to works by Villa-Lobos many years later that used similar instrumentation.

Nepomuceno was a supporter of Brazilian music on several fronts. He actively encouraged the use of the Portuguese language for Brazilian art songs, which before that time were considered inferior to Italian for bel canto singing, and he was an avid collector of Brazilian traditional songs. He was instrumental in the founding of the Instituto Nacional de Música (National Institute of Music) and worked as the director of that institution for many years, greatly influencing Brazilian music pedagogy. Under the aegis of his Sociedade de Concertos Populares (Society for Popular Concerts) in Rio de Janeiro, avant-garde music from Europe and new works by Brazilian composers were introduced to the public. In 1908, Nepomuceno produced a series of concerts that featured works by European and Brazilian composers,[11] laying the groundwork for the influential Semana de Arte Moderna of 1922. In 1910, he again scandalized elite audiences by sponsoring a concert at the Instituto Nacional de Música that included modinhas of Catulo da Paixão Cearense together with standard concert pieces. Popular music influenced Nepomuceno's works throughout his life, as evidenced in one of his last pieces, a work for solo piano written in 1919 called "A brasileira."

In many ways, Nepomuceno foreshadowed the nationalist stylistic tendencies of Brazilian composers in the decades to come. His incorporation of Brazilian percussion instruments into standard orchestration reveals a desire to rethink Brazilian classical music based on European standards, and his organic integration of the rhythms and melodies of Brazilian popular music into the classical idiom was a great advance from the superficial addition of a colorful title of earlier nationalist composers. Nepomuceno was also among the first to recognize the importance of Brazil's most famous composer, Heitor Villa-Lobos, and he did much to support the performance and publication of his countryman's music.

Gomes, da Cunha, Levy, Mesquita, and Nepomuceno are the names most recognized by musicologists as nationalist composers. There were, however, scores of amateur composers of popular and salon genres who, knowingly or unknowingly, incorporated the influences of choro and other popular genres into their works. In the 1850s, long before choro arose as a distinct style, clarinetist Jorge Henrique Klier composed what he called "light music," including the schottische "Sylphide" (1851). Manoel Joaquim Maria wrote the polka "Capenga não forma" ("Without a Limp") in 1867, and L. A. Dias's polka-lundu called "O careca tem chino" ("The Bald Man Has a Wig") achieved some popularity in the 1870s. Because many Brazilian composers and instrumentalists studied in France, some of these pieces lived on for a time in Paris, including J. Soares Barbosa's 1881 polka "Que é a chave?" ("What Is the Key?"). From these examples, it is clear that genres such as the polka were popular among all classes of cariocan society. What differentiated a specific piece as "classical" was often the style, instrumentation, and context at the moment of its performance.

Heitor Villa-Lobos (1887–1959)

Without doubt, the most important and famous Brazilian composer of the twentieth century is Heitor Villa-Lobos. No other Brazilian composer composed as prolifically as Villa-Lobos (some 800 works, according to the catalog of the Villa-Lobos Museum) or incorporated so thoroughly so many different aspects of the Brazilian musical soundscape. Villa-Lobos experimented with music throughout his life, scoring works for previously unheard-of combinations of instruments and pushing the boundaries of classical music. Today his compositions for solo guitar are considered to be a major part of the instrument's concert and pedagogical repertory. Many books and biographies have been written on Villa-Lobos, but few investigate the role and significant influence of choro on his works. Although there is a general consensus among musicologists that popular music figured heavily in Villa-Lobos's music, little effort has been made to ascertain how his early associations with popular music affected his subsequent compositional style.

Villa-Lobos's affinities for the guitar and choro were important motivating forces in many of his compositions. He was admittedly fascinated by choro, describing it as the "integral translation of the Brazilian soul in the form of music."[12] Villa-Lobos was a rebel and an iconoclast who enjoyed making outrageous claims. He asserted that his music was unique and without influence: "As soon as I feel someone's influence on me, I shake myself and jump out of it."[13] Although his music was clearly influenced by European musical trends, including the works of Debussy and Puccini, as well as by Brazilian folk music and choro, he would only ever admit to two influences: the music of J. S. Bach and the Brazilian guitar.

Villa-Lobos was introduced to Bach and the guitar in his youth. After the death of his father, the young composer left home to live with his Aunt "Zizinha" (Maria Carolina), a pianist who introduced the young composer to the music of Bach. Also at that time, unbeknown to his aunt, who would have been horrified at his activities, he started playing the guitar in a roda de choro that met at the Cavaquinho de Ouro. Later, when he was on his own, Villa-Lobos played the guitar in various brothels and clubs and cello in theater orchestras to make a living. He was known as the "classical guitarist" among his friends and fellow chorões, the one who encouraged the others to study legitimate music for the instrument. The influence of the guitar is apparent in many of his compositions, regardless of orchestration. The influence of the guitar was so important in Villa-Lobos's life that it deserves further examination.

The guitar has always held an important place in the choro tradition. It is preferred in numerous forms of Brazilian music for accompaniment and as a capable solo instrument. Choro guitar technique typically passed from master to novice; there were no methods devoted to the choro guitar until the 1930s. Villa-Lobos developed an idiomatic playing style that used all five fingers of the right hand (rather than the thumb, index, middle, and ring finger as in classical guitar technique) that to this day is considered to be outside the norm. When Villa-Lobos and the great guitarist Andres Segovia first met, he told the Spanish master that he was familiar with the European guitar methods of Fernando Sor, Mateo Carcassi, and Francisco Tárrega,[14] and he was undoubtedly acquainted with the Brazilian methods modeled after them, such as Miguel Viera's *Indocador dos accordos para violão* (1851) and José Barros's *Methodo de viola* (c. 1880).[15] However, Villa-Lobos never admitted to following any particular guitar school, and it is probable that he developed his technique from a variety of sources that included choro guitar players. Scholar Bruno Kiefer believes that Villa-Lobos went beyond the typical, saying that "as a creative artist, he did not limit himself to the usual practices of his [choro] colleagues."[16]

Villa-Lobos learned to master the guitar by observing the best choro guitarists of the time and by applying the rigid discipline he had learned from his father while studying cello and clarinet to his self-taught guitar technique. In this way, he quickly "mastered the technique of the instrument, to the point of being a virtuoso."[17] There is a good deal of evidence that this was no exaggeration. Donga, one of the great choro musicians of the twentieth century, said of Villa-Lobos's guitar-playing that he "was always an improviser. He was a great soloist on the guitar, great, great. He always played the difficult classics, things [requiring an accomplished] technique, and he constantly worked to improve his playing."[18] The most convincing evidence of Villa-Lobos's ability to play the guitar comes from the composer himself. In the late 1950s, when he was approaching 70 years of age and after more than thirty-five years without having seriously practiced the guitar, he made a home recording of two of his pieces, the "Choro típico" and the "Preludio No.1." These recordings, which were released on LP by the Villa-Lobos Museum,[19] demonstrate that although he was undoubtedly out of shape, Villa-Lobos played the guitar quite well.

Villa-Lobos's devotion to and ability on the guitar, as well as his years of participation in the choro tradition, greatly influenced his instrumental music in general and his guitar music in particular. For many nationalist scholars and critics, the popular guitar, like the black popular music Freyre discovered, was seen as an authentic expression of Brazilian culture. According to Carvalho:

Figure 9.1. Villa-Lobos and the guitar. Courtesy of the Museu Villa-Lobos. Used with permission.

It is certain that the Brazilian guitar unites all of the essential characteristics of our musical process. It was through the guitar that the mannerisms, subtleties, tendencies and musical characteristics were fixed. As an essentially popular instrument, it was chosen to retain and express that musical truth born of the people, which a classical composer has the express function of registering and translating. . . . The guitar also appears to be suggested in almost all of [Villa-Lobos's] works, from his symphonic pieces to his chamber production. . . . He rose because of popular music and breathed that atmosphere in order to shout his message.[20]

Villa-Lobos's exposure to and love for choro is evident in his frequent use of the guitar in his chamber works. In 1917, he wrote the *Sexteto mystico* (*Sextour Mistique*) for guitar, flute, oboe, saxophone, clarinet, harp, and celesta, the only piece he wrote for this particular ensemble. In the sextet, the guitar, harp, and celesta assume a rhythmic and harmonic function that is strikingly similar to that of the cavaquinho, guitar, and seven-string guitar in the choro ensemble, with the wind instruments playing the melody and countermelody. Given Villa-Lobos's experiences with choro ensembles, it is likely that he envisioned the ensemble as a classical version of the *regional*.

The only other piece in the catalogue of Villa-Lobos's music that calls for the guitar in its original chamber music scoring is "Distribuição das flores" for guitar and flute with an optional untexted women's choir.[21] The guitar in this case is used mostly for strumming chords while the flute plays the melody in a manner reminiscent of the modinha of the past century. The guitarist chosen to play for the work's first performance was the most famous and popular choro guitarist of the time, João Teixeira Guimarães, better known as João Pernambuco.[22]

Chopin's influence on Villa-Lobos is apparent in many of his dance forms, including the mazurka and the waltz, as well as in much of his piano music. Indeed, the piano work "Impressões seresteiras" ("Impressions of a Serenade") (1936) sounds as if the hand of the Polish master himself had touched it. To some degree, his guitar works also pay homage to Chopin, whose piano etudes were clearly the model for Villa-Lobos's estudos for guitar. These are true concert etudes for the guitar and, like the Chopin works, are meant for the stage; they are not limited to the status of mere pedagogical tools. Villa-Lobos's *Estudos* also represent an attempt, consciously or subconsciously, to legitimate the guitar as a concert instrument and raise it to the level of the piano, the prized instrument of the bourgeoisie. In doing so, however, he did not abandon the popular roots of the instrument; instead, he created a masterful blend of pedagogy, musicality, and popular sensibility embedded in a classical context.

The many typical choro devices present in Villa-Lobos's guitar music are integral components of the music, not superficial exoticism (see Example 9.4b–d). "He always preserved, in all his works for the instrument, that which to him seemed most characteristic of the Brazilian guitar; the special and unique inflections, the timbral variety not explored or found by any other."[23] The influence of choro is clearly apparent from his earliest extant compositions to the later *Estudos* and *Preludios* in harmony, structure, rhythm, melody, and bass line. Although Villa-Lobos's guitar music often incorporates a sophisticated harmonic palette, he never abandons completely the harmonic roots of choro, much of which was determined by performance practice. As an example, one often finds parallel chords (often a diminished-seventh chord) that are slid up and down the fingerboard of the guitar, as in "Preludio No. 1," "Estudo No. 1," and "Estudo No. 12." This harmonic device was a common technique that was idiomatic to the choro guitar and can be found in popular guitar pieces such as "Interrogando" and "Brasileirinho" by João Pernambuco. The constant sixteenth-note rhythm of choro is present in many of the guitar pieces, including "Preludio No. 2," and the guitar bass lines in "Preludio No. 2" and "Estudo No. 7" suggest the choro baixaria. Melodic construction consisting of arpeggiated chords connected by diatonic or chromatic scales, which is typical of choro, is evident in "Preludio No. 2" and "Estudo No. 2." Other, more lyrical melodies are based on the modinha (see Example 9.4a), in which the guitar assumes both the vocal and accompaniment parts, as in "Estudo No. 8" and "Preludio No. 1." Another aspect of the composer's guitar music that derives from choro performance practice is the use of strong portamento, often played without an attached slur and reattacked after the slide, as a melodic embellishment.

Example 9.4. Opening measures of several Villa-Lobos guitar pieces, demonstrating modinha ("Preludio #1") and choro influences ("Choro #1" ["Choro típico"], "Preludio #2," and "Estudo #1"). Written by: Heitor Villa-Lobos. © Les Editions Max Eschig (SACEM). All rights for the world on behalf of Les Editions Max Eschig (SACEM) administered by BMG Music Publishing France (SACEM). All rights for the US on behalf of BMG Music Publishing France (SACEM) administered by Careers–BMG Music Publishing, Inc. (BMI). Used with permission.

a. Preludio #1

b. Choro tipico

c. Preludio #2

d. Estudo #1

THE *BACHIANAS BRASILEIRAS*

The influence of the music of J. S. Bach on Villa Lobos is most evident in his series of nine works scored for various combinations of instruments titled *Bachianas brasileiras* (1938–1945). Nowhere are the classical and popular traditions better fused and the influences of Bach and Brazilian popular music more evident than in the *Bachianas brasileiras No. 5* (1938). The piece is scored for the unusual combination of soprano and eight cellos. It has two parts: The first is a lyrical piece subtitled "Ária (Cantilena)," which is reminiscent of the languid, melancholy modinhas of days past; the second part is a lively rhythmic dance subtitled "Dança (Martelo)." This piece is one of the most popular, and therefore the most commercially successful, pieces today by a Latin American classical composer. One indication of its popularity is the fact that it has been transcribed by the composer for many different instrumental and vocal combinations, including voice and piano, voice, cello and piano, and voice and guitar.[24]

The *Bachianas brasileiras No. 5* opens with two bars of introduction that Villa-Lobos himself said "defines the atmosphere of the plucking of the choro guitar." The accompaniment then moves to a rhythmic pattern reminiscent of choro, with a baixaria bass line and a constant sixteenth-note compound rhythm. While the pizzicato celli strongly suggest the choro guitar, the soaring lyrical melody references the modinha, at the same time proceeding with polyphony and voicing reminiscent of the "Air" from the *Orchestral Suite #3* by J. S. Bach (see Example 9.5). The middle section of the aria is a passionate recitative that slowly descends by steps, accompanied by an active improvisatory-sounding accompaniment like that of the recita-

Example 9.5. *Bachianas brasileiras No. 5*, arranged by composer for guitar. By Heitor Villa-Lobos. Copyright © 1947 (Renewed) by Associated Music Publishers, Inc. (BMI) International Copyright Secured. All Rights Reserved. Reprinted by Permission.

tive accompagnato, followed by a pedal in the voice supported by a syncopated accompaniment. The first section returns, this time pianissimo, and ends on the tonic, completing the aria.

Villa-Lobos later transcribed the first movement, entitled "Aria," for soprano and guitar at the request of Olga Praguer Coelho, for whom Villa-Lobos transcribed many pieces. Coelho was a guitarist as well as a soprano, and she was able to accompany herself while singing. She said of his music:

> Villa-Lobos has written for me some admirably well-adapted transcriptions from orchestral and piano versions of songs by himself. He was proud to be able to make the statement that he is the one contemporary composer to have written directly for the instrument, without any adaptations necessary to make the music playable. Here, Villa-Lobos's familiarity with the guitar as a *player* [emphasis in the original] was a great advantage.[25]

Many of these adaptations were realized by the composer but not formally notated; he taught these pieces to Praguer Coelho and they remained in her repertoire. Of the very few of these adaptations that were formally notated, the most famous is "Modinha," in its original form the fifth of fourteen serenades composed in Rio de Janeiro beginning in 1926. There are at least two editions of "Modinha": One was published by the *Guitar Review* in its 1957 issue;[26] the other, by Eschig, has the copyright date of 1975.[27]

Because of its suggestive title, musicologists and musicians generally assume that the *Bachianas brasileiras* were highly influenced by the music of Bach and by Baroque compositional techniques. There are undoubtedly some connections to Bach and the Baroque in this series, but the same can be said for a great deal of Villa-Lobos's music. Villa-Lobos was well known as an inventor of legend to promote himself and his work. He changed the dates of his compositions when he felt it was advantageous to do so and was able to move fluidly between compositional styles scholars associated with periods of his life, thus creating great difficulties for scholars concerned with arranging his works chronologically. He often worked quickly to meet deadlines and frequently used previously composed material. By the time he wrote the *Bachianas Brasileiras,* Villa-Lobos was an established composer, but he was always struggling to maintain his popularity and his freshness. It is very possible that he gave the series the title in order to spark renewed interest in his music and ensure his place in the musical marketplace rather than as a description of the work's inspiration.

THE *CHOROS*

The connection between choro and classical processes is most often discussed in relation to Villa-Lobos's series of seventeen pieces called *Choros,* which illustrate Villa-Lobos's delight in unusual instrumental combinations; the series ranges from

works for solo guitar to works for large orchestras with military bands and many instrumental combinations in between. The series was composed over many years,
from 1920 to the mid-1940s. Villa-Lobos's time in Paris—first in 1923 and later in
1928—influenced his composition of *Choros* and *Bachianas brasileiras*. In Paris, he
heard the work of (and at times conversed with) Europe's most important composers, including Stravinsky and the members of the group known as Les Six; these
interactions showed him new possibilities in terms of musical and nationalistic expression. According to Vasco Mariz, his new musical skills and his longing for home
"evoked powerful memories that were the basis for his series of *Choros*."[28] In the
series, and indeed in most of his music composed after 1928, there is a clear influence of Debussy in terms of harmony and structure. Although many of the rhythmic
patterns in the series strongly resemble Brazilian popular music, Stravinsky's influence is also apparent.

In *Choros,* Villa-Lobos incorporated a variety of influences from folk and popular music. The third choro uses Amerindian melodies, and several choros include
percussion instruments typically found in samba, including rêco-rêco, tamborim,
prato, surdo, chocalho, and cuíca. Instruments and ensemble types normally associated with popular choro are also used, including small ensembles of winds, guitars,
and percussion instruments; solo guitar and solo piano; and military bands, at times
with additional Brazilian percussion instruments. Did Villa-Lobos conceive of
Choros as a classical interpretation of the popular choro? Simon Wright suggests
that this is not necessarily so:

> This series embodies completely Villa-Lobos's vision of Brazil as a vast, teeming
> landscape, immense in its inclusivity, variety, and proportion. . . . [N]o European
> musical form was adequate to contain this vision, and so, like the *Ciranda,* the
> *Seresta,* and the *Poema,* in the *Choros* a new mold was born, in which the im-
> provisations and instrumental groupings of the chorões were merely a basis, a
> convenient name and embryo for a form which would eventually accommodate
> not only popular elements, but also stylizations of Indian and black music, and of
> natural sounds.[29]

Instead of incorporating the harmonic and formal structures of popular music, the
pieces in this series tend to explore the limits of composition within the classical
music idiom. These techniques included a certain degree of freedom within structures, continuous invention, polyphonic textures, and emphasis on ostinato in
rhythmic or melodic or a combination of lines.

Composers After Villa-Lobos

Villa-Lobos is the best-known twentieth-century composer to embrace Brazilian
popular music as a source for erudite music, but by no means is he the only one.

Choro and the Brazilian Classical Tradition

Popular music and specifically choro was a source of inspiration for many other composers, including contemporaries of Villa-Lobos. One such composer was Mozart Camargo Guarnieri (1907–1993), one of several siblings given the names of famous composers. As a young man, Guarnieri studied piano with Sá Pereira and Ernani Braga and composition with Lamberto Baldi[30] at the Conservatório Dramático e Musical (Dramatic and Musical Conservatory), where he later was a professor.

In 1928, he became acquainted with the musicologist, critic, and novelist Mario de Andrade, who guided the composer through the study of literature, sociology, criticism, philosophy, and art, thus establishing Guarnieri's sense of musical aesthetics. Andrade taught that each composer had to develop his own unique voice that expressed his national identity and that folk and popular music were a rich repository of national heritage. Andrade's teachings greatly impressed the second and third generations of nationalist composers, including Guarnieri. Andrade considered Guarnieri to be his principal disciple and later provided the text for many of Guarnieri's songs and for his opera *Pedro Malazarte*.

Guarnieri had established himself as a musician of importance in São Paulo when he was awarded a scholarship in 1938 to study in Paris. There he studied counterpoint and composition with Charles Koechlin (1876–1950) and conducting with Franz Rühlmann (1896–1945); he also worked with Nadia Boulanger. In 1942, the young composer was invited by the Pan-American Union to go to the United States, where time he received first prize from the Philadelphia Public Library for his *Concerto for Violin*. In the late 1950s, Guarnieri was named special assistant minister for music by the Ministério da Educação, a position he used to exert a significant influence on Brazilian classical music. Shortly before his death in 1993, he was awarded the Gabriela Mistral Prize from the Organization of American States as the "most important contemporary composer in the Americas."

Guarnieri embraced musical nationalism, and stylistically he belongs to a third generation of Brazilian composers, after the generations of Nepomuceno and Villa-Lobos, to fully incorporate national traits into a mature and often passionate musical language. Over time, Guarnieri became more and more interested in incorporating African rhythms into concert music, and in 1937 he served as a representative at a conference on Afro-Brazilian culture in Bahia. In 1950, in defense of what he saw as authentic Brazilian art, he wrote an open letter to the musicians and critics of Brazil denouncing the avant-garde *Música Viva* movement founded by Hans Joachim Koellreutter. This movement advocated the adoption of new European musical techniques such as dodecaphony and serialism. Guarnieri felt that these new compositional systems had destroyed the basic principles of European musical culture and threatened to do the same to Brazilian music. His views were passed on to his many notable students who were nationalist and postnationalist composers, including Marlos Nobre, Oswaldo Lacerda, and José Antônio de Almeida Prado.

Guarnieri deliberately incorporated choro and other African-based popular-music genres in his classical compositional process. Many pieces have choro in the title, including "Chôro for Piano and Orchestra" (1957), which won first prize for the second Festival Interamericano de Caracas, and a number of pieces scored for solo instrument or chamber group accompanied by orchestra, including the "Chôro for Violin and Orchestra" (1951), "Chôro for Clarinet and Orchestra" (1956), "Chôro for Cello and Orchestra" (1961), "Choro for Flute and Chamber Orchestra" (1972), "Choro for Viola and Orchestra" (1975), "Choro for Bassoon, Harp, Percussion and Orchestra" (1991). Choro is also present in his chamber works, including "Choro No. 1" and "Choro No. 3" for small chamber ensemble (1929), "Choro for Winds" (1933), both of which resemble a *regional* in instrumentation. Other choro-influenced works are the piano pieces "Choro torturado" (see Example 9.6), "Dança selvagem," and "Dança negra e toccata." He also composed a number of choros for piano and solo instruments and guitar music; titles for guitar include "Ponteio" (1944), "Valsa no. 2" (1986), and "Valsa-choro" (1954).

Example 9.6. "Choro torturado," by Camargo Guarnieri.

The music of Radamés Gnattali (1906–1988) represents a seamless blending of popular and classical traditions. His popular music is based on classical compositional procedures, and his classical music relies on his skills in popular music performance and composition. Even his earliest training reflects this dichotomy: He studied classical violin, piano, guitar, and cavaquinho, and by 1920 he was an accomplished performer on all four instruments. While a student, he began playing popular music at movie theaters and in dance orchestras and composing nationalist music inspired by popular music, most notably choro. Although he aspired to be a concert pianist, he made his living playing popular music. The combination of classical and popular was the hallmark of both his compositional and performing career; he indelibly linked classical form and structure with the nationalist aesthetic that was becoming increasingly important in Brazil.

Shortly before his graduation from the Instituto de Belas Artes in his home town of Porto Alegre (in the state of Rio Grande do Sul, the southernmost state in Brazil), he gave his debut in Rio de Janeiro at the Teatro Municipal, playing music by Liszt and Bach as well as Tschaikovsky's *First Piano Concerto* with an orchestra directed by maestro Francisco Braga. On that occasion he met Ernesto Nazaré, who had a tremendous impact on the young composer and pianist. Although he dedicated himself to the study of classical music, he continued playing piano in theaters and movie houses, and by 1928 he was making his living playing popular music at Rádio Clube do Brasil.

Dedicating himself to composition, he gave his first concert of his own music in 1930, in which he presented two pieces for piano, the second and third *Preludios*. That same year he moved permanently to Rio de Janeiro and began studies at the Instituto Nacional de Música. While establishing himself as a composer of serious music with pieces such his "Rapsódia brasileira," he continued to work in popular music as an arranger and orchestrator for *regionais* with such notable composers as Pixinguinha, Lamartine Babo, Costinha, and Cardoso de Menezes. He also worked as an arranger for the RCA recording company, arranging choros and sambas with *regional* accompaniment through the 1940s. At times he incorporated the American-style drum set in his arrangements, and later he embraced other contemporary influences outside of the *regional* tradition.

Gnattali's nationalist compositional style received great public support during the Vargas years. In 1931, he participated in a concert with Luciano Gallet and Heitor Villa-Lobos, which gave him an opportunity to have his music heard by a serious classical music audience, apparently with great success. This did not, however, lead to a way for him to make a living playing classical music; he continued to play piano in bars and theaters to earn his keep. Since classical music offered few moneymaking opportunities, he decided to continue to compose popular music.

Gnattali was known as a talented arranger and was hired by many of the best popular musicians and radio stations to produce arrangements, including some of the first arrangements of Brazilian popular music for symphony orchestra. He embraced the sounds of Glenn Miller and American swing and jazz and added American jazz harmonies to his sophisticated arrangements, to the disgust of hard-line critics who accused him of becoming "Americanized." He worked as an arranger for radio for thirty years and later worked for the Globo television network. His work expanded the scope of Brazilian popular music, encouraged young composers and arrangers, and added legitimacy to instrumental popular music.

Although his radio work focused on popular music, Gnattali continued to be active as a composer and performer of classical music. He once said, "I love popular music, but, if I could choose, I would work exclusively in classical music." He composed concerti that premiered with himself as soloist and continued to work with the greats of Brazilian classical music, including Villa-Lobos, Camargo Guarnieri, and Bidu Sayão. His music was performed by some of the great orchestras of the world, including the BBC Symphony, the Chicago Symphony, and the Philadelphia Orchestra. He was an innovative classical composer, and his works include *Concertino for Guitar and Orchestra, Suite da dança popular brasileira* for

Figure 9.2. Radamés Gnattali with Jacó do Bandolim. From the collection of Marco de Pinna.

electric guitar and piano, *Concerto for Accordion and Orchestra,* and *Concerto for Harmonica and Orchestra.* In a clear mix of choro and classical tradition, he dedicated his *Concerto #1* for guitar to choro great Dilermando Reis, who played the first performance and made the first recording. He also directed a popular music orchestra that played music that spanned the two traditions. Among his many compositions that blend the popular and the erudite is the series of pieces called *Brasiliana* for various instrumental combinations and *Suite popular brasileira* for electric guitar and piano. One of his best-loved pieces among choro musicians is the *Suite retratos* (*Portraits Suite*) for bandolim, string orchestra, and *conjunto regional,* which was dedicated to Jacó do Bandolim. Each of its four movements evokes the styles and images of great choro composers of the past such as Gonzaga and Medeiros.

Gnattali was a prolific composer of both classical and popular music. His popular music output includes numerous choros, including "Conversa fiada" (1933), "Dengoso" (1935), "Amoroso" (1936), "Batepapo" (1949), "Amigo Pedro" (1952), "Conversa mole" (1955), "Mulata Risoleta" (1945), "Cheio de malícia" (1956), "Zanzando em Copacabana" (1958), "Meu amigo Pixinga" (1969), "Capibaribe" (1985) (see Example 9.7), and many others. As an interpreter, Gnattali became known for his perfor-mances of the music of Ernesto Nazaré and Pixinguinha, through whose music he learned about choro and samba.

Example 9.7. "Capibaribe," by Radamés Gnattali.

Several other composers of the generation of Guarnieri and Gnattali embraced the same nationalistic ideal and used popular music, including choro, in their com-positions. One such composer was Francisco Mignone (1897–1986), who studied in Italy with Vincenzo Ferroni; much of his early music shows traits of Italian music. After further studies with Mario de Andrade, his work exhibited a blend of Euro-pean and Brazilian influences. He exerted great influence on classical and popular music in the 1930s as the artistic director of Parlophon, one of the larger recording companies in Brazil. He was an active teacher throughout his career, a founding member of the Brazilian Academy of Music and the Brazilian Conservatory of Music, and the chaired professor of conducting at the Instituto Nacional de Música for thirty years. In the 1960s, Mignone experimented with atonality, and his music of the period includes careful orchestration and harmonies that extended the Brazilian popular music palette.

Mignone's piano music has a virtuosic flair, and he is perhaps best remem-bered for his piano works, of which the "Choros for Piano," "Valsa-Choros," and "Valsas" embrace many choro characteristics. Mignone wrote modinhas and choros for other instruments as well, including several choros for guitar. Composer Mario Tavares said of Mignone: "He was the greatest creator and teacher after Villa-Lobos. He was always on the vanguard of what was happening, researching and in-novating. And he was principally concerned with the question of Brazilian music."[31]

Cesar Guerra-Peixe (1914–1993) is another composer whose work is firmly rooted in both the classical and popular traditions. Like Gnattali, he lived profes-sionally in both worlds: He played choro in bars and cafés and performed in sym-phony orchestras. He was educated in a music conservatory but made his living as

Example 9.8. "Choro No. 3," by Francisco Mignone.

199

a young man as a freelance popular musician. In the 1940s, Guerra-Peixe studied composition in the Conservatório Brasileiro de Música, where he was greatly influenced by Koellreutter and the *Música Viva* movement. He experimented with dodecaphonic music and other European techniques (exemplified in works such as his *Sinfonia No. 1*, *Nonetto*, and *Sonatina for Flute and Clarinet*) before returning to nationalist composition in the 1950s. In the 1940s, Guerra-Peixe worked as an arranger for radio *regionais* and published choros he composed and arranged for both the *regional* (see Example 9.9) and solo guitar. These pieces are firmly grounded in the choro tradition but demonstrate the skill of a well-trained classical composer.

Example 9.9. Piano reduction of "Rabo de galo," originally written for a *regional*, by Guerra-Peixe.

Other composers have embraced choro to varying degrees. Edino Krieger (b. 1928) was a student of Koellreutter, Krenek, and Peter Mennin; a colleague of Guerra-Peixe; and a member of the *Música Viva* movement. He experimented with dodecaphony and was deeply involved in the avant-garde movement in Brazil. Although he was never actively involved in choro, he recognized its place in Brazilian musical culture with his "Choro manhoso" for piano (1956) (see Example 9.10) and "Choro for Flute and Strings" (1952). José Vieira Brandão (b. 1911), an associate of Villa-Lobos and founding member of the Brazilian Academy of Music, composed a "Chôro for Woodwinds" (1944), dedicated to Villa-Lobos and modeled after Villa-Lobos's "Quinteto en forma de choros." Even bossa nova composer Antônio Carlos

Jobim composed a choro dedicated to Gnattali, entitled "Meu amigo Radamés" (1985), that Gnattali arranged for two pianos.

Example 9.10. "Choro manhoso," by Edino Krieger.

Current classical composers continue to rely on choro in their compositions. One such composer is Rio de Janeiro native Ricardo Tacuchian (b. 1939), who studied with Mignone. He experimented with minimalism and other techniques before the 1980s, when he developed a serial system of pitch control he calls Sistema T (the T System), which moves between tonality and atonality. Although much of his music is deeply embedded in classical processes, he could not resist the quintessential carioca genres in his *Série Rio de Janeiro* for solo guitar. The piece evokes images of and pays homage to Rio de Janeiro's culture with stylized versions of the modinha, maxixe, samba, waltz, choro, and bossa nova. The second movement, "Maxixando" ("Dancing the Maxixe"), is reminiscent of the maxixes of Nazaré, and his "Festas da Igreja da Penha" ("Cliff Church Feasts") (see Example 9.11) is much like the solo-guitar choros of Garoto and Dilermando Reis. The composer explains the inspiration for "Festas":

> The October and November celebration near the cliffside church [in the neighborhood of Penha], with stalls, choro players and guitars, bands of music, and the faithful paying their vows by climbing the 365-step staircase, are a landmark in the popular tradition of Rio de Janeiro. The composer sets his childhood memories when, every year, he used to participate in the festivities.[32]

In this chapter, we explored the use of choro as a rich resource for Brazilian classical music. Composers seeking a national voice found in choro an instrumental repertoire with distinctive melodic, harmonic, and rhythmic characteristics that could easily be assimilated into classical idioms. Brazilian composers before 1922 were strongly influenced by Italian opera and French music and culture. In the late nineteenth and early twentieth centuries, the desire to break away form European models led composers to seek alternative musical models and resources. Although indigenous themes played an important role in nationalist literary movements, indigenous musical culture was too strange for conservative Francophile composers and audiences, and many Brazilian composers turned instead toward incorporat-

Example 9.11. "Festas da Igreja da Penha" by Ricardo Tacuchian.   **201**

ing popular musics, including the modinha, lundu, maxixe, and choro, into their works.

The Semana de Arte Moderna of 1922 linked modernism and nationalism in the search for truly Brazilian artistic modes of expression, with Heitor Villa-Lobos leading the way for nationalist composers. The prolific works of Villa-Lobos represent a unique synthesis of the popular and the erudite, in which choro and the guitar play major roles. The blurring of the boundaries between classical and popular music is perhaps most striking in the works of composers such as Villa-Lobos, Gnattali, and Guerra-Peixe, all of whom worked professionally in both realms. The influence of musicologist and critic Mario de Andrade was also a significant factor in the incorporation of choro and other popular genres into twentieth-century Brazilian classical music. As Brazil's most distinctive instrumental genre, choro has proven to be more than a style and a genre. It is a spirited conversation that is taking place between the heart of Brazil and the world.

afoxé: Afro-Brazilian percussion instrument consisting of a gourd encased in a beaded net that is shaken and rubbed.

agogô: An Afro-Brazilian double-headed cowbell used in *samba* and *candomblé* music.

atabaque: Single-headed conical drum like the Cuban conga.

baixaria (from *baixo* = bass): The active bass line that distinguishes traditional *choro*. It is created using a number of stylistic resources: filling in the tonic and dominant chords with scalar runs, utilizing a walking bass (i.e., a stepwise motion that reinforces the beat), inserting melodic or rhythmic responses to the soloist or cavaquinho player, and improvising contrapuntal melodies, riffs, and pedal points. It also refers to associations with the lower class, which was a hallmark of early choro.

bandolim: The Brazilian version of the mandolin with an oval body, flat back, and four double strings. It is played with a pick made of tortoiseshell or plastic. Although the technique of tremolo, or passing the pick rapidly up and down to give the impression of a single sustained note, is used at times, the plucking of individual notes is more common. The bandolim is exclusively associated with *choro*.

barbeiros: Barbers of the late nineteenth century, most often former slaves or black freemen who, in addition to cutting hair, were associated with the first professional popular music ensembles, *música de barbeiros*.

batucada: Generic term used to refer to African-influenced rhythmic dances, such as *samba* and *lundu,* that were predominantly accompanied by drumming.

batuque: General term for a historical Afro-Brazilian dance consisting of a solo dancer or couple within a ring formed by people singing, playing instruments, and clapping; a generic term used in the past to designate any black dance accompanied by drumming.

berimbau: A musical bow of African origin capable of producing several different tones; used in and strongly associated with *capoeira.*

bolero: A slow, romantic ballad that arose in Cuba and has since become a pan-Latin style and genre.

bossa nova (lit. "new way"): A genre of popular music developed in the late 1950s that includes understated vocals, syncopated accompaniments derived from *samba,* and sophisticated harmonies from American jazz and classical music. Bossa nova was heralded as the first Brazilian musical export with universal appeal, and it quickly took the world by storm, generating numerous imitations and derivations.

branqueamento (lit. "whitening"): The Brazilian racial theory premised on the idea that deliberate and systematic miscegenation, or blending of the races, would eventually and inevitably produce a light-skinned Brazilian race. The theory is based on the racist notion that European blood was dominant and would dilute and civilize the African and Indian races.

cachaça: Brazilian liquor made from sugar cane, often referred to as white rum.

candomblé: Afro-Brazilian religion based on the Yoruban polytheistic system of deities called Orishás (*Orixás* in Portuguese). Ceremonies involve singing, dancing, and drumming. Similar to Cuban *Santeria.*

canja **(lit. "chicken soup"; colloquially "give it a whirl"):** Improvised performance, usually by a guest rather than a regular member of a roda.

capoeira: Afro-Brazilian dance and game involving two players in a ring of spectators and musicians. Music consists of singing accompanied by clapping, *atabaque* drums, *berimbaus, pandeiros,* and other percussion instruments. Developed by slaves as a means of fighting without weapons, it is also considered a martial art.

carioca: A person or thing native to the city of Rio de Janeiro.

Carnaval: The pre-Lenten festival celebrated in most Catholic countries. In Brazil, Carnaval involves *escolas de samba* ("samba schools"), large organizations involving hundreds of drummers, singers, and dancers and lavish costumes and floats.

cavaquinho: A small four-string guitar derived from the larger Portuguese *cavaco* (known in Hawaii as the ukulele); commonly used for accompaniment in *choro, samba,* and *pagode.*

charamela: Folk oboe from Spain and Portugal, also known as *choromela, charamel, charamelinha, charamita,* and *charumbela.* The instrument was common in colonial wind bands of Brazil and the Iberian peninsula.

chocalho: Wood or metal shaker used in *samba.*

chorão **(pl. *chorões*):** Skilled *choro* musician (female = *chorona*) or a valued participant (such as a host or fan) in the *choro* tradition.

choromeleiro: Afro-Brazilian musical tradition from the state of Minas Gerais, originally based on ensembles of *charamelas* and guitars. The term was later used to refer any ensemble with a wind instrument accompanied by guitars. Together with *música de barbeiros* and *fazenda* bands, it is one of the antecedents of *choro.*

corpo de bombeiros: Lit. firemens' corps, a reference to the Corpo de Bombeiros do Rio de Janeiro, which sponsored the famous band founded by Anacleto de Medeiros, Banda do Corpo de Bombeiros. It was one of the first ensembles to produce *choro* recordings (1902).

cuíca: Friction drum commonly associated with *samba.* The instrument is played by rhythmically rubbing the stick attached to the underside of the head with a damp cloth, causing friction that vibrates the skin, which is amplified by the shell.

fazenda **bands:** Afro-Brazilian slave bands of rural plantations, or *fazendas.* Plantation owners adopted urban fashions, including music, and their bands were expected to play the latest urban songs and dance music at rural parties. The size and skill of *fazenda* bands played an important role in the social status of plantation owners.

forró: Popular music genre from the northeast of Brazil, which features accordion, drums, and triangle.

lundu: Dance, song, and instrumental genre introduced to Brazil by Bantu slaves; popular in the early eighteenth century. As it developed in Brazil, it became the earliest Brazilian popular music genre to combine African rhythm with European harmony, melody, and instrumentation.

malícia: Stylistic marker of early *choro;* an attitude of spirited competition in which one outwits the other. Found in other Afro-Brazilian cultural expressions, including *samba* and *capoeira.*

modinha: Lyrical sentimental song genre that developed in Brazil and Portugal in the eighteenth century. The upper-class version was accompanied by piano, and the lower-class version was accompanied by the guitar. A musical antecedent of *choro.*

MPB: *Música popular brasileira,* a generic term for popular music in Brazil that developed after bossa nova and combined a variety of local and transnational stylistic elements. Representative artists include Caetano Veloso, Gilberto Gil, Chico Buarque, and Milton Nascimento.

música nordestina: Music from the northeast of Brazil that includes genres such as *forró*, *baião*, *frevo*, and others.

ophicleide: Obsolete brass instrument designed to play in the bass register that was common in early *rodas de choro*. It had keys that allowed for chromaticism, similar to a saxophone. It was replaced in function by the tuba.

pagode: Originally a term designating a party with live music, usually *choro;* currently used to refer to a popular form of *samba*.

pandeiro: Percussion instrument similar to the tambourine. It became the primary percussion instrument in *choro* in the 1920s.

pianeiro: A piano player, as opposed to a pianist; usually associated with popular genres such as *choro* and *maxixe*.

pianista: A pianist; usually associated with classical music.

pirão: Common dish of polenta made with manioc flour, term refers to a party with music and to good food and drink in abundance.

***povo* (lit. "people"):** Term used to refer to the masses; associated with popular culture.

prato e faca: Plate and knife, commonly used as a percussion instrument in *samba* and in *rodas de choro*.

rêco-rêco: A scraper that produces sound by drawing a stick across corrugated grooves of a bamboo tube. Used in a variety of African-Brazilian traditions in both rural and urban contexts.

***regional* (pl. *regionais*):** A professional *choro* ensemble based on the *terno* that includes a melody instrument (usually flute), *cavaquinho*, guitars (six- and seven-string), and *pandeiro*. The *regional* was one of the most important types of ensemble from the 1930s through the 1950s in radio and recording.

samba-canção: Slow sentimental type of *samba* that emphasizes the voice over the accompaniment.

samba de morro: A type of *samba* associated with the *favelas*, the hillside slums of Rio de Janeiro, in contrast to *samba-canção*. Accompanied by guitar, *cavaquinho*, *pandeiro*, and/or other percussion.

seresta: Serenade; music performed out of doors.

sertão: The arid backlands of northeastern Brazil.

***surdo* (lit. "deaf"):** Large drum, played with a stick, that is associated with *samba;* provides the bass sound in a *samba* ensemble.

tamborim: Small hand-held drum played with a three-pronged stick; commonly used in *samba*.

tango brasileiro: Euphemism for *choro* and *maxixe;* used before the 1920s to minimize the association with black culture.

tenor guitar: Four-string guitar popular in the first half of the twentieth century. Used primarily as a solo instrument; in Brazil it functions like the *cavaquinho*.

viola: Small five-course guitar used in *samba* and early *choro*.

violão: Six-string Spanish guitar; used in classical and popular genres.

violão de sete cordas: Seven-string guitar with an additional bass string for playing extended *baixarias*.

Notes

1. Introduction

1. The pandeiro, now considered an integral part of the traditional choro ensemble, was not used regularly until the early twentieth century. Before this time, the rhythmic line was assumed and embellished by the center and bass roles and reinforced by the melody line, which was often subdivided into sixteenth notes, the basic rhythmic unit of choro.

2. The degree of freedom of a soloist is related to the performing context and type of music played. In the roda, all the players take a great deal of liberty. In concerts of choro music, however, which rely on precise arrangements, the soloist is expected to play what is written.

3. Interview of Jacob Bittencourt (Jacó do Bandolim) by Ricardo Cravo Albim, Sergio Bittencourt, and Sérgio Cabral, 1967, Archive of Jacó do Bandolim, Museu da Imagem e do Som, Rio de Janeiro.

4. The ensemble in this recording consists of flute (melody), piano (center), and guitar (bass); Chiquinha Gonzaga is the pianist.

5. This piece was originally intended for the ensemble known as the terno (flute, cavaquinho, and two guitars), but as ternos generally learned new choros aurally, it was never published other than in piano score. Comparisons of several editions of the piece yielded the edition Thomas Garcia used for this study.

6. See J. Lowell Lewis, *Ring of Liberation: Deceptive Discourse in Brazilian Capoeira* (Chicago: University of Chicago Press, 1992) for a detailed examination of the art of capoeira. Lewis analyzes the role played by deception, or malícia, as one of the fundamental driving forces of the capoeira game and art.

7. Lewis, *Ring of Liberation*, 31–32, 236.

8. See Lisa Shaw, *The Social History of the Brazilian Samba* (Aldershot, UK: Ashgate Publishing, 1999) for a detailed analysis of the lyrics of Ataúlfo Alves, Noel Rosa, and Ari Barroso.

9. Most published choros do not include an extensive *baixaria;* even to this day, guitarists are expected to improvise a bass line.

10. Erudite choro refers to choros composed or arranged in the Western classical music tradition or performed by ensembles associated with classical music. In performance, erudite choro is often distinguished from popular choro by close adherence to a written-out arrangement or performing score.

2. Race, Class, and Nineteenth-Century Popular Music

1. For studies of African influences and retentions in Brazilian music, see Melville J. Herskovits, *The New World Negro: Selected Papers in Afroamerican Studies,* ed. Francis Herskovits (Bloomington: Indiana University Press, 1966); José Jorge de Carvalho, "Music of African Origin in Brazil," in *Africa in Latin America: Essays on History, Culture, and Socialization,* ed. Manuel Moreno Fraginals, trans. Leonor Blum (New York: UNESCO, 1984); Ger-

had Kubik, *Angolan Traits in Black Music, Games and Dances of Brazil: A Study of African Cultural Extension Overseas* (Lisbon: Junta de Investigações Científicas do Ultramar, 1979); Peter Fryer, *Rhythms of Resistance: African Musical Heritage in Brazil* (Hanover, N.H.: Wesleyan University Press, 2000); and John Storm Roberts, *Black Music of Two Worlds* (Tivoli, N.Y.: Original Music, 1972).

2. E. Bradford Burns, *A History of Brazil* (New York: Columbia University Press, 1993), 43.

3. Thomas E. Skidmore, *Black into White: Race and Nationality in Brazilian Thought* (New York: Oxford University Press, 1974), 41. According to Skidmore, 1,081,174 of Brazil's total population of 3,598,132 were slaves in 1819.

4. Donald Pierson, *Negroes in Brazil: A Study of Race Contact in Brazil* (Carbondale: Southern Illinois University Press, 1942), 118. According to Pierson, in 1819, there were 628,000 mixed-bloods or mulattos to 843,000 whites.

5. The Brazilian government encouraged immigration from Europe as early as 1819, when the government helped approximately 2,000 Swiss to establish a colony at Novo Friburgo in the province of Rio de Janeiro. Subsequent government immigration programs between 1850 and 1888 attracted German settlers (primarily to Rio Grande do Sul and Paraná), Italians, Portuguese, and Spaniards as well as Russian, French, English, Syrian, and Austrian settlers in smaller numbers. In 1888, the annual arrival of European immigrants reached 133,253. European immigrants were valued by the Brazilian government both as a cheap source of labor and for their contributions to the process of "whitening," through which it was believed their blood would dilute and civilize the black and Indian races. E. Bradford Burns, *A History of Brazil*, 3rd ed. (New York: Columbia University Press, 1993), 217.

6. Dulce Tupy, *Carnavais de guerra: O nacionalismo no samba* (Rio de Janeiro: ASB, 1985), 18. Census takers relied on self-identification with racial groups. As a result, the number of "whites" refers to the number of people who identified themselves as white by a number of criterion, including but not limited to skin color. Arabs considered themselves white in order to distinguish themselves from the African slave population.

7. The theory of racial mixing as the basis of Brazilian national identity was set forth in 1888 in Sílvio Romero's *História da Literatura Brasileira*. His ideas were not generally accepted, however, until the publication of Gilberto Freyre's *Casa Grande e Senzala* in 1933. See Renato Ortiz, *Cultura brasileira e identidade nacional* (S;alao Paulo: Editora Brasiliense, 1983).

8. Arthur Gobineau, *Essai sur l'inégalité des races humaines*, 4th ed. (Paris: Librairie de Paris, 1900).

9. Georges Vacher de Lapouge, *L'Aryen: son rôle social* (Paris: A. Fontemoing, 1899).

10. Manoel Bonfim, *A America Latina*, 2nd ed. (Rio de Janeiro: A. Noite, 1939). Bonfim continued this line of argument in several other books, including *O Brasil na América: caracterização da formação brasileira* (Rio de Janeiro: 1929).

11. Graça Aranha, *Canaã* (Rio de Janeiro: H. Garnier, 1901).

12. Oliveira Viana, *Populações meridionaes do Brasil: historia, organização, psicologia*, 3rd ed. (São Paulo: Companhia Editora Nacional, 1900).

13. Vianna Moog, *Bandeirantes and Pioneers*, trans. L. L. Barrett (New York: George Braziller, 1964), 13.

14. Quoted in Thomas E. Skidmore, *Black into White*, 68–69.

15. In the 1960s and 1970s, black power movements in the United States inspired similar movements in Brazil and initiated a dialogue about the racial democracy myth. See Charles Perrone, "Axé, Ijexá, Olodum: The Rise of Afro-and African Currents in Brazilian Popular Music," *Afro-Hispanic Review* 11, nos. 1–3 (1992): 42–50; and Larry N. Crook, "Black Consciousness, Samba Reggae, and the Re-Africanization of Carnival Music in Brazil," *The World of Music* 35, no. 2 (1993): 90–106.

16. Carl N. Degler, *Neither Black nor White: Slavery and Race Relations in Brazil and the United States* (Madison: University of Wisconsin Press, 1971), 191.

17. Gérard Béhague, "Popular Musical Currents in the Art Music of the Early Nationalistic Period in Brazil, Circa 1870–1920" (Ph. D. diss., Tulane University, 1966), 68.

18. José Ramos Tinhorão, *Pequena história da música popular* (São Paulo: Círculo do Livro, 1980), 9.

19. Mozart de Araújo, *A modinha e o lundu no século XVIII—uma pesquisa bibliográfica* (São Paulo: Ricordi Brasileira, 1963), 15.

20. The Moors occupied southern Portugal for several hundred years, and as a result many aspects of Portuguese culture reveal Moorish traits. Portuguese music is strongly influenced by Moorish music, particularly in terms of rhythm.

21. After 1870 and before the First World War, Italian immigrants outnumbered those from Portugal and the rest of Europe. According to Burns, Italians made up 34.1 percent of the approximately 3.5 million immigrants that arrived in Brazil between 1820 and 1930. Like many immigrants suffering economic hardship in their native countries, Italians were drawn to Brazil by the prospects of wealth, work, and land. E. Bradford Burns, *A History of Brazil*, 3rd ed. (New York: Columbia University Press, 1993), 315.

22. Arvellos was a famous composer of modinhas, lundus, and polkas and was the music teacher of Dom Pedro I, first emperor of Brazil.

23. In 1822, Brazil declared its independence from Portugal and Pedro I was proclaimed Emperor. The First Empire came to a close in 1831 with the abdication of Pedro I. The period of the Second Empire was initially characterized by a series of chiefs of state rising from the Brazilian plantation-owning elite. Provincial rebellions and unrest led to the demand that the young Pedro II assume the crown in 1840. Pedro II ruled until he was dethroned by the army in 1889 and Brazil was declared a republic.

24. Tinhorão, *Pequena história,* 33–34.

25. Alexandre Gonçalves Pinto, *O Choro: reminiscencias dos chorões antigos* (Rio de Janeiro: Edição FUNARTE, 1978), 57. This publication is a facsimile of the 1936 original. See chapter 3 for a detailed discussion of the book.

26. The Velha Guarda (Old Guard) was a group of the most respected chorões before the turn of the century; it included Chiquinha Gonzaga, Anacleto de Medeiros, Juca Vale, Saturnino, and many others. In 1932, Pixinguinha called his group the "Velha Guarda," even though the musicians were young, to imply that they were linked with the old choro musicians of the past.

27. Pinto, *O Choro.* Some of these were listed exclusively as singers; others were instrumentalists who were also known for their singing ability.

28. Flausino Rodrigues Valle, *Elementos de folk-lore musical brasileiro* (São Paulo: Editora Nacional, 1936), 85.

29. Fryer suggests that the snapping of fingers (perhaps in imitation of Spanish castanets) and stamping of feet were likely influences of the fandango, "the most popular dance among Europeans in the [Brazilian] colony [under Spanish rule, 1581–1640]." Peter Fryer, *Rhythms of Resistance: African Musical Heritage in Brazil* (Hanover, N.H.: University Press of New England for Wesleyan University Press, 2000), 118.

30. The umbigada functioned to invite someone to dance or to end a dance; the act in itself had no inherent erotic significance. The choreographic movement was incorporated into a number of Brazilian popular dances.

31. According to Fryer, the lundu continues to be danced on the island of Marajó in the mouth of the Amazon River; *Rhythms of Resistance,* 125–126.

32. A rare first-hand account of lyrics accompanying the lundu dance describes them as "bantering [gouailleur], disorderly, stunning [abracadabrant], as often as not with a sting

of coarse irony." Fryer, *Rhythms of Resistance*, 125, citing an 1889 description by French writer F. J. de Santa-Anna Nery. Very little is known about the lyrics accompanying the dance.

33. de Araújo, *A Modinha e o lundu*, 11.

34. Tinhorão, *Pequena História*, 54. *Entremezes*, or intermezzi, were entertainments between acts of plays.

35. Anonymous poem in F. A. Pereira da Costa, *Vocabulário pernambucano* (Recife, 1937), quoted in Jota Efegê, *Maxixe—A dança excomungada* (Rio de Janeiro: Conquista, 1974), 34.

36. Fryer, *Rhythms of Resistance*, 154.

37. Tinhorão, *Pequena História*, 59.

38. In Portuguese, "*x*" and "*ch*" have the same sound. Words tend to contain one or the other, but confusion in spelling is not uncommon. In other words, the orthography may be affected by a word's pronunciation. As words are invented, they are spelled as they sound, not necessarily preserving the spelling of the original word. Thus, "*machiche*" could be spelled "*maxixe*." "*Machiche*" gives clues to its origin, whereas "*maxixe*" may not.

39. Mário de Andrade, *Dicionário musical brasileiro* (Belo Horizonte: Itatiaia, 1989).

40. Tinhorão, *Pequena História*.

41. Arthur Ramos, *O folclore Negro do Brasil*, 2nd ed. (Rio de Janeiro: Livraria-Editora da Casa do Estudante do Brasil, 1964), 136.

42. Ramos, *O Folclore Negro*, 131.

43. *O Globo Ilustrado* of Rio de Janeiro, quoted in Efegê, *Maxixe*, 20.

44. These dances include lundu and samba, which were viewed as lewd, even though they were not partner dances with close contact.

45. Francisca Hedwiges ("Chiquinha") Gonzaga (1847–1935) was one of the most popular pianists and composers of her generation. Her work is discussed in chapter 4.

46. Ary Vasconcelos, *A nova música da república velha* (Rio de Janeiro: Ary Vasconcelos, 1985), 14.

47. Tupy, *Carnavais de guerra*, 25.

48. Efegê, *Maxixe*, 84. This theater was named after the opera composer Antônio Carlos Gomes (1836–1896) and was one of the most important theaters in turn-of-the-century Rio de Janeiro.

49. Fred Astaire danced a very stylized Hollywood version of the maxixe in the film *Flying Down to Rio* (RKO Pictures, 1933). Reflecting the general ignorance of Americans concerning cultures south of the Mexican border, the movie lumps Hollywood versions of samba and maxixe together with Cuban rumba and Argentine tango, all supposedly set in the city of Rio de Janeiro. The costumes also followed this line; some actors were dressed in the style of Carmen Miranda with fruit baskets on their heads, others in Cuban and Mexican clothing styles. In the 1950s, the Apache was danced on an episode of *I Love Lucy* by the characters Fred and Ethel, probably because it was a popular vaudeville stage dance.

50. Mário de Andrade, *Música, doce música* (São Paulo: Editora Martins/Instituto Nacional do Livro, 1976), 124.

51. Baptista Siqueira, *Origem do termo samba* (Rio de Janeiro: IBRASA/MEC, 1978), 19.

3. The Roda de Choro

1. The vignette was constructed from descriptions of rodas in Alexandre Gonçalves Pinto's *O choro: reminiscencias dos chorões antigos* (Rio de Janeiro: Edição FUNARTE, 1978) and from biographies of early choro musicians. It is also based on information gleaned from

past, as well as the authors' experiences in contemporary rodas.

2. The concept of participatory music is the theoretical framework for this chapter; the theory informs much of the book. Participatory music is defined as music in which the degree and quality of participation determines to a large extent the evaluation of the event in which the music is played. In music performed on a stage presented to a passive listening audience, the music event is judged by the perfection of the sound product. In participatory music, a combination of factors, including engagement of participants (whether they are playing an instrument, singing, dancing, or clapping), the proportion of skilled to novice participants, and feelings of group synchronization often described as "being in the groove" determine whether or not the music event was a success. The concept's originator, Thomas Turino, argues that because the goals of participatory music are different from staged or presentational forms of music, participatory music should be considered a distinct art form. Turino developed the theory in the course of his work in Peru, Zimbabwe, and the United States. Turino, "Participatory Music as a Separate Art: Peruvian and Zimbabwean Case Studies," unpublished paper, 1995, and in *Nationalists, Cosmopolitans, and Popular Music in Zimbabwe* (Chicago: University of Chicago Press, 2000), 52–59. The framework is also discussed and used by Tamara Livingston in "Choro and Music Revivalism in Rio de Janeiro, 1973–1995" (Ph.D. diss., University of Illinois at Urbana-Champaign, 1999), 280–282, and "Brazilian Choro as Participatory Music," paper presented to the Society for Ethnomusicology, Pittsburgh, Pennsylvania, October 1997.

3. Pinto, *O choro*.

4. Pinto, *O choro*, 13–14, 78, 95, and passim.

5. *Tia* means "aunt," but it is also used as a sign of respect; these women from Bahia in northeastern Brazil were often powerful social and religious figures in the Afro-Brazilian community. Social gatherings of the middle classes of society at that time typically had different musical events going on at the same time: choro was found in the salon or front room while samba was played in the yard. For more on this subject, see Roberto Moura, *Tia Ciata e a pequena África no Rio de Janeiro* (Rio de Janeiro: FUNARTE, 1982).

6. The ophicleide was an alto or bass brass instrument invented in 1817; the bass ophicleide was a common instrument in military bands of the 1830s and 1840s. Don Michael Randel, ed., *The New Harvard Dictionary of Music* (Cambridge: Harvard University Press, 1986).

7. Another name for *cachaça*, the most popular Brazilian liquor.

8. Pinto uses the term "chorões" interchangeably with "seresteiros," another indication of their similarity in terms of musical function and social perception. Pinto, *O choro*, 107.

9. Pinto, *O choro*, 96–97.

10. In *Música popular: um tema em debate* (Rio de Janeiro: Saga, 1966), José Ramos Tinhorão fixes the number of musicians Pinto counted at 300. There are indeed 300 biographical entries, but many entries mention more than one chorão.

11. Villa-Lobos, "Qu'est-ce qu'un choros?" lecture at the Club de Trois Centres, Paris, May 29, 1958, Record 29.V.1958, EMI (France), 1959.

12. Pinto, *O choro*, 94.

13. Gonzaga is discussed in greater detail in chapter 4.

14. Pinto, *O choro*, 78. It would not be surprising to discover that Durvalina was either a prostitute or a madam and that her house was popular because of this as well as the abundance of good choro. Brothels were common gathering places for chorões, and some musicians were able to make a living performing in brothels. Although there is no documentary proof, it has been suggested by Olga Prauger de Coelho and other friends of Villa-Lobos that the composer supported himself as a teenager in part by playing guitar choros in a brothel.

15. Vasco Mariz, *Heitor Villa-Lobos: Life and Work of the Brazilian Composer* (Washington, D.C.: Brazilian American Cultural Institute, 1970), 37.

16. Manoel Antonio Barroso, "Bide: da Velha Guarda aos chorões de Brasília," *Cultura* 8, no. 29 (1978): 24.

17. Horondino da Silva, interview by Tamara Livingston-Isenhour, Rio de Janeiro, September 13, 1995.

18. See Ingrid Monson, *Saying Something: Jazz Improvisation and Interaction* (Chicago: University of Chicago Press, 1996); and Paul Berliner, *Thinking in Jazz: The Infinite Art of Improvisation* (Chicago: University of Chicago Press, 1994).

19. It is very possible that prejudice against female players is most prevalent among male players of the older generation. As younger musicians continue to become involved in choro, the prejudice against women musicians seems to be diminishing.

20. This view of presentational music was developed from the theoretical framework discussed in endnote 2 of this chapter.

4. From the Plantation to the City

1. David Appleby, *The Music of Brazil* (Austin: University of Texas Press, 1983), 72.

2. Baptista Siqueira, *Três vultos históricos da música brasileira* (Rio de Janeiro: MEC, 1969), 141.

3. Flautist Josías, interviewed by Thomas Garcia, Rio de Janeiro, November 11, 1994. In Brazil, it is common for a musical genre to assume the name of the social occasion where it is played.

4. Gérard H. Béhague, "Popular Musical Currents in the Art Music of the Early Nationalistic Period in Brazil, Circa 1870–1920" (Ph.D. diss., Tulane University, 1966), 95.

5. Renato Almeida, *História da Música Brasileira* (Rio de Janeiro: F. Briguiet & Cia, 1956), 122.

6. Ary Vasconcelos, *Carinhoso, etc.: história e inventário do choro* (Rio de Janeiro: Grafico Editora, 1984), 17. The "*-eiro*" ending in Portuguese refers to a profession (e.g. one who plays choromela is a *choromeleiro,* and one who repairs *sapatos* [shoes] is a *sapateiro.*)

7. Francisco Curt Lange, a musicologist who conducted one of the earliest studies of the choromeleiro, also stresses the relationship between choro and choromeleiro: "[F]rom these choromeleiros came, without doubt, the tradition of serenades in the open air, on the streets or at the big houses of the fazendas because the word choro or seresta, which was kept alive in professional and amateur groups until the beginning of this century, has the same origin." Lange, "A organização musical durante o período colonial brasileiro," *Actas do V Colóquio Internacional de Estudos Luso-Brasileiros* (Coimbra, 1966), 24.

8. From the journals of French priest Courte de la Blanchardière, 1748, quoted in José Ramos Tinhorão, *Música popular dos Indios, Negros e Mestiços* (Petropolis, Rio de Janeiro: Vozes, 1972), 72.

9. Peter Fryer, *Rhythms of Resistance: African Musical Heritage in Brazil* (Hanover, N.H.: University Press of New England for Wesleyan University Press, 2000), 140.

10. *Fado* is a nineteenth-century style of popular song of Portuguese origin; *tirana* is a Brazilian song and dance of Spanish origin; *fandango* is a generic name for a variety of circle dances that use the Spanish tapping of feet, or *sapateado.*

11. José Ramos Tinhorão, *Música popular: um tema em debate* (Rio de Janeiro: Editora Saga, 1966), 110–111.

12. Alexandre Gonçalves Pinto, *O choro: reminiscencias dos chorões antigos* (Rio de Janeiro: Edição FUNARTE, 1978), 111. Some prominent examples are Jacó do Bandolim

Guimarães).

13. In 1960, the new capital city of Brasília was inaugurated.

14. *Embolada* refers to a poetic and musical form sung by northeastern folk musicians characterized by a verse-refrain structure, improvised verses, and a fast tempo. *Toada* is a melancholy song that is also popular in the northeast of Brazil.

15. June E. Hahner, *Poverty and Politics: The Urban Poor in Brazil, 1870–1920* (Albuquerque: University of New Mexico Press, 1986).

16. E. Bradford Burns, *A History of Brazil*, 3rd ed. (New York: Columbia University Press, 1993), 199. See also Hahner, *Poverty and Politics*, 300–302 for a summary of the literature concerning the Brazilian middle class.

17. Initially, choro players did not like the diminutive and resented the implications that choro players were not to be taken seriously. However, it came to be used as an affectionate way of referring to the genre. In today's usage, "chorinho" often refers to slow pieces and "choro" to faster-paced pieces.

18. Charles Hamm, "The Early Songs of Irving Berlin," in *Putting Popular Music in Its Place* (Cambridge: Cambridge University Press, 1995), 380.

19. Saturnino is quite possibly the first chorão to be known for his solo guitar-playing. Calado, Gonzaga, and Saturnino constituted part of the Velha Guarda.

20. Brazilian music conservatories have traditionally restricted their activities to orchestral and band instruments. It was only recently that studying classical guitar became an option at some institutes of higher education.

21. Portamento refers to a continuous movement from one pitch to another without the intervening pitches sounding discretely; it is similar to a glissando. Don Michael Randel, ed., *The New Harvard Dictionary of Music* (Cambridge: Harvard University Press, 1986).

22. Tadeo Coelho, phone interview by Thomas Garcia, February 25, 1997. Tadeo Coelho is a Brazilian flautist and professor of flute at the North Carolina School of the Arts. He has written extensively on historical Brazilian flute-playing.

23. Pinto, *O choro*, 12.

24. Pinto, *O choro*, 11.

25. The saxophone was not popular in the early days of choro. Pinto dismisses the saxophone as an instrument that came into fashion only because of the popularity of American music. It became increasingly popular in the 1930s and 1940s.

26. Villa-Lobos wrote a series of fifteen choros for various combinations of instruments that incorporate many popular choros as well as the stylistic characteristics of the choro genre. See chapter 9.

27. Lieutenant Colonel Eugênio Rodriguez Jardim requested that a band be formed. Ministry of Justice Aviso 1.225, October 30, 1896, Arquivo Nacional, Rio de Janeiro.

28. Jota Efegê, *Figuras e coisas da música popular brasileira*, vol. 1 (Rio de Janeiro: FUNARTE, 1978), 179.

29. Jota Efegê, "Dudu, O Bombeiro Boêmio," *O Jornal*, March 7, 1966, reprinted in Jota Efegê, *Figuras e coisas*, 179.

30. Efegê, *Figuras e coisas*, 218.

31. Humbert M. Francesci, *A Casa Edison e seu tempo* (Rio de Janeiro: Sarapuí, 2003).

32. Pinto, *O choro*, 60.

33. Gilberto Freyre, *Ordem e progresso*, vol. 1 (Rio de Janeiro: Livraria José Olympio Editora, 1962), 105.

34. The Brazilian Republic was established in 1889 when the army dethroned Emperor Pedro II in a bloodless revolution. The constitution of 1891 provided for a centralized federal

republican form of government, led by an elected president. Historians distinguish between the Old Republic, the period before Getúlio Vargas rose to power, and the New Republic, ushered in by the military coup in 1930.

35. The revolution that led to the Republic of Brazil was caused by widespread discontent with the monarchy among the military, the clergy, the coffee barons, and members of the urban middle class. With backing from civilian groups, military officers carried out a successful coup on November 15, 1889.

36. Hermínio Bello de Carvalho, *O canto do Pajé: Villa-Lobos e a música popular brasileira* (Rio de Janeiro: Editora Espaço e Tempo, 1988), 166.

37. As Béhague points out, "[H]is knowledge of and predilection for Chopin had a significant role in his pianistic writing. This influence is felt in the melodic and harmonic aspects of some of his compositions." Gérard H. Béhague, "Popular Musical Currents in the Art Music of the Early Nationalistic Period in Brazil, Circa 1870–1920" (Ph.D. diss., Tulane University, 1966), 141.

38. From the turn of the century through the 1950s, Chopin was so popular that most Brazilian states had a Chopin piano competition. Winners were invited to a national competition, which was sponsored at times by the federal government. The winner of the first prize at the national level was then sponsored to concertize in Europe and to compete in international piano competitions, most notably the Chopin Competition in Warsaw. As Brazilian nationalism became a strong cultural force in the 1920s and 1930s, there were many attempts to break the hold of the French, especially Chopin, on Brazilian music conservatories and replace them with Brazilian composers such as Villa-Lobos, Carmargo Guarnieri, Frutuoso Viana, and Enrique Oswaldo.

39. Beatriz Leal Guimarães, "Ernesto Nazareth—Pianista e compositor de gênio," reprinted in *Ernesto Nazareth; album de violão* (São Paulo: Editôra Arthur Napoleão, n.d.), signed text appearing on the inside cover of published sheet music. Villa-Lobos composed a series called *Choros* consisting of numbered, separate works for various instrumental combinations. These works are discussed in chapter 9.

40. See chapter 5 for more about the Semana de Arte Moderna.

5. From the Terno to the *Regional*

1. As quoted in Herman Vienna, *The Mystery of Samba: Popular Music and National Identity in Brazil*, edited and translated by John Charles Chasten. Chapel Hill: University of North Carolina Press, 1999), 8.

2. Gilberto Freyre, *Orem e progresso*, vol. 1 (Rio de Janeiro: Livraria José Olympia Editora, 1962), 107.

3. Thomas E. Skidmore, *Black Into White: Race and Nationality in Brazilian Thought* (New York: Oxford University Press, 1974), 146.

4. Futurism was a literary movement founded in Italy in 1909 with a manifesto by Filippo Tommaso Marinetti, "Le Futurisme." It was profoundly influenced by the rapid industrialization and militarization that Italy had recently undergone. It rejected the celebration of the individual in Italian romanticism in favor of the inhuman structures that appeared to control society, which included embracing the machine technologies of war, transportation, and communication. Luigi Russolo (author of the highly influential musical manifesto "Musica Futurista" advocating the incorporation of noise into musical compositions) was a representative composer of the movement. German expressionism was a movement in the visual arts that arose in Germany in 1905. It advocated that artists convey the inner state of the artistic subject through brilliant color and lines rather than through realistic portrayal. It was influenced by other artistic movements, including symbolism and cubism. Leading ex-

pressionist artists are Wassily Kandinsky, Franz Marc, and Amadeo Modigliani. Dada was an artistic and literary movement founded in 1915 in Zürich, Switzerland. The purpose of the movement was to expose the pretensions of society before the First World War by relying on the elements of chance, nonsense, and the absurd to inform artistic works. It is generally regarded as the precursor to surrealism. Representative artists were sculptor Jean Arp and Marcel Duchamp.

5. The events of the Semana de Arte Moderna occurred at the Teatro Municipal in São Paulo on February 13, 15, and 17 of 1922. The event was organized by Emiliano Di Cavalcanti, and participants included Anita Malfatti, Antônio Alcântara Machado, Antônio Gômide, Graça Aranha, Guilherme de Almeida, John Graz, Lasar Segall, Manuel Bandeira, Mário de Andrade, Menotti del Picchia, Oswald de Andrade, Ronald de Carvalho, Tarsila do Amaral, Vicente do Rêgo Monteiro, Heitor Villa-Lobos, and Vitor Brecheret. One of the financial backers, René Thiollier, was a modernist painter and sculptor who exhibited his works during the event.

6. The term "*conjunto regional*" refers to a professional choro ensemble typically consisting of flute or other melody instrument, cavaquinho, guitars, and pandeiro; they were employed by radio stations or recording studios in the 1930s until the 1950s. These ensembles provided accompaniment for singers and performed instrumental numbers.

7. In Brazil it was common for certain civil service positions to be assigned as favors or gift; in some cases employees received paychecks without ever having to appear on the job.

8. Olga Prauger de Coelho, interview by Thomas Garcia, Rio de Janeiro, January 14, 1995.

9. Ary Vasconcelos, *Carinhoso, etc.: historian e inventoried does choro* (Rio de Janeiro: Graphic Editor, 1984), 27.

10. Hermínio Bello de Carvalho, *O canto do Pajé: Villa-Lobos e a música popular brasileira* (Rio de Janeiro: Editora Espaço e Tempo, 1988), 166.

11. From a publication by the Cavaquinho de Ouro music store, quoted in José de Souza Leal and Artur Luiz Barbosa, *João Pernambuco: arte de um povo* (Rio de Janeiro: FUNARTE, 1982), 27.

12. There is some controversy surrounding this piece: Pernambuco claimed to have written the melody but was accused of having used a folk song from the northeast. He denied this allegation, insisting that he had indeed composed the melody. Villa-Lobos was his strongest defender in this controversy and went on to arrange the modinha for his grand concerts of tens of thousands of voices held in soccer stadiums in the 1930s and 1940s. In fact, Villa-Lobos published an arrangement of this modinha in the daily newspaper *Correio de Manha* (Rio de Janeiro), October 12, 1937.

13. Leal and Barbosa, *João Pernambuco*, 47.

14. Leal and Barbosa, *João Pernambuco*, 47.

15. Sevcenko cites a notice in the newspaper *Jornal do Commercio* of 1901 that calls for police repression of serenaders and guitar-players. Nicolau Sevcenko, *Literatura como missão: tensões sociais e criação cultural na Primeira República* (São Paulo: Brasiliense, 1983), 32 and 69.

16. Donga, quoted in Hermínio Bello de Carvalho, *O canto do Pajé*, 29.

17. Ratinho, Sivuca, Canhoto de Paraíba, and Francisco Soares are just a few chorões from the northeast.

18. Ary Vasconcelos, *Carinhoso*, 37.

19. As cited in Alcino Santos, Gracio Barbalho, Jairo Severiano, and M. A. Azevedo, *Discografia brasileira, 78 rpm, 1902–1964* (Rio de Janeiro: FUNARTE, 1982), ii.

20. According to Vasconcelos, Malaquias was a composer, clarinetist, and conductor who was born in 1870 (?) and died in 1940 (?). Pinto states that he learned clarinet as a

member of the Corpo de Marinheiros and that Figner admired his playing. Ary Vasconcelos, *Panorama da música popular brasileira na "Belle Epoque"* (Rio de Janeiro: Sant'Anna, 1977), 262.

21. As employees of radio stations, musicians were documented workers entitled to benefits, including pension plans, a rare commodity among popular musicians.

22. The name comes from Pizindim, "good boy" in one of the African languages spoken in Brazil. He was later called Bexiguinha (i.e., "Little Bladder"), and his ultimate nickname is a mixture of the two.

23. Several sources give Pixinguinha's birth year as 1897, others as 1898.

24. His collection included many genres of popular and classical music. Although several sources state that this was a collection of choro scores, they were for the most part lead sheets—melody and basic harmony. Sebastião Godinho, son of chorão Godinho, godson of Pixinguinha, and acquaintance of Alfredo de Rocha Vianna, Sr., interview by Thomas Garcia, Cabo Frio, Brazil, August 15, 1996.

25. In her history of the samba, Dulce Tupy claims that his first recording was with his brother Henrique and Calado's Choro Carioca for Casa Faulhaber. Dulce Tupy, *Carnavais de guerra: o nacionalismo no samba* (Rio de Janeiro: ASB, 1985), 35.

26. In 1933 he was nominated a *funcionário público,* one who worked for the bureau of street-cleaning. As was the case with Quincas Laranjeiras, it is unlikely that he ever worked a day in that capacity. It did give him the right to a government pension, and his popularity encouraged the government to look the other way.

27. The group was comprised of Pixinguinha, flute and (later) saxophone; Ernesto dos Santos (aka Donga), six- and seven-string guitar; Nélson dos Santos Alves (aka Nélson Boina), cavaquinho; Pixinguinha's brother Otávio Vianna ("China"), guitar and vocals; José Alves, bandolim and ganzá (an Afro-Brazilian percussion instrument); Raul Palmieri, guitar; Jacó Palmieri, pandeiro; and Luís de Oliveira, bandola (a large bandolim) and rêco-rêco.

28. Guinle also sponsored Villa-Lobos's first trip to Paris in 1923. Duque and Gaby were a famous dance duo responsible for the maxixe dance craze in Paris during the early twentieth century. Duque (Antônio Lopes de Amorim Diniz) was formerly a dentist from Bahia, and Gaby was a Parisian dancer. They were influential in convincing the philanthropist Arnaldo Guinle to finance the Oito Batutas's trip to Paris as a demonstration of the "progress" of Brazilian popular music.

29. Catulo da Paixão Cearense felt that he was the true representative of *sertanejo* (rural) Brazil and worried that Pixinguinha would mix his modinhas with *bobagens* [nonsense]. Sérgio Cabral, *Pixinguinha: vida e obra* (Rio de Janeiro: FUNARTE, 1978), 37.

30. This is a reference to the current Avenida Rio Branco, at that time the location of prestigious cafes and theaters patronized by the elite, who preferred foreign music.

31. Casa Mozart and Arthur Napoleão were large music publishing houses in Rio de Janeiro.

32. The full text is given in Marília T. Barbosa da Silva and Arthur L. de Oliveira Filho, *Filho de ogum bexiguento* (Rio de Janeiro: FUNARTE, 1979), 199–200.

33. Barbosa da Silva, *Filho de ogum bexiguento,* 199–200.

34. Cabral, *Pixinguinha,* 57.

35. *Oito Batutas,* Projeto Revivendo RVCD-064 (1993).

36. Composed and registered by Donga, a member of several of Pixinguinha's groups, and recorded by Casa Edison 121.312, featuring the Banda Odeon. The piece bears little resemblance to contemporary samba and rhythmically was heavily influenced by the maxixe.

37. Since Pixinguinha invariably conducted his own arrangements, he did not bother to prepare a full score.

38. Cabral, *Pixinguinha,* 59.

39. Getúlio Vargas first rose to a position of power in 1930. After losing a presidential election, he led a revolt that resulted in his assumption of the presidency. In November of 1937, President Getúlio Vargas terminated the scheduled presidential election process, dismissed Congress, and assumed unlimited powers. He called the new administration the Estado Novo, or New State, which endured until 1945, when he was deposed by the military.

40. In 1935 the *escolas de samba,* or samba schools, began to receive subsidies from the City of Rio de Janeiro in exchange for adhering to certain rules and regulations. See Alison Raphael, "From Popular Culture to Microenterprise: The History of Brazilian Samba Schools," *Latin American Music Review* 11, no. 1 (1990): 73–83.

41. Lourival Fontes, *Voz do rádio,* February 20, 1936, as quoted in Luiz Carlos Saroldi and Sonia Virginia Moreira, *Rádio Nacional: o Brasil em sintonia* (Rio de Janeiro: Martins Fontes/FUNARTE, 1984), 13.

42. "For one hour, from 8 to 9 at night, all radio stations in the country were required to broadcast this program from the government's official radio station. This program . . . was a collection of praises and hosannas to the administrative genius of Vargas, to the magnificent public works, and above all to the generosity of the dictator and his intense love for the 'workers of Brazil.' It wasn't long before the listening audience began to grow tired of this program and exactly at eight o'clock when it would begin, everyone would turn off their radios. The irreverence of the carioca came to call the 'Hour of Brazil' the 'Hour of Silence.' " Affonso Henriques, *Ascensão e queda de Getúlio Vargas,* vol. 2, *Vargas e o Estado Novo* (Rio de Janeiro: Record, 1966), 265–266. The Departamento de Imprensa e Propaganda was created by presidential decree in December 1939.

43. According to Tinhorão, only two Brazilians, singer Amorim Filho and a pandeiro player, were part of the cast that produced the biweekly show. José Ramos Tinhorão, *Música popular: um tema em debate* (Rio de Janeiro: Saga, 1966).

44. The fall of the monarchy in 1889 left control of the nation in the hands of the military, which was supported by powerful coffee planters and the urban middle class. In the new republic, the powers of church and state were separated, but considerable power was given to the states, specifically those cultivating coffee, Brazil's most important export in the nineteenth century. The succession of presidents before Vargas had little real power, as they depended on the elite cadre of landowners who had elected them.

45. Martha Gil-Montero, *Brazilian Bombshell: The Biography of Carmen Miranda* (New York: Donald I. Fine, 1989), 54.

46. From an information sheet published by the Museu Carmen Miranda, Rio de Janiero, Brazil, and confirmed by the director of the Museu in communication with Thomas Garcia, July 1996.

47. For more on this subject see John Storm Roberts, *The Latin Tinge: The Impact of Latin American Music on the United States,* 2nd ed. (New York: Oxford University Press, 1999).

48. The music was actually Cuban *son,* and the "rhumba" dance was an American invention that had no relationship to the Cuban *rumba.*

49. It would not be until the 1960s that "traditional samba," the samba that was often sung in a rough fashion accompanied by guitar, cavaquinho, and pandeiro, and was associated with poor Afro-Brazilian communities, would reach a wide Brazilian audience.

50. For more on the life of Carmen Miranda, see Gil-Montero, *Brazilian Bombshell;* see also the biographical film *Carmen Miranda: Bananas Is My Business,* directed by Helena Solberg (Fox Lorber Studio, 1995).

51. According to Daniella Thompson, the film *It's All True* was intended to consist of a series of episodes documenting different aspects of Brazilian life. The project was plagued by disasters, including an incident resulting in the hospitalization of the great Brazilian actor

Grande Otelo (Sebastião Bernardo de Souza Preta) and a drowning death that interrupted the filming of the episode recreating an historic 1,650 mile voyage made by four fishermen from Ceará. The film was presumed lost for many years until footage was found in a vault. It was edited and released in 1993. See Daniella Thompson, "Stalking Stokowski," *Brazzil*, February 2000. *Brazzil* is an electronic magazine available at http://www.brazzil.com/musfeb00.htm.

52. According to Daniella Thompson, in 1940 Columbia Records released seventeen of the forty pieces recorded aboard the *Uruguay* under the title *Native Brazilian Music* (2 albums, each with four 78-rpm discs). Thompson, "Stalking Stokowski."

6. The Velha Guarda in the New Brazil

1. Liner notes from recording entitled *Paraguassú*, on the Continental label, no copies available.

2. Abel Cardoso Junior, *Carmen Miranda: a cantora do Brasil* (São Paulo: Abel Cardoso Junior, 1978), 136.

3. The acetate tapes were restored and the tracks were released on a compact disc in 1993. *Viva Garoto*, CD 107.225, Projeto Memória Brasileira.

4. As quoted on the liner notes of compact disc *Viva Garoto*.

5. A samba school, or *escola de samba*, is a social organization that plans and carries out the annual Carnaval parade, including composing the school's theme song, preparing the costumes, and rehearsing the dancers and musicians. A fundamental part of the samba school is the drum and percussion section, called the *bateria*.

6. Samba-canção is a lyrical form of samba that emphasizes the voice. It is typically accompanied by *conjunto regional* or *orquestra*.

7. Charles Perrone, *Masters of Contemporary Brazilian Song: MPB 1965–1985* (Austin: University of Texas Press, 1989), xxvi.

8. Robert Myers, "Brazilian Popular Music in Bahia: 'The Politics of the Future,' An Interview with Gilberto Gil," *Studies in Latin American Popular Culture* 9 (1990): 300. *Tropicália* was a radical artistic movement in the late 1960s. The musical component was led by iconoclasts Caetano Veloso, Gilberto Gil, and other popular singers, who advocated the juxtaposition of a variety of foreign and domestic musical sources (including aspects of rock-and-roll) in the creation of an authentic modern Brazilian popular music.

9. Myers, "Brazilian Popular Music in Bahia," 302–303.

10. Some critics, notably Jose Ramos Tinhorão, denounced bossa nova as a bourgeois imitation of American jazz. See José Ramos Tinhorão, *Música popular: um tema em debate* (Rio de Janeiro: Saga, 1966).

11. Collector's Editora Ltda., *Catálogo geral: Collector's No. 1* (Rio de Janeiro). Many of these Old Guard composers composed choros, among other genres.

12. As transcribed and translated from the radio show *O Pessoal da Velha Guarda*, vol. 1, October 15, 1947, released by Collector's Editora, Rio de Janeiro.

13. Bryan McCann, "The Invention of Tradition on Brazilian Radio," in *The Brazil Reader: History, Culture, Politics*, ed. Robert M. Levine and John J. Crocitti (Durham, N.C.: Duke University Press, 1999), 474–482.

14. The chorões that came from Rio de Janeiro for the festival were Jacó do Bandolim, Pixinguinha, Donga, João do Baiano, Mozart de Araújo, Alfredinho de Flautim, Caninha, Patrício Teixeira, Benedito Lacerda, Bide de Flauta, Léo Viana (brother of Pixinguinha), Bororó (the 15-year-old grandson of Donga), guitarist Sidney dos Santos Silva, and 15-year-old guitarist Baden Powell; Cabral, *No tempo de Ari Barroso*.

15. *O Estado do São Paulo*, April 23, 1954, 10.

17. The Museu da Imagem e do Som (Museum of Image and Sound, MIS) was originally founded to house the extensive popular music collection of radio personality/singer Almirante that was purchased by the state of Guanabara. The museum was inaugurated in 1965.

18. It is unclear whether the show was actually produced. The documents consulted in the Archive of Jacó do Bandolim at the MIS consist of typed program notes, which were preceded by a cover letter from the Rádio Sociedade Guanabara Departamento Comercial Publicidade addressed to "Dear Announcer." The text of the note is as follows: "The program which we are offering you, in addition to its other striking characteristics, will frame the presentation of an artist who on his own merits guarantees complete success. Jacob, the best Brazilian mandolinist, in whom the public trusts and remains loyal to, a public which buys monthly approximately 30,000 discs recorded by Jacob! There are, therefore, 30,000 guaranteed listeners for the program, 30,000 potential consumers who will be influenced by the advertisements on the station, besides the regular listeners of PRE-8."

19. Modern choro bandolims often have five courses. The additional lower course enables artists to play more-sophisticated solo arrangements.

20. Ermelinda A Paz, *Jacob de Bandolim* (Rio de Janeiro: Funarte, 1997), 106.

21. The group founded by Déo Rian, who replaced Jacó as soloist for Época de Ouro after his death, is named Noites Cariocas in honor of his mentor.

22. Later, Jorge Jose da Silva (Jorginho do Pandeiro) replaced D'Ávila.

23. Lúcio Rangel, *Sambistas & chorões: aspectos e figuras da música popular brasileira* (Rio de Janeiro: Editora Francisco Alves, 1963), 69.

24. *Baião* is a northeastern song and a dance that is accompanied by accordion, triangle, and large *zabumba* drum. Melodies often incorporate a raised fourth and/or a flat seventh (called the *sétima nordestina*). The genre was popularized by Luis Gonzaga, who introduced it to Rio de Janeiro in the late 1940s.

25. MPB, or *música popular brasileira,* arose in the late 1960s as a nationalistic reaction to imitations of foreign popular genres. It is characterized by the use of acoustic instruments, carefully crafted lyrics that are often poetic or political, and references in lyrics and in music to Brazilian culture. Well-known MPB artists include Chico Buarque, Edu Lobo, Milton Nascimento, Gilberto Gil, Gal Costa, Ivan Lins, and Caetano Veloso.

26. It appears that in the 1960s, the middle class conceived of samba de morro as political in terms of economics and class rather than in terms of race. This would change in the 1970s with the emergence of black power movements and musics in Rio de Janeiro and Salvador. See Larry N. Crook, "Black Consciousness, Samba Reggae, and the Re-Africanization of Carnival Music in Brazil," *The World of Music* 35, no. 2 (1993): 90–106; John Burdick, "Brazil's Black Consciousness Movement," *Report on the Americas* 24, no. 4 (1992): 23–29; and Charles Perrone, "Axé, Ijexá, Olodum: The Rise of Afro-and African Currents in Brazilian Popular Music," *Afro-Hispanic Review* 11, no. 1–3 (1992): 42–50.

27. *Opinião* was written and produced by Oduvaldo Viana Filho, Armando Costa, and Paulo Pontes. It featured singer Nara Leão and sambistas Zé Keti and João do Vale.

28. The Cinema Nova movement was spearheaded by filmmakers Nelson Pereira dos Santos, Glauber Rocha, Carlos Diegues, and Leon Hirszmann. These filmmakers set their Films in slums, or favelas, the arid harsh sertão of the northeast, and in other areas of misery and poverty as political statements of their dedication to social justice. Using minimal technology and low budgets, they felt they were creating an anticolonial art form because they used the resources at hand instead of depending on borrowed materials and borrowed cash. See Randal Johnson, *The Film Industry in Brazil: Culture and the State* (Pittsburgh: University

of Pittsburgh Press, 1987); and Randal Johnson and Robert Stam, eds., *Brazilian Cinema* (Rutherford, N.J.: Fairleigh Dickinson University Press, 1982).

7. The Choro Revival

1. Canhoto de Paraíba is the nickname of Francisco Soares de Araújo (b. 1928), a left-handed guitarist from the state of Paraíba. *Canhoto* in Portuguese means "left-handed."

2. The concert was recorded live and released by RCA as *O Fino da música: música brasileira num espetáculo que marcou época,* RCA 107-0270, 1977. Quotes taken from liner notes to LP written by J. E. Homem de Mello.

3. *Jornal do Brasil,* September 10, 1977, B:4.

4. For a detailed discussion of music revivals and a theoretical model, see Tamara E. Livingston, "Music Revivals: Towards a General Theory," *Ethnomusicology* 43, no. 1 (Winter 1999): 66–85.

5. Ruy Fabiano, "Os novos chorões: os jovens descobrem no choro o jazz brasileiro," *Jornal de música e som* (November 11, 1976): 5–6.

6. Literally "salon," a reference to elite society of the past.

7. The Choro Club of Rio de Janeiro was the first choro club established in Brazil. It was founded in 1975 by Paulinho da Viola, Sérgio Cabral, musicologist and government official Mozart de Araújo, and producers Albino Pinheiro and Juarez Barroso. The purpose of this and subsequent choro clubs was to preserve and disseminate choro as a valuable part of Brazilian cultural history. To this end, clubs sponsored and organized concerts and events commemorating choro musicians of the past, and some provided space for regular rodas.

8. *Veja,* October 25, 1995.

9. Fabiano, "Os novos chorões." The groups were Os Carioquinhas, Galo Preto, Cinco Companheiros, Levanta Poeira, Anjos de Madrugada, Eramos Felizes, and Fina Flor do Samba.

10. As quoted in *O Globo,* October 3, 1993, 11.

11. As quoted by Fabiano in "Os novos chorões," 5.

12. The Jovem Guarda were mid-1960s rock groups whose style was greatly influenced by the Beatles and other British and American groups.

13. Ruy Fabiano, "Os novos chorões," 5.

14. Ary Vasconcelos, *Carinhoso etc: história e inventário do choro* (Rio de Janeiro: Ary Vasconcelos, 1984), 40.

15. Diana Aragão and Lena Frias, "Com Sotaque e Giria," *Jornal do Brasil,* September 2, 1977, 10.

16. Jorge Simas, interview by Tamara Livingston, Rio de Janeiro, October 9, 1995.

17. According to Cabral, the club disbanded in 1978. Records of the club housed in the Museu da Imagem e do Som suggest that it re-formed in 1979 and lasted until 1993.

18. Araújo served as the first president of the club.

19. The state of Rio de Janeiro as it exists today was formed in 1975.

20. Manoel Antonio Barroso, "Bide: da Velha Guarda aos chorões de Brasília," *Cultura* 8, no. 29 (1978): 18–19, 20–29.

21. Roberto Fernandes, "Brasília, capital do choro: quando os chorões buscam bons empregos," *Jornal do Brasil,* August 12, 1983, section B.

22. Godofredo ("Godo") Viana Dudman, saxophonist, arrived in Brasília in 1975 with his sixteen children. In 1981, Figueiredo made him a government "official."

23. Marcus Pereira, *Música: está chegando a vez do povo 1. A história de "O Jogral"* (São Paulo: HUCITEC, 1976).

24. Although the disc was originally released under the label name Jogral, Pereira re-

labeled them in 1973 under the label of Discos Marcus Pereira to take advantage of the name recognition he had achieved with *Música popular do Nordeste*. Pereira, *Música: está chegando*.

25. The musicians were Manuel Gomes, flute; Benedito Costa, cavaquinho; Adauto Santos, guitar, Geraldo Cunha, guitar; and Fritz, pandeiro.

26. Marcus Pereira, *Música: está chegando*. *Música sertaneja* is Brazilian country music, often sung by male duos accompanying themselves on guitars. The repertoire consists of a blend of rural music genres from the southeast of Brazil and urban popular music.

27. His discs in this series are dedicated to the memory of Brazil's first musicologist, Mário de Andrade.

28. MEC evolved from the Ministry of Education and Public Health Affairs (Ministério dos Negócios de Educação e Saúde Pública), which was created in 1930. The agency was re-named in 1937 as the Ministry of Education and Health (Ministério da Educação e Saúde), and in 1953 the agency assumed responsibility for cultural affairs and was renamed the Min-istry of Education and Culture. The agency ceased to exist in 1990, and cultural affairs were placed under the Secretary of Culture of the Presidency of the Republic in 1990. In 1992, this agency was again called the Ministry of Culture. The choro revival depended in large part on subsidies from the MEC to support its activities.

29. Tarik de Souza, "Ataque de choro," *Veja*, October 12, 1977, 99–100.

30. Regina Echevarria, "The Same Old Choro: For Now, Nothing New. What Will Fol-low?" *Veja*, October 11, 1978, 100–102.

31. Rossini Ferreira was a bandolinist from Recife. Os Ingênuos is a group from Sal-vador.

32. Although many other groups participated, the Department of Culture listed only a few by names of members and the instruments they played.

33. The father of Maurício M. de Carvalho ("Mu") was "Dodo." Dodo and Osmar were the first to present an electric form of the Carnaval genre *frevo* from a flatbed truck in the 1950s in Salvador. In 1951 they added a third instrument, and the term "*trio elétrico*" came into use. Chris McGowan and Ricardo Pessanha, *The Brazilian Sound: Samba, Bossa Nova and the Popular Music of Brazil* (Philadelphia: Temple University Press, 1998), 123.

34. Frevo is a fast syncopated march from Recife, often danced during Carnaval.

35. As quoted in the *Jornal do Brasil*, October 28, 1978, B:4.

36. At one point in his career, Dino was obliged to play electric guitar in a dance band in order to make a living. The seven-string guitar, however, remains his preferred instrument.

37. As quoted in Luiz Henrique Romagnoli, "Depois o festival, o debate: choro que te quero ou é preciso mudar?" *Jornal do Brasil*, October 28, 1978, B:4.

38. José Ramos Tinhorão, "Elites musicais começam a implicar com o choro," *Jornal do Brasil*, October 21, 1978, B:4.

39. Echevarria, "The Same Old Choro," 100–102.

40. Although some choro musicians played there regularly, most were unenthusiastic about the ambience. Like the imitation Sovaco de Cobra, the roda at the planetarium was seen as contrived, one that did not pay attention to the details that make a physical space conducive to good music-making.

41. Roberto Schwarz, *Misplaced Ideas: Essays on Brazilian Culture*, edited by John Gledson (London: Verso, 1992), 138.

42. In 1964, President João Goulart was deposed by the military, ushering in a period of military rule until 1985. Military leaders and the conservative opposition were concerned with leftist actions undertaken by Goulart, including his radical agrarian reform plan and his refusal to break a strike by naval enlisted officers. Convinced he was planning to instigate a leftist dicta-torship, the military staged a rebellion and Goulart went into exile. For the military and conser-

vatives, the coup was necessary to restore order; they called the action the "Revolution of 1964." At first the coup was supported by the middle class, whom Goulart had alienated with his radical reforms. The leaders of the rebellion who took charge of the government instituted drastic reforms to counteract Goulart's actions, swinging the government strongly to the right. Soon after the fall of Goulart, the new regime began mass arrests of those suspected of subversion or communist activities and suspended the political rights of former government officials. In the years to come, as random arrests, censorship, and torture began to be a part of daily life under the dictatorship, very few still believed that the coup was a revolution and that the military government was a temporary one. Democracy was eventually restored, but the nation was governed by a series of military officials for twenty one years. These were: Humberto Castelo Branco (1964–1967), Artur Costa e Silva (1967–1969), Emílio Garrastazú Medici (1969–1974), Ernesto Geisel (1974–1979), and João Baptista de Oliveira Figueiredo (1979–1985). In 1985, the military regime relinquished its control and democracy was restored.

43. As quoted in Margarida Autran, " 'Renascimento' e descaracterização do choro," in *Anos 70*, vol. 1, *Música Popular* (Rio de Janeiro: Europa, 1980), 68.

44. The *Real* Plan was the brainchild of Fernando Henrique Cardoso, finance minister under President Itamar Franco. Cardoso ran for president in 1995 and won the election, largely on the success of the *Real* Plan.

45. FUNARTE, the National Foundation of Art (Fundação Nacional de Arte) was created in 1975 as a division of the Ministry of Education and Culture. The agency was responsible for the research into, promotion of, and support of the areas of popular and classical music and the visual and plastic arts. The agency was disbanded by President Collor in 1990, and its activities were assumed by the Brazilian Institute of Art and Culture (IBAC), a division of the Secretary of Culture of the Presidency of the Republic (which again became the Ministry of Education and Culture in 1992). In 1994, the IBAC assumed the name FUNARTE.

EMBRAFILME, a national foundation supporting Brazilian filmmakers (Empresa Brasileira de Filmes), was established in 1969. It was dissolved in 1990.

46. FUNARJ is a state government department that funds and promotes artistic and cultural affairs within the state of Rio de Janeiro. In 1960, the nation's capital moved from Rio de Janeiro to Brasília. At that time the Federal District within the state of Rio de Janeiro became the state of Guanabara. In 1975 the state of Guanabara merged with and became part of the state of Rio de Janeiro, and FUNARJ was established as part of the new state government.

47. The term "*axé* music" refers to Afro-Bahian popular music.

8. Contemporary Choro

1. Jacó do Bandolim, interview by Ricardo Cravo Albim, Sergio Bittencourt, and Sergio Cabral, Archive of Jacob Bittencourt, Museu da Imagem e do Som, Rio de Janeiro, 1967.

2. Pedro Amorim, interview by Tamara Livingston, Rio de Janeiro, September 19, 1995.

3. Valdinha Barbosa and Anne Marie Devos, *Radamés Gnattali: o eterno experimentador* (Rio de Janeiro: FUNARTE, 1985), 67–68.

4. Ozeas Duarte and Paulo Baia, "Choro: continuidade e renovação: entrevista com Maurício Carrilho," *Teoria & Debate* 37 (Feb/Mar/Apr 1998).

5. Pedro Amorim, interview by Tamara Livingston-Isenhour, Rio de Janeiro, September 10, 1995.

6. Luciana Rabello, electronic mail interview by Tamara Livingston-Isenhour, October 1, 1998.

7. As quoted in Duarte and Baia, "Choro: continuidade e renovação."

8. As quoted in Ozeas Duarte and Paulo Baia, "Choro: continuidade e renovação."

Others have noted the similarities between choro and ragtime. See especially Thomas Garcia's dissertation on the history of choro, "The Brazilian Choro: Music, Politics and Performance" (Ph.D. diss., Duke University, 1997). Garcia does an extensive social and musical comparison of ragtime and choro.

9. The Sharp Prize is an award given by a Japanese company, Sharp Electronics, a major company in Brazil, for the best new music recording in several categories including popular and classical music.

10. *Trio elétrico* refers to music traditionally played on electric instruments aboard a flatbed truck during Carnaval in Bahia.

11. This trend parallels the direction taken by Brazilian instrumental music in general. Although there is still a concern about remaining true to one's national identity, it is no longer the primary preoccupation. For more, see Andrew Connell, "Jazz brasileiro?: Música Instrumental Brasileira and the Representation of Identity in Rio de Janeiro" (Ph.D. diss., University of California Los Angeles, 2001).

12. http://www.tirapoeira.hpg.ig.com.br/TPgrupo.htm.

13. Tamara Livingston-Isenhour, personal communication with organizer Tânia Amorim of MIS, Rio de Janeiro, November 24, 1995.

14. Enor Paiano, "Gov't Plan May Hinder Brazil's Music Industry," *Billboard* 109 (Nov. 29, 1997): 1+.

15. For example, Eldorado contracted with Sony for distribution.

16. Marisa Monte, *Rose & Charcoal (Verde Anil Amarelo Cor de Rosa e Carvão)*, Blue Note Records, 5GYB (1994). Época de Ouro participated on Arnaldo Antunes's "De Mais Ninguém."

17. Interview with Mario de Aratanha. See also Kuarup website, http://www.kuarup.com.br/sitekuarup/index.asp.

18. *Villa por chorões;* Various Artists, Kuarup KCD166.

19. This recording was also released in the United States as *Rio Nights* on the Milan label, CD 73138 35648-2 (1993).

20. Quoted on the Kuarup website, http://www.kuarup.com.br.

21. Thomas Garcia was the North American contributor to the magazine.

22. Charles Perrone, " 'Chiclete com Banana': Internationalization in Brazilian Popular Music," in *Brazilian Popular Music and Globalization,* ed. Charles A. Perrone and Christopher Dunn (New York: Routledge, 2002), 7.

23. Teldec Classics International 3984-25736-2 and Teldec Classics International 0630-19899-2, respectively.

24. Concord Picante CCD-4320.

25. From Mike Marshall's website, http://www.mikemarshall.net/bio.html.

26. *Obrigado Brazil,* Sony Classical CD SK89935 (2003). Most of the arrangements are by Jorge Calandrelli.

27. Korman maintains a website at http://www.cliffkorman.com.

28. From the website http://www.chorotime.com. Accessed Spring 2004.

9. Choro and the Brazilian Classical Tradition

1. Sivuca (Severino Dias de Oliveira), interview by Thomas Garcia, Rio de Janeiro, January 3, 1995.

2. E. Bradford Burns, *A History of Brazil* (New York: Columbia University Press, 1993), 201.

3. Gerard H. Béhague, "Popular Musical Currents in the Art Music of the Early Nationalistic Period in Brazil, circa 1870–1920" (Ph.D. diss., Tulane University, 1966).

4. José Martiniano de Alencar, *O Guaraní: romance brasileiro* (Rio de Janeiro: B. L. Garnier, 1901); *Ubirajara* (São Paulo: Editora Atica, 1993); *Iracema: lenda do Ceará* (São Paulo: Editora FTD, 1991).

5. Mário de Andrade lists a number of other dances that were influenced by Amerindian culture, including the cateretê, the cururu, the cabloquihos, and the caiapós. He cites the nasal vocal quality used in the caipira (the rural areas of central Brazil) singing voice and a variety of subjects for songs (in contrast to the domination of love songs in the Portuguese tradition) as Amerindian influences. The fetishist rituals with a large musical component (catimbó, pajelança) of Amerindian culture was another inspiration. The movement of vocal lines probably arises from the influence of Gregorian chant that the Indians learned from the priests. Cited in Oneyda Alvarenga, *Música popular brasileira, coleção o baile das quatro artes* (São Paulo: Livraria Duas Cidades, 1982), 13.

6. For two landmark English-language studies of the music and culture of indigenous peoples in Brazil, see Ellen Basso, *A Musical View of the Universe: Kalapalo Myth and Ritual Performance* (Philadelphia: University of Pennsylvania Press, 1985); and Anthony Seeger, *Why Suyá Sing: A Musical Anthropology of an Amazonian People* (Cambridge: Cambridge University Press, 1987).

7. In subsequent years, this label was used quite often on instrumental pieces (usually salon versions of choro or lundu) that were influence by or suggested African-based popular music.

8. The most famous *quilombo* was Quilombo das Palmares, which existed as a self-governing entity for more than 100 years.

9. Béhague suggests that the importance of this piece has been overestimated, in part because it was the only nationalistic piece by an amateur composer who had little influence on later nationalist developments in Brazil. Béhague, "Popular Music Currents," 169.

10. Béhague, "Popular Music Currents," 195.

11. Music by Brazilian composers Leopoldo Miguez (1850–1902), Henrique Oswald (1852–1923), Francisco Braga (1868–1945), João Gomes de Araújo (1846–1943), Barroso Neto (1881–1941), and Glauco Velásquez (1884–1914) was featured in these concerts.

12. Hermínio Bello de Carvalho, *O canto de pajé: Villa-Lobos e a música popular brasileira* (Rio de Janeiro: Espaço e Tempo, 1988), 152.

13. Quoted by Vasco Mariz in *Heitor Villa-Lobos: Life and Work of the Brazilian Composer* (Washington, D.C.: Brazilian American Cultural Institute, 1970), 64.

14. Recorded by Hermínio Bello de Carvalho, cited by Turíbio Santos, *Heitor Villa-Lobos e o violão* (Rio de Janeiro: Museu Villa-Lobos, 1975), 17.

15. Miguel Jose Rodrigues Viera, *Indocador dos accordos para violão* (Pernambuco: Typographo Imparcial da Viuva Roma, 1851); and José Antonio Pelsoa de Barros, *Methodo de violão (guia material) para qualquer pessoa aprender em muito pouco tempo independente de mestre e sem conhecimento algum de música* (Rio de Janeiro: H. Laemmert, c. 1880).

16. Bruno Kiefer, *Música e dança popular: sua influência na música erudita* (Porto Alegre: Editora Movimento, 1979), 34.

17. Adhemar Nóbrega, *Os choros de Villa-Lobos* (Rio de Janeiro: Museu Villa-Lobos 1973), 102.

18. Carvalho, *O canto do pajé*, 30.

19. *Villa-Lobos O Interprete,* Museu Villa-Lobos/Ministério da Cultura, Album MVL-002.

20. Carvalho, *O canto do pajé*, 162.

21. *Distribuiçã das flores* is rarely performed with the choral parts.

22. Santos, *Heitor Villa-Lobos e o violão*, 8.

23. Carvalho, *O canto do pajé*, 154.

24. For example, the *Bachianas brasileiras No. 5* was recorded by legendary chorões on the recording *Noites Cariocas: os maiores do choro ao vivo no Municipal* (Kuarup KCD040).

25. Olga Praguer Coelho, "The Guitar in Brazil . . . and Some Reminiscences," *Guitar Review* 22 (1958): 16–17.

26. Published in *Guitar Review* 21 (1957): 11–13. Praguer Coelho was a friend of the Augustines, the publishers of *Guitar Review.*

27. Heitor Villa-Lobos, *Modinha* (Paris: Editions Max Eschig, 1975).

28. Vasco Mariz, *Heitor Villa-Lobos.*

29. Simon Wright, *Villa-Lobos* (Oxford: Oxford University Press, 1992), 61.

30. Lamberto Baldi (1895–1979) was an Italian composer conductor and teacher who had studied in Paris with Isador Philip. Much of his career was spent in Uruguay and Brazil, where he was music director of the Orquestra Sinfónica do Brasil.

31. Mário Tavares, *Globo,* February 20, 1986.

32. Ricardo Tacuchian, explanatory notes in sheet music of "Festas da Igreja da Penha."

Bibliography

Adamo, Sam. "Race and Povo." In *Modern Brazil: Elites and Masses in Historical Perspective,* ed. Michael L. Conniff and Frank D. McCann. Lincoln: University of Nebraska Press, 1989.

Alencar, Edigar de. *O carnaval carioca através da música.* 2 vols. Rio de Janeiro: Freitos Bastos, 1965.

————. *O fabuloso e harmonioso Pixinguinha.* Rio de Janeiro: Cátedra, 1979.

————. *Nosso Sinhô do samba.* 2nd ed. Rio de Janeiro: FUNARTE, 1981.

Alencar, José Martiniano de. *O Guarany: romance brasileiro.* Rio de Janeiro: B. L. Garnier, 1901.

————. *Iracema: Lenda do Ceará.* São Paulo: Editora FTD, 1991. First published in 1865.

————. *Ubirajara.* São Paulo: Editora Ática, 1993. First published in 1874.

Almeida, Renato. *Compéndio de história da música brasileira.* Rio de Janeiro: F. Briguiet, 1956.

————. *História da música brasileira.* Rio de Janeiro: F. Briguiet, 1942.

Almirante. *No tempo de Noel Rosa.* 2nd ed. Rio de Janeiro: Francisco Alves, 1977.

Alvarenga, Oneyda. *Música popular brasileira.* Rio de Janeiro: Globo, 1950.

————. *Música popular brasileira, coleção o baile das quatro artes.* São Paulo: Livraria Duas Cidades, 1982.

Andrade, A. C. *Methodo para violão: com 24 tons e duas inversões em cada ton.* Rio de Janeiro: Cavaquinho de Ouro, 1930.

Andrade, Mário de. *Aspectos da música brasileira.* São Paulo: Martins, 1965.

————. *Danças dramaticas do Brasil.* São Paulo: Martins, 1959.

————. *Dicionário musical brasileiro.* Belo Horizonte: Itatiaia, 1989.

————. *Ensaio sobre a música brasileira.* Brasília: Martins:MEC, 1972.

————. *Modinhas imperiais.* Belo Horizonte: Itatiaia, 1930.

————. *Música, doce música.* São Paulo: Editora Martins/ Instituto Nacional do Livro, 1976.

Andrade, Oswald de. *Obras completas.* Vol. 6. Rio de Janeiro: Civilização Brasileira, 1978.

————. *Anos 70.* 7 vols. Rio de Janeiro: Europa Editora, 1980.

Antonio, Irati, and Regina Pereira. *Garoto: sinal dos tempos.* Rio de Janeiro: FUNARTE, 1982.

Anunciação, Luiz Almeida da. *A percussão dos ritmos brasileiros: pandeiro.* Rio de Janeiro: Escola Brasileira de Música, n.d.

Appleby, David P. *Heitor Villa-Lobos: A Bio-bibliography.* Bio-bibliographies in Music no. 9. New York: Greenwood Press, 1988.

————. *The Music of Brazil.* Austin: University of Texas Press, 1989.

Aragão, Diana, and Lena Frias. "Com sotaque e giria." *O Jornal do Brasil,* September 2, 1977.

Aranha, Graça. *Canaã.* Rio de Janeiro: H. Garnier, 1901.

Araújo, Mozart de. *A modinha e o lundu no século XVIII: uma pesquisa histórica e bibliográfica.* São Paulo: Ricordi Brasileira, 1963.

————. "Ernesto Nazaré." *Revista brasileira de cultura* 4, no. 14 (1972): 13–28.

————. *Preservação da cultura violonística do Ceará.* Fortaleza, Brazil: Imprensa Oficial do Ceará, 1986.

228 ————. *Rapsódia brasileira: textos reunidos de um militante do nacionalism o musical.* Fortaleza, Ceará: Universidade Estadual do Ceará, 1994.

Araújo, Samuel Mello, Jr. "Acoustic Labor in the Timing of Everyday Life: A Critical Contribution to the History of Samba in Rio de Janeiro." Ph.D. diss., University of Illinois at Urbana-Champaign, 1992.

Autran, Margarida. " 'Renascimento' e descaracterização do choro. " In *Anos 70,* vol. 1, *Música popular.* Rio de Janeiro: Europa, 1980.

————. "Samba, artigo de consumo nacional." In *Anos 70,* vol. 1, *Música popular.* Rio de Janeiro: Europa, 1980.

Azevedo, Fernando. *Segrédo do acompanhamento.* 12th ed. Rio de Janeiro: Edições Fernando Azevedo, n.d.

Bahiana, Ana Maria. "A 'linha evolutiva' prossegue—a música dos universitários." In *Anos 70,* vol. 1, *Música popular.* Rio de Janeiro: Europa, 1980.

————. "Importação e assimilação: rock, soul, discotheque." In *Anos 70,* vol. 1, *Música popular.* Rio de Janeiro: Europa, 1980.

————. "Música instrumental—o caminho do improviso brasileiro." In *Anos 70,* vol. 1, *Música popular.* Rio de Janeiro: Europa, 1980.

Bandeira, Manuel. "Literatura de violão." *Ariel* II, no. XIII (1924): 463–468.

————. "Literatura de violão." *Revista de música popular* 12 (April 1956): 8–10.

Barbosa, Orestes. *Samba: sua história, seus poetas, seus músicos e seus cantores.* Rio de Janeiro: FUNARTE, 1933.

Barbosa, Valdinha, and Anne Marie Devos. *Radamés Gnattali: o eterno experimentador.* Rio de Janeiro: FUNARTE, 1985.

Barbosa da Silva, Marília T. "Pelos caminhos do choro." In *Notas musicais cariocas,* ed. João Baptista M. Vargens. Petrópolos: Vozes, 1986.

Barbosa da Silva, Marília T., and Arthur L. de Oliveira Filho. *Filho de ogum bexiguento.* Rio de Janeiro: FUNARTE, 1979.

————. *Paulo da Portela: traço de união entre duas culturas.* Rio de Janeiro: FUNARTE, 1979.

Barrense-Dias, Jose, ed. *Les guitaristes bresiliens: pour guitare.* Vols. 1 and 2. Paris: Editions Musicales Transatlantique, 1976.

Barros, José Antonio Pelsoa de. *Methodo de violão (guia material) para qualquer pessoa aprender em muito pouco tempo independente de mestre e sem conhecimento algum de música.* Rio de Janeiro: H. Laemmert, n.d. (c. 1900).

Barroso, Manoel Antonio. "Bide: da Velha Guarda aos Chorões de Brasilia." *Cultura* 8, no. 29 (1978): 18–19, 20–29.

Basso, Ellen. *A Musical View of the Universe: Kalapalo Myth and Ritual Performance.* Philadelphia: University of Pennsylvania Press, 1985.

Bastide, Roger. *African Civilizations in the New World.* New York: Harper & Row, 1971.

Batista, Marta Rossetti, Telé Porto Ancona Lopez, and Yone Soares de Lima, eds. *Brasil: primeiro tempo modernista-1917/29: documentação.* São Paulo: Instituto de Estudos Brasileiros, 1972.

Béhague, Gérard. *The Beginnings of Musical Nationalism in Brazil.* Detroit Monographs in Musicology no. 1. Detroit: Information Coordinators, 1972.

————. "Biblioteca da Ajuda (Lisbon) MSS 1595/1596: Two Eighteenth-Century Anonymous Collections of Modinhas." *Yearbook Interamerican Institute for Musical Research* (1968): 44–81.

————. "Bossa and Bossas—Recent Changes in Brazilian Urban Popular Music." *Ethnomusicology* 17, no. 2 (1973): 209–233.

————. "Brazilian Musical Values of the 1960s and 1970s: Popular Urban Music from Bossa Nova to Tropicália." *Journal of Popular Culture* 13, no. 3 (1980): 47–452.

————. *Heitor Villa-Lobos: The Search for the Brazilian Musical Soul.* Austin: University of Texas Press, 1994.

————. *Music in Latin America: An Introduction.* Englewood, N.J.: Prentice-Hall, 1979.

————. "Notes on Regional and National Trends in Afro-Brazilian Cult Music." In *Tradition and Renewal,* ed. Merlin H. Forster. Urbana: University of Illinois Press, 1975.

————. "Popular Musical Currents in the Art Music of the Early Nationalistic Period in Brazil, circa 1870–1920." Ph.D. diss., Tulane University, 1966.

Berliner, Paul. *Thinking in Jazz: The Infinite Art of Improvisation.* Chicago: University of Chicago Press, 1994.

Bispo, Antonio Alexandre. "O Século XIX na pesquisa histórico-musical brasileira: necessidade de sua reconsideração." *Latin American Music Review* 2 (Spring 1981): 131–142.

Boff, Ruy Celso. "Les 'Choros' de Heitor Villa-Lobos (1887–1959)—La 'Transfiguration' de l'élément populaire." Licence, Université Catholique de Louvain (Institut Superieur d'Archeologie et d'Histoire de l'Art), n.d.

Bonfim, Manoel. *A America Latina.* 2nd ed. Rio de Janeiro: A. Noite, 1939.

Borges, Beatriz. *Música popular brasileira.* São Paulo: Edição Beatriz Borges, 1990.

Brandão, Assis. "O il festival da Velha Guarda." *Revista de Música Popular* 7 (1955): 20–23.

Britto, Jomard Muniz de. *Do modernismo à bossa nova.* Rio de Janeiro: Civilização Brasileira, 1966.

Brody, Elaine. *Paris: The Musical Kaleidoscope 1870–1925.* New York: George Braziller, 1987.

Burdick, John. "Brazil's Black Consciousness Movement." *Report on the Americas* 24, no. 4 (1992): 23–29.

Burns, E. Bradford. *A History of Brazil.* 3rd ed. New York: Columbia University Press, 1993.

Cabral, Sérgio. *ABC do Sergio Cabral: um desfile dos craques da M.P.B.* Rio de Janeiro: Codecri, 1979.

————. *No tempo de Almirante: uma história do rádio e da MPB.* Rio de Janeiro: Francisco Alves, 1988.

————. *No tempo de Ari Barroso.* Rio de Janeiro: Lumiar, 1990.

————. *Pixinguinha: vida e obra.* Rio de Janeiro: FUNARTE, 1978.

————. "Um som que sobrevive sem fazer conçesões a tecnologia." *O Estado de São Paulo,* September 17, 1995, Section 2: D-3.

Calado, Carlos. "Produtor Mapeou a Música do Pais." *Folha de São Paulo,* April 2, 1994, 5:1.

Campos, Augusto de. *Balanço da bossa.* São Paulo: Ed. Perspectiva, 1968.

Caparelli, Sergio. *Televisão e Capitalismo no Brasil.* Porto Alegre: L&PM, 1982.

Cardoso, Abel, Jr. *Carmen Miranda: a cantora do Brasil.* São Paulo: Símbolo, 1978.

Carlevaro, Abel. *Technique, Analysis and Interpretation of: The Guitar Works of Heitor Villa-Lobos; 5 Preludes [1940] Choro No. 1 [1920].* Abel Carlevaro Guitar Masterclass. Heidelberg: Chanterelle, 1987.

————. *Technique, Analysis and Interpretation of The Guitar Works of Heitor Villa-Lobos: 12 Studies.* Abel Carlevaro Guitar Masterclass. Heidelberg: Chanterelle, 1988.

Carneiro, Edison. *Carta do samba.* Rio de Janeiro: Ministério da Educação e Cultura, 1962.

————. *Samba de Umbigada.* Rio de Janeiro: Ministério da Educação e Cultura, 1961.

Carrilho, Maurício. "Camuflagem do genero e recurso comum." *O Estado de São Paulo,* Sept. 17, 1995, section B.

————. "O Choro e a modernidade: o choro vai Muito Bem, obrigado. . . ." *Roda de Choro,* Nov.–Dec. 1995, 7–10.

Carvalho, Hermínio Bello de. *O canto do pajé: Villa-Lobos e a música popular brasileira.* Rio de Janeiro: Espaço e Tempo, 1988.

Carvalho, Luiz Fernando Medeiros de. *Ismael Silva: samba e resistência.* Rio de Janeiro: José Olympio, 1980.

Cazes, Henrique. *Escola moderna do cavaquinho*. Rio de Janeiro: Lumiar, 1998.

———. "Radio e a fixação do 'regional.' " *Roda de Choro* 5, no. 13 (1997).

Chaves, Edgard de Brito, Jr., and Enos da Costa Palma. *As Bachianas brasileiras de Villa-Lobos*. Rio de Janeiro: Companhia Editora Americana, 1971.

Coelho, Olga (Prauger). "The Guitar in Brazil . . . and Some Reminiscences." *Guitar Review* 22 (1958): 16–18.

Conrad, Robert Edgar. *Children of God's Fire: A Documentary History of Black Slavery in Brazil*. Princeton, N.J.: Princeton University Press, 1983.

———. *The Destruction of Brazilian Slavery, 1850–1888*. Berkeley: University of California Press, 1972.

———. *World of Sorrow: The African Slave Trade to Brazil*. Baton Rouge: Louisiana State University Press, 1986.

Corrêa de Azavedo, Luiz Heitor. *150 anos de música no Brasil (1800–1950)*. Rio de Janeiro: Livraria José Olympio Editora, 1956.

———. "O compositor Latino-Americano e o universo sonoro deste fim de século." *Latin American Music Review* 7 (Fall/Winter 1986): 249–253.

———. "Music and Musicians of African Origin in Brazil." *World of Music* 24 (1982): 53–63.

———. *A música brasileira e seus fundamentos*. Translated by Elizabeth M. Taylor and Mercedes de Noura Reis. Washington, D.C.: Pan American Union/ Division of Music and Visual Arts, Department of Cultural Affairs, 1948.

Coutinho, Carlos Nelson. "Cultura e democracia no Brasil." *Encontros com a Civilização Brasileira* 17 (1979).

Crook, Larry N. "Black Consciousness, Samba Reggae, and the Re-Africanization of Carnival Music in Brazil." *The World of Music* 35, no. 2 (1993): 90–106.

Degler, Carl N. *Neither Black nor White: Slavery and Race Relations in Brazil and the United States*. Madison: University of Wisconsin Press, 1986.

Doderer, Gerhard, ed. *Modinhas Luso-Brasileiras*. Portugaliae Musica, vol. 44. Lisbon: Fundação Calouste Gulbenkian, 1984.

Druesedow, John. *The Chamber Works for Wind Instruments by Villa-Lobos*. Bloomington: Latin American Music Center, Indiana University, 1963.

Duarte, Ozeas, and Paulo Baia. "Choro: continuidade e renovação : entrevista com Maurício Carrilho." *Teoria & Debate* 37 (Feb./Mar./Apr. 1998).

Dulles, John W. F. *Vargas of Brazil: A Political Biography*. Austin: University of Texas Press 1962.

Echevarria, Regina. "The Same Old Choro: For Now, Nothing New. What Will Follow?" *Veja*, October 11, 1978.

Efegê, Jota [João Ferreira Gomes]. *Figuras e coisas da música popular brasileira*. Rio de Janeiro: FUNARTE, 1978.

———. *Maxixe—a dança excomungada*. Rio de Janeiro: Conquista, 1974.

Eneida. *História do carnaval carioca*. Rio de Janeiro: Civilização Brasileira, 1958.

Epaminondas, Antonio. *Brasil brasileirinho*. Rio de Janeiro: Livraria Editora Cátedra, 1982.

Evans, Peter. *Dependent Development: The Alliance of Multinational, State, and Local Capital in Brazil*. Princeton, N.J.: Princeton University Press, 1979.

Fabiano, Ruy. "Os carioquinhos no choro." LP liner notes. Rio de Janeiro: Som Livre.

———. "Os novos chorões: os jovens descobrem no choro o jazz brasileiro." *Jornal de Música e Som* (November 11, 1976): 5–6.

Faria, Nelson. *The Brazilian Guitar Book*. Petaluma: Sher Music, 1995.

Faria, Nelson, and Cliff Korman. *Inside the Brazilian Rhythm Section*. Petaluma: Sher Music, 2001.

Feintuch, Burt. "Musical Revival as Musical Transformation." In *Transforming Tradition: Folk Music Revivals Examined*, ed. Neil Rosenberg. Urbana: University of Illinois Press, 1993.

Feith, Roberto. "Villa-Lobos: O Indio de Casaca." Rio de Janeiro: Manchete Video, 1980.

Fernandes, Roberto. "Brasília, Capital do Choro: Quando os Chorões Buscam bons Empregos." *Jornal do Brasil*, August 12, 1983, section B.

Fink, Siegfried. *Percussion Brasil*. Frankfort: Zimmerman, 1978.

Fleischmann, Hugo R. "É música contemporanea a expressão do nosso tempo?" *Revista Brasileira de Música* VI, no 1 (1939): 21–28.

Francesci, Humbert M. *A Casa Edison e seu tempo*. Rio de Janeiro: Sarapuí, 2003.

Freitag, Léa Vinocur. *Momentos de música brasileira*. São Paulo: Nobel, 1985.

Freitas e Castro, Enio de. "Em Caminho para a música brasileira." *Boletim Latino Americano de Musica* II (1936): 163–167.

Freyre, Gilberto. *Casa-grande e senzala*. Rio de Janeiro: Editora Record, 1992.

———. *The Masters and the Slaves (Casa-grande & senzala): A Study in the Development of Brazilian Civilization*. New York: Knopf, 1946.

———. *Ordem e progresso*. Rio de Janeiro: Livraria José Olympio Editora, 1962.

Fryer, Peter. *Rhythms of Resistance: African Musical Heritage in Brazil*. Hanover, N.H.: University Press of New England for Wesleyan University Press, 2000.

Galinsky, Philip. "Co-option, Cultural Resistance, and Afro-Brazilian Identity: A History of the Pagode Samba Movement in Rio de Janeiro." *Latin American Music Review* 17, no. 2 (1995): 120–149.

Garcia, Thomas George Caracas. "The Brazilian Choro: Music, Politics and Performance." Ph.D. diss., Duke University, 1997.

———. "Villa-Lobos and the Guitar: Perspectives on the Early Guitar Music." Master's thesis, University of Massachusetts, 1991.

Gilman, Bruce. "Choro, chorinho, chorão." *Brazzil* (electronic magazine), February 1996. Available online at http://www.brazzil.com/musfeb96.htm.

———. "Crying High: Choro with a Mike Marshall Taste." *Brazzil* (electronic magazine), November 1997. Available online at http://www.brazzil.com/musnov97.htm.

Gil-Montero, Martha. *Brazilian Bombshell: The Biography of Carmen Miranda*. New York: Donald I. Fine, 1989.

Gobineau, Arthur, comte de. *Essai sur l'inégalité des races humaines*. 4th ed. Paris: Librairie de Paris, 1900.

Goldwasser, Maria Julia. *Palácio do samba*. Rio de Janeiro: n.p., 1975.

Gomes, Lu. "Jovem Guarda." *Som Tres* 81 (September 1985): 97–98.

Guilbault, Jocelyne. "On Redefining the 'Local' through World Music." *The World of Music* 35, no. 2 (1993): 33–47.

Haberly, David T. *Three Sad Races: Racial Identity and National Consciousness in Brazilian Literature*. Cambridge: Cambridge University Press, 1983.

Hahner, June E. *Poverty and Politics: The Urban Poor in Brazil, 1870–1920*. Albuquerque: University of New Mexico Press, 1986.

Hamm, Charles. *Putting Popular Music in Its Place*. Cambridge: Cambridge University Press, 1995.

Henriques, Affonso. *Ascensão e queda de Getúlio Vargas*. Vol. 2, *Vargas e o Estado Novo*. Rio de Janeiro: Record, 1966.

Herold, Cacilda M. "The 'Brazilianization' of Brazilian Television: A Critical Review." *Studies in Latin American Popular Culture* 7 (1988): 41–58.

Holanda, Nestor. *Memórias do Café Nice: subterrâneo da música popular e da vida boêmia do Rio de Janeiro*. Rio de Janeiro: Conquista, 1969.

Ianni, Octavio. *A ideia de Brasil moderno*. São Paulo: Brasiliense, 1992.

232   Itiberê, Brasilio. "A Obra de Villa-Lobos e o problema folclórico." *Música Viva* 1 (January–February 1941): 4–5.

J., C. "Flauta e violão." *Ariel* Anno 2 (February 1925): 24–25.

Jacomino, Americo (Canhoto). *Methodo prático de violão: dedicado aos meus discipulos, contendo todas as tonalidades e acompanhando com sete acordes em cada tom (nova edição).* Rio de Janeiro: A Guitarra de Prata, n.d. (c. 1925).

Jansen, David A., and Trebor Jay Tichenor. *Rags and Ragtime: A Musical History.* New York: Dover, 1978.

Johnson, Randal. *The Film Industry in Brazil: Culture and the State.* Pittsburgh: University of Pittsburgh Press, 1987.

———. "Popular Culture and the Political Transition in Brazil." *Studies in Latin American Popular Culture* 7 (1988): 1–16.

———. "Regarding the Philanthropic Ogre: Cultural Policy in Brazil, 1930–45/1964–90." In *Constructing Culture and Power in Latin America,* ed. Daniel H. Levine. Ann Arbor: University of Michigan Press, 1993.

Johnson, Randal, and Robert Stam, eds. *Brazilian Cinema.* Rutherford, N.J.: Fairleigh Dickinson University Press, 1982.

Kehl, Maria Rita. "As novelas, novelinhas e novelões: mil e uma noites para as multidões." In *Anos 70,* vol. 5, *Televisão.* Rio de Janeiro: Europa, 1980.

———. "Um só povo, uma só cabeça, uma só nação." In *Anos 70,* vol. 5, *Televisão.* Rio de Janeiro: Europa, 1980.

Kiefer, Bruno. *Música e dança popular: sua influência na música erudita.* Porto Alegre: Editora Movimento, 1979.

———. *Villa-Lobos e o modernismo na música brasileira.* Porto Alegre: Editora Movimento, 1986.

Krich, John. *Why Is This Country Dancing? One-Man Samba to the Beat of Brazil.* New York: Simon & Schuster, 1993.

Kubik, Gerhard. *Angolan Traits in Black Music, Games and Dances of Brazil: A Study of African Cultural Extension Overseas.* Lisbon: Junta de Investigações Científicas do Ultramar, 1979.

———. "Drum Patterns in the 'Batuque' of Benedito Caxias." *Latin American Music Review* 11 (December 1990): 115–181.

Lange, Francisco Curt. "A organização musical durante o período colonial brasileiro." In *Actas do V Colóquio Internacional de Estudos Luso-Brasileiros.* Coimbra, 1966.

Lange, Humberto. *Violão é facil.* São Paulo: Fermata do Brasil, 1963.

Lapouge, Georges Vacher de. *L'Aryen: son rôle social.* Paris: A. Fontemoing, 1899.

Lauerhass, Ludwig, Jr. *Getúlio Vargas e o triunfo do nacionalismo brasileiro.* Belo Horizonte: Itatiaia, 1986.

Leal, José de Souza, and Artur Luiz Barbosa. *João Pernambuco: arte de um povo.* Rio de Janeiro: FUNARTE, 1982.

Leite, Dante Moreira. *O carater nacional brasileiro: história de uma ideologia.* 4th ed. São Paulo: Pioneira, 1982.

Levine, Robert M. "Elite Conceptions of the Povo." In *Modern Brazil: Elites and Masses in Historical Perspective,* ed. Michael L. Conniff and Frank D. McCann. Lincoln: University of Nebraska Press, 1989.

———. "Elite Intervention in Urban Popular Culture in Modern Brazil." *Luso-Brazilian Review* 21, no. 2 (1984): 9–22.

Lima, Luis Felipe de. "Os instrumentos no choro: violão de 7." *Roda de Choro* 2 (1996): 6.

Lira, Mariza. *Chiquinha Gonzaga: grande compositora popular brasileira.* 2nd ed. Rio de Janeiro: FUNARTE, 1978.

Livingston, Tamara. "Brazilian Choro as Participatory Music." Paper presented at the Society for Ethnomusicology, Pittsburgh, Pennsylvania, October 1997.

———. "Choro and Music Revivalism in Rio de Janeiro, 1973–1995." Ph.D. diss., University of Illinois at Urbana-Champaign, 1999.

———. "Music Revivals: Towards a General Theory." *Ethnomusicology* 43, no. 1 (Winter 1999): 66–85.

Lopes, Nei. *O negro no Rio de Janeiro e sua tradição musical.* Rio de Janeiro: Pallas, 1992.

Lyra, Abdon. *O Carioca: Methodo pratico de violão (Contendo todos os tons com posições claras ao alcance de todos que desejam aprender sem professor).* Rio de Janeiro: n.d. (c. 1925).

———. *Methodo prático para aprender a tocar o violão sem mestre.* Rio de Janeiro: I. Bevilacqua, n.d. (c. 1930).

Machado, Afonso. *Método do bandolim brasileira.* Rio de Janeiro: Escola Brasileira de Música, 1986.

Machado, Maria Cecilia. *H. Villa-Lobos; Tradição e renovação na música brasileira.* Rio de Janeiro: Francisco Alves, 1987.

Marcondes, Marco Antonio. *Enciclopédia da musica brasileira: erudita, folclórica e popular.* 2 vols. São Paulo: Art Editora, 1977.

Mariz, Vasco. "As canções de Villa-Lobos." *Revista de Academia Nacional de Música* 1 (1990): 15–24.

———. *Heitor Villa-Lobos: compositor brasileiro.* 6th ed. Rio de Janeiro: Ministério da Cultura, Museu Villa-Lobos, 1978.

———. *Heitor Villa-Lobos: el nacionalismo musical brasileño.* Bogota, Columbia: Siglo Veintiuno Editores, 1987.

———. *Heitor Villa-Lobos: Life and Work of the Brazilian Composer.* Washington, D.C.: Brazilian American Cultural Institute, 1970.

———. *História da música no Brasil.* Brasilia: MEC, 1981.

Masur, Gerhard. *Nationalism in Latin America: Diversity and Unity.* New York: Macmillan, 1966.

Matos, Claudia. *Acertei no milhar: malandragem e samba no tempo de Getúlio.* Rio de Janeiro: Paz e Terra, 1982.

Máximo, João and Carlos Didier. *Noel Rosa: uma biografia.* Brasília: Universidade de Brasília, 1990.

McGowan, Chris, and Ricardo Pessanha. *The Brazilian Sound: Samba, Bossa Nova and the Popular Music of Brazil.* Philadelphia: Temple University Press, 1998.

Monson, Ingrid. *Saying Something: Jazz Improvisation and Interaction.* Chicago: University of Chicago Press, 1996.

Moog, Vianna. *Bandeirantes and Pioneers.* Translated by L. L. Barrett. New York: George Braziller, 1964.

Moraes, Raul de. "Francisco Mignone." *Ariel* 11 (August 1924): 395–397.

Morais, Eduardo Jardim de. *A Brasilidade modernista: sua dimensão filosófica.* Rio de Janeiro: Edições Graal, 1978.

Mota, Carlos Guilherme. *Ideologia da cultura brasileira: pontos de partida para uma revisão histórica.* São Paulo: Atica, 1977.

Moura, Roberto. *Tia Ciata e a pequena África no Rio de Janeiro.* Rio de Janeiro: FUNARTE, 1982.

Mukuna, Dazadi wa. *Contribuão Bantu na música popular brasileira.* São Paulo: Global Editora, 1976.

Muniz, Jose, Jr. *Do Batuque a escola de samba: asubsidios para a história do samba.* São Paulo: Edições Simbolo, 1976.

234   Muricy, Andrade. "Villa-Lobos." *Bulletin of the Pan American Union* 79 (January 1945): 1–9.

Museu da Imagem e do Som. *As vozes desassombradas do museu: ciclo de música popular brasileira, 1: Pixinguinha—João da Baiana—Donga*. Rio de Janeiro: MIS, 1970.

———. Typescript of interview of Jacob Bittencourt, conducted by Ricardo Cravo Albim, Sergio Bittencourt, and Sergio Cabral. Archive of Jacob Bittencourt, Museu da Imagem e do Som, Rio de Janeiro, 1967.

Museu Villa-Lobos, ed. *Villa-Lobos: sua obra*. 3rd ed. Rio de Janeiro: Museu Villa-Lobos, 1989.

Myers, Robert. "Brazilian Popular Music in Bahia: 'The Politics of the Future.' An Interview With Gilberto Gil." *Studies in Latin American Popular Culture* 9 (1990).

Nasser, David. *Parceiro da glória: 45 anos na música popular*. Rio de Janeiro: José Olympio, 1983.

Nóbrega, Adhemar. *As Bachianas brasileiras de Villa-Lobos*. Rio de Janeiro: Museu Villa Lobos, 1971.

———. *Os choros de Villa-Lobos*. 2nd ed. Rio de Janeiro: Museu Villa-Lobos, 1973.

Nunes, Wilso da Silva. *Violão sem mestre*. Rio de Janeiro: Edições de Ouro, 1971.

Ohtake, Ricardo, ed. *Instrumentos musicais brasileiros*. Rio de Janeiro: Rhodia, 1988.

Ortiz Oderigo, Nistor. *La presencia del Negro en la música del Brasil*. Buenos Aires: Servicio de Extension Cultural, Dirección General de Obra Social, Secretaria de Estado de Obras Publicas, 1965.

Ortiz, Renato. *Cultura brasileira e identidade nacional*. São Paulo: Editora Brasiliense, 1983.

Paiano, Enor. "Brazil '97: Medium Hot: TV's Tops For Exposing New Acts." *Billboard* 109 (November 8, 1997): 50+.

———. "Brazilian Indies Flex Their Muscle." *Billboard*, October 1996, 68+.

———. "Gov't Plan May Hinder Brazil's Music Industry." *Billboard* 109 (November 29, 1997): 1+.

———. "The Recovery Gets Real." *Billboard*, December 10, 1994, 56+.

Paraguassú. *Método prático para violão sem mestre (Nova Edição)*. São Paulo: Irmãos Vitale, 1932.

———. *O serenatista: método prático para violão para aprender a tocar sem mestre*. São Paulo: Ricordi Brasileira, n.d. (c. 1930).

———. *O seresteiro: novo e completo moderno método prático para violão*. São Paulo: Fermata do Brasil, n.d. (c. 1945).

Passos, Claribalte. *Vultos e temas da música brasileira*. Rio de Janeiro: Paralelo, 1972.

Paz, Ermelinda A. *Jacob de Bandolim*. Rio de Janeiro: Funarte, 1997.

Pellegrini, Tania. "Brazil in the 1970s: Literature and Politics." *Latin American Perspectives* 21, no. 1 (1994): 56–71.

Peppercorn, Lisa. *Villa-Lobos: Collected Studies by L. M. Peppercorn*. Cambridge: Scholar Press, 1992.

———. *Villa-Lobos, the Music: An Analysis of His Style*. Translated by Stefan de Haan. White Plains, N.Y.: Kahn & Avrill, 1991.

Pereira, Marco. *Heitor Villa-Lobos: sua obra para violão*. Brasília: Editora Musimed, 1984.

Pereira, Marcus. *Música: está chegando a vez do povo 1. A história de "O Jogral."* São Paulo: HUCITEC, 1976.

Pereira, Paulo. "Pixinguinha." *Revista de Música Popular* 12 (April 1956): 22–24.

Perrone, Charles. " 'Chiclete com Banana': Internationalization in Brazilian Popular Music." In *Brazilian Popular Music and Globalization*, ed. Charles A. Perrone and Christopher Dunn, 1–38. New York: Routledge, 2002.

———. *Masters of Contemporary Brazilian Song: MPB 1965–1985*. Austin: University of Texas Press, 1989.

Perrone, Charles A., and Christopher Dunn, eds. *Brazilian Popular Music and Globalization.* New York: Routledge, 2002.

Pinto, Alexandre Gonçalves. *O choro: reminiscencias dos chorões antigos.* Rio de Janeiro: MEC, 1978. Facsimile of 1936 edition.

Pixinguinha and Donga. *As vozes desassombradas do Museu.* Rio de Janeiro: Museu da Imagem e do Som, 1970.

Priolli, Gabriel. "A Tela Pequena no Brasil Grand." In *Televisão & Video.* Rio de Janeiro: Jorge Zahar, 1985.

Rabello, Luciana. "Os instrumentos no choro: cavaquinho." *Roda de Choro* 4, no. 6 (1996).

Rangel, Lucio. *Sambistas e chorões: aspectos e figuras da música popular brasileira.* Rio de Janeiro: Francisco Alves, 1962.

Rennó, Carlos, Luiz Chagas, and J. C. Bruno, eds. *Luiz Gonzaga.* São Paulo: Martin Claret, 1990.

Ricardo, Sérgio. *Quem quebrou meu violão: uma análise da cultura brasileira nas décadas de 40 a 90.* Rio de Janeiro: Editora Record, 1991.

Roberts, John Storm. *Black Music of Two Worlds.* Tivoli, N.Y.: Original Music, 1972.

———. *The Latin Tinge: The Impact of Latin American Music on the United States.* 2nd. ed. New York: Oxford University Press, 1999.

Rocha, Jesus. "Do Ameno Resedá ao Pedacinho de Ceu." *Última Hora,* November 26, 1975, rev. 5.

Rodriques, Wilson Woodrow. *Folclore coreográfico do Brasil.* Rio de Janeiro: Publicitan Editora, 1952.

Romagnoli, Luiz Henrique. "Depois o festival, o debate: choro que te quero ou é preciso mudar?" *Jornal do Brasil,* October 28, 1978, B:4.

Ruiz, Roberto. *Araci Cortes: Linda flor.* Rio de Janeiro: FUNARTE, 1984.

Sampaio, Mario Ferraz. *Historia do rádio e da televisão no Brasil e no mundo.* Rio de Janeiro: Achiame, 1984.

Santa Cruz, Maria Aurea. *A musa sem máscara: A imagem da mulher na música popular brasileira.* Rio de Janeiro: Editora Rosas dos Tempos, 1992.

Santos, Alcino, Gracio Barbalho, Jairo Severiano, and M. A. Azevedo. *Discografia brasileira, 78 rpm, 1902–1964.* 5 vols. Rio de Janeiro: FUNARTE, 1982.

Santos, Turíbio. *Heitor Villa-Lobos and the Guitar.* Translated by Victoria Forde and Graham Wade. Gurtnacloona, Ireland: Wise Owl Music, 1985.

———. *Heitor Villa-Lobos e o violão.* Rio de Janeiro: Museu Villa-Lobos, 1975.

Sardinha, Annibal Augusto [Garoto]. *Cacique: método prático para violão.* São Paulo: Irmãos Vitale, 1943.

Saroldi, Luiz Carlos, and Sonia Virginia Moreira. *Rádio Nacional: o Brasil em sintonia.* Rio de Janeiro: Martins Fontes/FUNARTE, 1984.

Schafer, William J., and Johannes Riedel. *The Art of Ragtime: Form and Meaning of an Original Black American Art.* Baton Rouge: Louisiana State University Press, 1974.

Schneider, Ronald. *"Order and Progress": A Political History of Brazil.* Boulder, Colo.: Westview Press, 1991.

Schreiner, Claus. *Música Brasileira: A History of Popular Music and the People of Brazil.* New York: Marion Boyars, 1993.

———. *Música Popular Brasileira: Handbuch der Folkloristischen und der Popularen Musik Brasiliens.* Darmstadt: Tropical Music, 1985.

Schwarz, Roberto. *Misplaced Ideas: Essays on Brazilian Culture.* Edited by John Gledson. London: Verso, 1992.

Seeger, Anthony. *Why Suyà Sing: A Musical Anthropology of an Amazonian People.* Cambridge: Cambridge University Press, 1987.

236   Segovia, Andres. "I Meet Villa-Lobos." *Guitar Review* 22 (1958): 22–23.

Sevcenko, Nicolau. *Literatura como missão: tensões sociais e criação cultural na Primeira República.* São Paulo: Brasiliense, 1983.

Sève, Mário. *Vocabulário do choro.* Rio de Janeiro: Lumiar, 1999.

Severiano, Jairo. *Getúlio Vargas e a música popular.* Rio de Janeiro: Fundação Getúlio Vargas, 1983.

Silva, Alberto de Castro Simoens da (Bororó). *Gente da madrugada: flagrantes da vida noturna.* Rio de Janeiro: Guavira Editores, 1982.

Silva, José. Rebello da. *Methodo prático para violão.* Rio de Janeiro: Rodrigues & Cia, 1931.

Silva, Marilia T. Barboza da. "Pelos caminhos do choro." In *Notas musicais cariocas,* ed. João Baptista M. Vargens. Petrópolis: Vozes, 1986.

Silva, Marilia T. Barboza da, and Arthur L. de Oliveira Filho. *Filho de Ogum bexiguento.* Rio de Janeiro: Funarte, 1979.

Simantos, Eduardo. "Projeto resgata obra de Marcus Pereira: colaboradores do publicitário, morto em 82, reativam o trabalho de documentação de música brasileira." *Folha de São Paulo* (April 2, 1994): 5:1.

Simões, Ronoel. "The Guitar in Brazil." *Guitar Review* 22 (1958): 6–7.

Siqueira, Baptista. *Modinhas do passado.* 2nd ed. [Rio de Janeiro]: Folha Carioca, 1979.

———. *Origem do termo samba.* Rio de Janeiro: IBRASA/MEC, 1978.

———. *Três vultos históricos da musica brasileira.* Rio de Janeiro: MEC, 1969.

Skidmore, Thomas E. *Black into White: Race and Nationality in Brazilian Thought.* New York: Oxford University Press, 1974.

———. *Politics in Brazil, 1930–64.* New York: Oxford University Press, 1967.

———. "Racial Ideas and Social Policy in Brazil 1870–1940." In *The Idea of Race in Latin America, 1870–1940,* ed. Richard Graham. Austin: University of Texas Press, 1990.

Soares, Dirceu. "Toca-Disco." *Folha de São Paulo,* October 6, 1977, 40.

Sodré, Muniz. *Samba, o dono do corpo.* Rio de Janeiro: Codecri, 1979.

Souza, Maria das Graças Nogueira de, et al. *Patápio, músico erudito ou popular?* Rio de Janeiro: FUNARTE, 1983.

Souza, Tarik de. "Cultura vende?" *Veja,* August 25, 1976, 101

———. "Ataque de choro." *Veja,* October 12, 1977, 99–100.

Straubhaar, Joseph D. "The Development of the Telenovela as the Pre-Eminent Form of Popular Culture in Brazil." *Studies in Latin American Popular Culture* 1 (1982): 139–140.

Tarasti, Eero. *Heitor Villa-Lobos e a Música dos Indios Brasileiros.* 1976.

Taylor, Julie M. "Carnival, Media, and Regional Traditions: Integration and Manipulation in Brazil." *Studies in Latin American Popular Culture* 7 (1988).

Teixeira, Patrício. *Método unico.* São Paulo: Irmãos Vitale, 1936.

Tinhorão, José Ramos. "Elites musicais começam a implicar com o choro." *Jornal do Brasil,* October 21, 1978, B:4.

———. *História social da música popular brasileira.* Lisbon: Caminho, 1990.

———. *Música popular: do gramafone ao rádio e TV.* São Paulo: Atica, 1981.

———. *Música popular: os sons que vêm da Rua.* Rio de Janeiro: Edições Tinhorão, 1976.

———. *Música popular: teatro & cinema.* Petrópolis: Vozes, 1972.

———. *Música popular: um tema em debate.* Rio de Janeiro: Saga, 1966.

———. *Pequena história da música popular: da modinha à canção do protesto.* São Paulo: Circulo do Livro, 1980.

Treece, David. "Guns and Roses: Bossa Nova and Brazil's Music of Popular Protest, 1958–68." *Popular Music* 16, no. 1 (1996).

Tupy, Dulce. *Carnavais de guerra.* Rio de Janeiro: ASB, 1985.

Turino, Thomas. *Moving Away from Silence: Music of the Peruvian Altiplano and the Experience of Urban Migration*. Chicago: University of Chicago Press, 1993.

————. *Nationalists, Cosmopolitans, and Popular Music in Zimbabwe*. Chicago: University of Chicago Press, 2000.

————. "Participatory Music as a Separate Art: Peruvian and Zimbabwean Case Studies." Unpublished paper, 1995.

Vasconcelos, Ary. *Carinhoso etc: história e inventário do choro*. [Rio de Janeiro]: [Ary Vasconcelos], 1984.

————. *A nova música da republica velha*. Rio de Janerio: By the Author, 1985.

————. *Panorama da música popular brasileira*. São Paulo: Martins, 1972.

————. *Panorama da música popular brasileira na "Belle Epoque."* Rio de Janeiro: Sant'Anna, 1977.

————. *Raízes da música popular brasileira*. Rio de Janeiro: Rio Fundo, 1991.

Vassberg, David E. "African Influences on the Music of Brazil." *Luso-Brazilian Review* 13, no. 1 (1976): 77–94.

Velloso, Mônica Pimenta. *As tradições populares na Belle Époque carioca*. Rio de Janeiro: Funarte, 1988.

Vianna, Hermano. *The Mystery of Samba: Popular Music and National Identity in Brazil*. Edited and translated by John Charles Chasteen. Chapel Hill: University of North Carolina Press, 1999.

Villa-Lobos, Heitor. *Qu'est-ce Qu'un Choros?* Lecture at the Club de Trois Centres, Paris, May, 29, 1958. Record 29.V.1958. EMI (France), 1959.

Vivacqua, Renato. *Música popular brasileira*. São Paulo: João Scortecci Editora, 1992.

Walden, Stephen Thomas. "Brasilidade: Brazilian Rock Nacional in the Context of National Cultural Identity." Ph.D. diss., University of Georgia, Athens, 1996.

Weco. *Methodo Weco para violão*. Rio de Janeiro: Carlos Whers & Cia, 1933.

Wright, Simon. *Villa-Lobos*. Oxford: Oxford University Press, 1992.

Select Discography of Choro Recordings

20 músicas do seculo XX. Altamiro Carrilho. Millennium 546 118-2.

À moda brasileira. Orquestra de Violões de Brasília. Independent release OVB CD 02.

Abel Ferreira & filhos. Abel Ferreira & Filhos. Marcus Pereira MP-10052.

Abismo de rosas. Dilermando Reis. Continental/Warner 903178892-2.

Abre alas. Brasília Brasil. Caravelas 270.045.

Ademilde Fonseca, vol. 2. Ademilde Fonseca. RGE Discos 6105 2.

Adeus batucada: Dussek canta Carmen Miranda. Eduardo Dussek. Kuarup CVA002.

Agua de Moringa. Agua de Moringa. Kuarup A001.

Altamiro Carrilho. Altamiro Carrilho. Millenium 546 118-2.

Alvaro Carrilho. Alvaro Carrilho. Acari Records AR1.

Anacleto de Medeiros. Rogério Duprat. Eldorado Memória 584-099.

Ao vivo. Baden Powell, Phillippe Baden Powell, Louis Marcel Powell. Luxo CD00156/4.

Ao vivo nos EUA. Joel Nascimento and Sexteto Brasileiro. Kuarup KCD093.

Arquivo Sigla: Copinha. Jubileu de Ouro. Copinha Gala/Som Livre 4194-2.

Arranca-toco. Jorginho do Pandeiro, Maurício Carrilho, Nailor Azevedo "Proveta," and Pedro Amorim. Acari Records AR 5.

Arthur Moreira Lima interpreta Ernesto Nazareth, vol. 1. Arthur Moreira Lima. Marcus Pereira 10021.

Arthur Moreira Lima interpreta Ernesto Nazareth, vol. 2. Arthur Moreira Lima. Marcus Pereira MPA-9364/5.

Ases do choro. Various artists. BMG 743216827329.

Ases do choro, vol. 2. Various artists. BMG 743216827428.

Baden, João Pernambuco e o sertão. Baden Powell. SESC São Paulo 199.008.497.

Bandolim & violão. Afonso Machado and Bartholomeu Wiese. Leblon LB 067.

Beatles 'n' choro. Henrique Cazes, Hamilton de Holanda, et al. DeckDisc 11006-2.

Beatles 'n' choro 2. Henrique Cazes, Hamilton de Holanda, et al. DeckDisc 7898324300486.

Bem Brasil. Altamiro Carrilho. Phillips 848-849-2.

Bem-te-vi. Galo Preto. Leblon LB.012.

Brasil (Duets). Mike Marshall. Earthbeat R2 71674.

Brasil revive o chorinho 2. Grupo Vou Vivendo. Movieplay BS-201.

Brasil, sax e clarineta. Abel Ferreira. Marcus Pereira MP10042.

Brasil, seresta. Carlos Poyares. Marcus Pereira MP10041.

Brasil, trombone. Raul de Barros. Marcus Pereira MPL9304.

Brasileirinho. Paula Robison. Omega OCD 3016.

Brazil Choro: Saxophone, Why Cry? Various artists. EMI Hemisphere, 1999.

Brésil Choro-Samba-Frevo 1914-1945. Various artists. Frémeaux & Associés FA 077.

Café Brasil. Conjunto Época de Ouro. Elektra/Asylum 82368.

Café Brasil 2. Conjunto Época de Ouro. Elektra/Asylum B000087RHR.

Canção da lua. Gilson Peranzzetta with David Chew. Marari Discos MR 002.

Canhoto da Paraíba: Walking on Coals. Canhoto da Paraíba. Milestone MCD-9230-2.

Carimbó do Moura (Confusão urbana, suburbana e rural). Paulo Moura. Música Latina MLMB 9-51024.

Chiquinha Gonzaga, a maestrina, vols. 1 and 2. Banda da Casa Edison, Almeida Cruz, Bahiano, Grupo Chiquinha Gonzaga, et al. Revivendo RVCD-138/1-2.

Chorando baixinho e chorinhos da pesada. Abel Ferreira e Os Chorões. EMI 829031-2.

Chorando baixinho: um encontro histórico. Arthur Moreira Lima, Abel Ferreira, and Época de Ouro. Kuarup KCD005.

Chorando de verdade. Joel Nascimento. Kuarup KCD069.

Chorinho. Grupo Som de Ouro. Novo Esquema CD 772452-2.

Chorinhos e chorões. Various artists. Gravações Elétricas 1-07-800-015.

Choro: 1906-1947. Pixinguinha, Ernesto Nazareth, Custódio Mesquita, Benedito Lacerda, Jacob do Bandolim, João Pernambuco, Luperce Miranda, Canhoto, et al. Frémeaux & Associés F&A 166.

Choro do quintal ao municipal. Various artists. Kuarup KCD107.

Chôro novo, Disco 1. Various artists. Marcus Pereira CDM-0025.

Choros. Various artists. EMI 4931 23 2.

Choros & jazz baroque. O Trio. Kardum KAR 262.

Choros & Waltzes of Brazil. Paulo Bellinati. Guitar Solo Publications 1005CD.

Choros dos mestres. Evandro e seu Regional. Movieplay do Brasil BR 1117.

Choros from Bahia. Fred Dantas and Ailton Reiner. Nimbus NI 5404.

Clássicos do choro. Various artists. EMI 364 793308 2.

Convida. Quintetto Villa-Lobos et al. Kuarup RD029.

Convite para ouvir choros, chorinhos, chorões. Os Coroas. RGE CD-344-6035.

Cristal. Gilson Peranzzetta. Marari Discos MR005

Desde que o choro é choro. Henrique Cazes and Família Violão. Kuarup MKCD071.

Destroçando a macaxeira. Grupo Dois de Ouro. Velas PN 003.

Disfarça e chora. Zé Nogueira. MP, B Warner Brothers Brasil, Ltda. M063012959-2.

Dois em um: Revivendo Patápio + A Bordo do Vera Cruz. Altamiro Carrilho. EMI 524529 2.

Dois em um: Rio Antigo + Chôros Imortais. Altamiro Carrilho. EMI 499601 2.

Dois irmãos. Paulo Moura and Raphael Rabello. Kuarup KCD112 (also Milestone MCD 9203-2).

Doutores em samba. Billy Blanco and Radames Gnattali. Kuarup K 068.

Ele e eu. Zé da Velha and Silvério Pontes. Independent release ZVSP 1-2000.

Elegia. Marco Pereira. Channel Crossings CCS 7695.

Enciclopédia musical brasileira 18: Waldir Azevedo. Waldir Azevedo. Warner/Continental 857381735-2.

Eu e eles. Hermeto Pascoal. Rádio MEC JABOUR99RMEC.

Flauta maravilhosa. Altamiro Carrilho. MoviePlay BS 269.

Gafieira etc & tal. Paulo Moura. Kuarup KCD024.

Gargalhada. Paulo Sérgio Santos Trio. Kuarup KCD155.

Gênios do violão. Garoto and Luiz Bonfá. EMI 837940 2.

Ginga de gafieira. Raul de Barros. Kuarup KCD119.

Gotas de ouro. Déo Rian. Revivendo RVCD-134.

Grandes choros e chorinhos. Various artists. RGE CD-342-6046.

Guerra-Peixe: música popular orquestra de salão. Tira o Dedo do Pudim. Independent release OSTDP9798.

Guitar Works of Garoto. Paulo Bellinati. Guitar Solo Publications 1002CD (also Velas 270-138).

Guitar Workshop in Rio. João Bosco, Raphael Rabello, et al. Movieplay JCD 30010.

Henrique Annes & Oficina de Cordas de Pernambuco. Henrique Annes and Oficina de Cordas de Pernambuco. Kuarup KCD085.

Henrique Cazes toca Waldir Azevedo, Pixinguinha, Hermeto & Cia. Henrique Cazes. Kuarup K055.

História de um bandolim. Luperce Miranda. Marcus Pereira 10076.

In Memoriam. Jacob do Bandolim. BMG 743211 323321.

Índio do Cavaquinho. Índio do Cavaquinho. Acari Records AR 4.

Inéditos de Jacob do Bandolim. Déo Rian and Conjunto Noites Cariocas. Eldorado 584.096.

Jacaré: choro frevado. Jacaré. Atração/Acervo Funarte ATR 32058.

Jacob do Bandolim (3-CD box). Jacob do Bandolim and Conjunto Época de Ouro. BMG 7432179712-2.

Jacob do Bandolim Original Classic Recordings, vol. 1. Jacob do Bandolim. Produced by David Grisman. Acoustic Disc ACD-3.

Jacob do Bandolim Original Classic Recordings, vol. 2. Jacob do Bandolim. Produced by David Grisman. Acoustic Disc ACD-13.

Jeitinho brasileiro (Escultor dos Ventos). Carlos Malta. Malandro Records MAL 71004.

João Pernambuco. Antonio Adolfo & Nó em Pingo d'Água. Atração/Acervo Funarte ATR 32010 (also Kuarup K055).

Leite de coco. Dirceu Leite. Kuarup C4008 (also Milestone MCD 9231 2).

Leonardo Miranda toca Joaquim Callado. Leonardo Miranda. Acari Records AR2.

Luciana Rabello. Luciana Rabello et al. Acari Records AR3.

Maogani. Quarteto de Violões. Quarteto Maogani. Rob Digital RD-CD-010.

Maurício Carrilho. Maurício Carrilho, Altamiro Carrilho, et al. Acari Records AR 6.

Memórias 2. Paulinho da Viola, César Faria, Chiquinho Faria, Copinha, Cristóvão Bastos, Dininho, Chaplin, and Hercules. EMI 852510 2.

Metamorfose. Gilson Paranzzetta. Marari Discos MR 003.

Mistura e manda. Paulo Moura. Kuarup KCD017.

Mulheres do choro. Various artists. Acari AR7.

Music of the Brazilian Masters. Almeida/Barbosa-Lima/Byrd. Concord Picante CCD-4389.

Naquele tempo. Choros e valsas. Pixinguinha, Benedito Lacerda, Custódio Mesquita e Orquestra, Garoto, Carolina Cardoso de Menezes. Revivendo RVCD-016.

Nó na garganta. Nó em Pingo d'Água. Rob Digital 803680061725.

Noites cariocas. Various artists. Kuarup K040.

O maior legado escrito de Pixinguinha. Orquestra Brasilia. Milan Sur 873 007.

O Trio. Maurício Carrilho, Pedro Amorim, and Paulo Sergio Santos. Kuarup S8000.

O violão brasileiro tocado pelo avesso. Canhoto da Paraíba. Marcus Pereira MP-10049.

Oboé no choro. Marco de Pinna and Harold Emert. Pro Vibrações 2001.

Obrigado, Brazil. Yo-Yo Ma and Friends. Sony Classical SK 89935.

Oito Batutas. Oito Batutas. Revivendo RVCD-064.

Orquestra Brasília (O maior legado escrito de Pixinguinha). Orquestra Brasília. Kuarup KCD035.

Orquestra de Cordas Brasileiras. Orquestra de Cordas Brasileiras. Kuarup K039.

Orquídea: Choro e samba em Niterói. Guinga, Nó em Pingo d'Água, Trio Madeira Brasil, Zé da Velha, Jorginho do Pandeiro, Quarteto Maogani, Eduardo Neves, et al. Rob Digital RD 027.

Os bambas da flauta. Atamiro Carrilho et al. Kuarup KCD180.

Os grande sucessos de Waldir de Azevedo. Waldir de Azevedo et al. EMI 795337 2.

Os Ingênuos play Choros from Brazil. Os Ingênuos. Nimbus Records NI 5338.

Os pianeiros: Antonio Adolfo abraça Ernesto Nazareth. Antonio Adolfo. Kuarup AR3007.

Patápio Silva. Altamiro Carrilho, Luiz Eça, Galo Preto, Banda do Corpo de Bombeiros do Estado de Rio de Janeiro. Atração/Acervo Funarte ATR 32021.

Pé na cadeira. Isaias and Seus Chorões. Kuarup KCD122.

Pedro Amorim interpreta Luperce Miranda. Pedro Amorim. Kuarup S8070.

Pernambuco's Music. Oficina de Cordas. Nimbus NI 5398.

Pingolé: choros. Gilson Peranzzetta. Marari Discos MR 004.

Pisando em brasa. Canhoto da Paraíba. Kuarup KCD114 (also Milestone MCD 9230-2).

Pixinguinha. Orquestra Brasilia. Kuarup K035.

Pixinguinha 100 anos. Pixinguinha, Benedito Lacerda, Orlando Silva, et al. RCA/BMG 7432146286 2.

Pixinguinha alma e corpo. Carlos Malta and Quarteto de Cordas. 500 Anos de Som 500-002.

Pixinguinha de bolso. Henrique Cazes and Marcello Gonçalves. Kuarup KCD142.

Pixinguinha. Marco de Pinna. Universidade Estácio do Sá EM 16089801.

Pixinguinha. Paulo Moura. Blue Jacket Entertainment BJAC 5019-2.

Pixinguinha. Paulo Moura and Os Batutas. Rob Digital RD 018.

Pixinguinha: No tempo dos Oito Batutas. Pixinguinha and Os Oito Batutas. Revivendo RVCD-064.

Pixinguinha/70 Jacob do Bandolim. Conjunto Época de Ouro, Radamés Gnattali, et al.. MIS/Rob Digital 199.001.525.

Princípios do choro 1 (3-CD set). Various artists. Acari/Biscoito Fino BF600-101, BF600-102 BF600-103.

Princípios do choro 2 (3-CD set). Various artists. Acari/Biscoito Fino BF600-104, BF600-105, BF600-106.

Princípios do choro 3 (3-CD set). Various artists. Acari/Biscoito Fino BF600-107, BF600-108, BF600-109.

Princípios do choro 4 (3-CD set). Various artists. Acari/Biscoito Fino BF600-110, BF600-111, BF600-112.

Princípios do choro 5 (3-CD set). Various artists. Acari/Biscoito Fino BF600-113, BF600-114 BF600-115.

Quinteto Pixinguinha. Quinteto Pixinguinha. Novas Direções ND002P002000

Rabo de Lagartixa (Quebra-Queixo). Rabo de Lagartixa. Kuarup/Malandro Records RDL 1998 (also Malandro Records MAL 71014).

Radamés Gnattali: retratos. Chiquinho do Acordeon, Raphael Rabello, Beto Cazes, and Orquestra de Cordas Brasileiras. Kuarup KCD044.

Radamés interpreta Radamés. Radamés Gnattali et al. RGE 6100 2.

Raízes do Samba: Pixinguinha. Pixinguinha, João da Baiana and Clementina de Jesus. EMI 522658 2.

Raphael Rabello & Dino 7 Cordas. Raphael Rabello and Dino 7 Cordas. Kuarup C4013 (also Milestone MCD-9221-2).

Raphael Rabello: todos os tons. Raphael Rabello et al. BMG 74321-10049-23.

Receita de Samba. Nó em Pingo d'Água. Visom 7219-2.

Reco do Bandolim & Choro Livre. Reco do Bandolim and Choro Livre. Kuarup KCD106.

Reflexões. Paulinho Nogueira. Malandro Records MAL 73001.

Relendo Dilermando Reis. Raphael Rabello. RGE 6130 2.

Relendo Waldir Azevedo. Henrique Cazes. RGE 6095 2.

Retratos: Jacob e seu Bandolim. Radamés Gnattali e Orquestra. Columbia 866.028/2.

Rio Days, Rio Nights. Paula Robison. Arabesque Too Y2002.

Rio Nights. Featuring the greatest stars of Choro Music. BMG/Milan 73138 35648-2.

Rua Marari. Gilson Peranzzetta. Marari Discos MR001.

Salvador. Nó em Pingo d'Água. Visom VICD00091.

Samba e choro negro. Paulinho da Viola and Ensemble. World Network WDR 55.834.
Saracoteando. Água de Moringa. Malandro Records MAL 71007.
Saxofone, por que choras? Luiz Americano. InterCD Records R 21017.
Segura ele. Paulo Sérgio Santos. Kuarup KCD064.
Sempre Anacleto. Art Metal Quinteto and Banda de Câmara Anacleto de Medeiros. Kuarup KCD123.
Sempre Chiquinha. Antonio Adolfo, Olivia Hime, Roberto Szidon, and Banda Anacleto de Medeiros. Kuarup KCD124.
Sempre Jacob. Déo Rian, Joel Nascimento, Afonso Machado, Nó em Pingo D'Água, Orquestra de Cordas Brasileiras. Kuarup KCD077.
Sempre Nazareth. Maria Teresa Madeira and Pedro Amorim. Kuarup KCD095.
Sempre Pixinguinha. Chiquinho, Joel Nascimento, Henrique Cazes, Odette Dias, Paulo Sérgio Santos, João Carlo Assis Brasil. Kaurup KCD076.
Shades of Rio. Romero Lubambo and Raphael Rabello. Chesky Records JD85.
Só gafieira! Zé da Velha and Silvério Pontes. Kuarup MKCD073.
Só Paulinho da Viola. Galo Preto. Leblon LB 067.
Tira poeira. Tira Poeira. Biscoito Fino BF535.
Todo o choro. Abel Ferreira, Altamiro Carrilho, et al. Marcus Pereira MPL 9362.
Tributo a Garoto, Radamés Gnattali, e Raphael Rabello. Atração/Acervo Funarte ATR 32081.
Trio Madeira Brasil. Trio Madeira Brasil (Ronaldo do Bandolim, José Paulo Becker, and Marcello Gonçalves). TMB/Kuarup TMB-98.
Trombone do Brasil. Roberto Marques. Rob Digital RD 015.
Um alô para o Six, Rossini Ferreira. Kuarup KCD098.
Uma chorada na casa do Six. Carlos Poyares. Kuarup KCD086.
Uma rosa para Pixinguinha. Elizeth Cardoso, Radamés Gnattali & Camerata Carioca. Atração/Acervo Funarte ATR 32018.
Valsas e choros. Turíbio Santos. Kuarup K001.
Vê se gostas. Ademilde Fonseca, Jacob do Bandolim, Waldyr Azevedo. Revivendo RVCD-145.
Villa por Chorões. Various artists. Kuarup KCD166.
Villa-Lobos: obra completa para violão solo. Turíbio Santos. Kuarup K028.
Villa-Lobos: os choros de camara. Various artists. Kuarup K002.
Viva Garoto. Gravações originais. Garoto. Núcleo Contemporâneo Memória Brasileira 107.225.
Violão carioca. Duda Anizio and Nelson Caiado. Suite Brasil SBP 001/2001.
Vivaldi & Pixinguinha. Radamés Gnattali & Camerata Carioca. Atração/Acervo Funarte ATR 32014.

Internet Resources

Recordings, Books, and Instruments for Sale

Acari Records (includes history, photos, and other information)
http://www.acari.com.br

Brazilian Percussion.com
http://www.brazilianpercussion.com/instrumentos/instrumentos.asp

The Brazilian Sound (Brazilian music, books, film, and culture)
http://www.thebraziliansound.com

BrazilianMusic.com (Brazilian music CDs)
http://www.brazilianmusic.com

Kuarup Discos (in English)
http://www.kuarup.com.br/english/index.asp

Lumiar (music books and records)
http://www.lumiar.com.br

Luso-Brazilian Books (Brazilian sheet music and books about Brazilian music)
http://www.lusobraz.com

Modern Sound Mega Music Store
http://www.modernsound.com.br/intro.asp

Putumayo World Music
http://www.putumayo.com

Clubs, Schools, and Institutions

Brazilian Academy of Music
http://www.abmusica.org.br

Le Club de Choro (Paris)
http://www.maisondubresil.org/Culturel/clubchoro.htm

Clube do Choro (Juiz de Fora, Minas Gerais, Brazil; site includes schedule, history, rodas, and workshops)
http://www.clubedochorojf.com.br

Clube do Choro de Brasília
http://www.clubedochoro.com.br

Endereços de Música
http://www.ufrgs.br/faced/slomp/musica.htm

Escola de Chôro Jorge Cardoso
http://geocities.yahoo.com.br/escolachorojorge/escolachorojorgecardoso.html

Escola de Choro Raphael Rabello (schedule, student lists, and groups)
http://www.clubedochoro.com.br/escola.htm

Instituto Jacob do Bandolim (a virtual institute)
http://www.jacobdobandolim.com.br

Latin American Music Center, School of Music, Indiana University
http://www.music.indiana.edu/som/lamc

Villa-Lobos Museum
http://www.museuvillalobos.org.br

Groups, Soloists, and Histories of Performers

Amarelindo
http://www.amarelindo.com/_FR/ChoroFR.html

Cheiro de Choro
http://www.artagenda.be/art/cheiro

Choro Club
http://www.sonymusic.co.jp/Music/Arch/SR/ChoroClub

Choro Ensemble
http://www.choroensemble.com/paginas/about_choro.html

Cliff Korman
http://www.cliffkorman.com

Crying High
http://www.cryinghigh.com/homepage/2.html

Dois de Ouro
http://www.doisdeouro.com

Ernesto Nazaré
http://www153.pair.com/bensav/Compositeurs/Nazareth.E.html

Flor de Abacate
http://sites.uol.com.br/flordeabacate/cd.html

Garoto
http://tinpan.fortunecity.com/sensible/732

Marco de Pinna
http://www.marco.pinna.mus.br

Maria-Brazil: Carmen Miranda
http://maria-brazil.org/carmen.htm

Marilynn Mair
http://www.marilynnmair.com/cds.shtml

Nó de Pingo D'Agua
http://noempingodagua.com.br

"Pixinguinha," entry on Center for Black Music Research website   **247**
http://www.cbmr.org/pubs/pixinguinha.htm

Receita de Choro
http://www.liaa.ch.ufpb.br/receitadechoro

Tira Poeira
http://www.tirapoeira.hpg.ig.com.br/TPgrupo.htm

General Information

Agenda do Samba & Choro
http://www.samba-choro.com.br

AllBrazilianMusic
http://www.allbrazilianmusic.com/en/Styles/Styles.asp?Status=MATERIA&Nu_Materia=894

Cafemusic
http://www.cafemusic.com.br

O Choro em Brasília
http://www.persocom.com.br/chorodebrasilia

Choro history and discography
http://www.brazzil.com/musfeb96.htm

Hot100Br@sil (Brazilian music charts from 1902 to the present)
http://www.hot100brasil.com

Maria-Brazil
http://www.maria-brazil.org/choros.htm

Página do Choro
http://www7.ocn.ne.jp/choronao

Sambossa
http://www.sambossa.com.br

Sovaca de Cobra
http://www.sovacodecobra.com.br

TAMARA ELENA LIVINGSTON-ISENHOUR is University Archivist and Assistant Professor of Music at Kennesaw State University in Georgia. She has a Ph.D. in ethnomusicology from the University of Illinois at Urbana-Champaign.

THOMAS GEORGE CARACAS GARCIA is Assistant Professor of Ethnomusicology at Miami University of Ohio.